SIX LIVES / SIX DEATHS

SIX LIVES
SIX DEATHS

Portraits from Modern Japan

Robert Jay Lifton
Shūichi Katō
and
Michael R. Reich

New Haven and London
Yale University Press

Designed by Christopher Harris
and set in VIP Janson type.
Printed in the United States of America by
Vail-Ballou Press, Binghamton, N.Y.

Library of Congress Cataloging in Publication Data
Lifton, Robert Jay, 1926–
    Six lives, six deaths.

    Bibliography: p.
    Includes index.
    1. Death—Psychological aspects—Case studies.
2. National characteristics, Japanese. 3. Japan—
Biography. I. Katō Shūichi, 1919–   joint author.
II. Reich, Michael, 1950–   joint author. III. Title.
[DNLM: 1. Medicine in literature. 2. Attitude to
death. 3. Death. 4. Culture. 5. Philosophy.
6. Psychology, Social—Japan. BD444 L722s]
BF789.D4L54   155.9'37'0926   78-11926
ISBN 0-300-02266-2; 0-300-02600-5 pbk.

The authors are grateful to the following publishers for
permission to use photographs of the six men: Iwanami shoten
(Chōmin, Ogai, and Kawakami), Yoshikawa kōbunkan (Nogi),
Shinchōsha (Hakuchō), and Asahi shinbun (Mishima).

12 11 10 9 8 7 6 5 4 3

For B. J., Midori, and Rose Hannah

CONTENTS

PREFACE

It may be that authors always lead double lives in connection with their books—one of careful planning and preparations as they take hold of their project, the other of surprise, excitement, and precariousness as their project takes hold of them. That certainly was our experience with this book.

Our collaboration developed from personal friendships. Katō and Lifton met originally in Japan at a conference on Japanese modernization in 1960, and although much stimulated by each other's ideas met only a few times over the next fourteen years. Katō and Reich met in Japan while Reich was doing research there between 1971 and 1974, and in the fall of 1974 they came to Yale as visiting professor and graduate student with the hope of working together. Aware of Lifton's work on East Asia and on issues around death, they approached him with the suggestion of giving a course together on modern Japanese attitudes toward death, with the possibility of then collaborating on a book. Lifton, attracted by the possibility of renewing and deepening a personal and intellectual relationship with Kato, agreed to the project. Our collaboration began to take shape.

The beginning materials for the project were developed during the fall semester of 1974, when Katō taught a small advanced seminar, in which Reich was both teaching assistant and student. Under Katō's supervision, the students translated a series of brief statements made by a number of prominent modern Japanese about their impending deaths, including last testaments, diaries, stories, and descriptions of how they felt about dying and about death itself. Then in the spring, Katō and Lifton began their joint course, with Reich as coordinator. We announced the course as an experiment. Yet those who joined us—medical students, graduate students in East Asian Studies or psychology, and various undergraduates—shared our sense of excitement in exploring modern Japan through individual lives and deaths and contributed to the vitality of the enterprise in ways that searching students always do.

For this book, Reich first worked with Katō in preparing a detailed outline on each individual, portraying experiences in each life that had bearing on death attitudes. Lifton then made interpretative suggestions, at first mainly focusing on additional information required for informed psychological (or psychohistorical) statements. Katō and

Reich then prepared an initial draft of the case study, to which Lifton responded with detailed written suggestions for revision and expansion. The three of us then reformulated the case study from beginning to end. On the basis of these discussions Reich prepared and Katō and Lifton revised drafts that became finished chapters.

What started out as an intellectual encounter between two senior authors became in every sense a three-way collaboration. At first it was Lifton prodding Katō for cultural and historical associations, Katō prodding Lifton for psychological meanings, and Reich pulling together these various currents. But eventually each of us proposed psychological principles as well as cultural and historical perspectives. Of course, divisions of labor remained. Chapter 1 contains one section presenting the contours of Lifton's paradigm of death and continuity and another outlining Katō's analysis of the Japanese world view and society. These two approaches are blended in the remaining chapters as we interpret our six subjects and their psychological patterns in sociohistorical terms. Reich had responsibility for interweaving the approaches and styles of Katō and Lifton, which meant contributing a great deal of his own to the fabric. In the commentaries that follow each study Lifton and Katō speak in their own voices to suggest various psychological and historical points in speculative ways that carry the discussion beyond the data at hand. And each chapter begins with selected and translated excerpts from works by our subjects that express their thoughts and personal feelings about death.

Our approach in this study emerged from Lifton's psychological paradigm around death and continuity and Katō's sociocultural views on group behavior and transcendental values. We realize that there are other perspectives we could have used and that studying individual lives and deaths is just one of many approaches to Japanese society. But we believe this framework has at least the potential advantage of combining death-linked principles of individual motivation with necessary social and historical "space."

We selected the six men in this book for a variety of reasons. We wanted people who had written about their deaths in concrete terms and whose lives were well recorded in biographical or autobiographical materials. These criteria limited our choice to men who belonged to the elite in modern Japan. We also wanted to explore various ways in which people had died, so we included two cases of suicide on the model of *seppuku*, or *harakiri* as commonly referred to in the West

(Nogi Maresuke and Mishima Yukio), two men who died of illness at the peak of their creative lives (Mori Ogai and Nakae Chōmin), and two who died looking back from advanced old age (Kawakami Hajime and Masamune Hakuchō).

We also sought different approaches toward social change: Nogi and Mishima died seeking to restore images of the past, Nakae and Kawakami seeking to transform Japan according to imagery of the future, and Mori and Masamune oriented toward accommodating themselves to a complex present. Their relationships to political power also differed: Nogi and Mori were within the oligarchy, if not at its center at least in its radius; Chōmin and Kawakami consistently opposed the government and met with severe oppression; Mishima was drawn to the military and political elite without really belonging to them; and Masamune neither opposed nor approached political power, preferring to keep his distance and tend his own garden. And we wanted the six men to span the period of Japanese history from the mid-nineteenth century until the present. Thus three of our subjects (Nogi, Mori, and Nakae) lived during Japan's first great modern transition, the Meiji Restoration of 1868; and the other three (Kawakami, Masamune, and Mishima) lived during Japan's second great modern transition, around and following the defeat in the Second World War in 1945.

Our final criterion was that of differing approaches, in life and death, to the Japanese intellectual tradition of emphasizing individual integration into an immediate group rather than personal commitment to a transcendental value or religious or philosophical world view. Three (Nogi, Mori, and Mishima) had no religious faith and subscribed to no philosophical system; one (Masamune) explicitly stated a pragmatic skepticism that was deeply rooted in the daily-life–centered world of the majority of the people; and two represent a small minority of Japanese intellectuals in their firm commitment to political ideologies and metaphysical stances that they considered as the absolute "truth." Nakae believed in an atheistic materialism and Kawakami in a religious system with Buddhistic overtones. Partly by accident and partly by design, our chronological ordering of the six cases has a certain symmetry, beginning with Nogi's seppuku and ending with Mishima's.

We are aware that the absence of women in our study is a major limitation. We had hoped to include one or more women, but could find none who met two of our basic requirements—writing about her own death, and a life sufficiently well recorded for us to reconstruct it. While this failure may reflect our own male shortcomings, we are convinced it is primarily a consequence of public male dominance in Japanese society. Still, studies of women and death, in Japan and elsewhere, can and should be undertaken.

Throughout this book we are intentionally speculative and subjective. But we try to base our speculation in evidence and to bring discipline to our subjectivity. That kind of balance seems appropriate for all psychological and historical work, as opposed to claims of neutrality and incontestable conclusions which tend to dehumanize and distort in the name of scientific accuracy. Our work together is grounded in a shared sensibility about many elements in Japanese and American culture, including a political position that is—broadly speaking—of the independent left. We see our efforts as part of a "natural history" approach now evolving in psychological work that borders on both literature and science, which in the end claims relationship to a modified area of scientific tradition.

We are grateful to the Council on East Asian Studies and the Committee on Sumitomo Faculty Research Grants of Yale University for the award that made this book possible. John W. Hall, Edwin McClellan, and Hugh Patrick provided valuable support to the project. Carol Gluck read portions of the manuscript and made important suggestions. Yajima Midori, while preparing her sensitive translation of the work into Japanese, offered comments and corrections that improved the English manuscript as well; as did Dianne Zolotow with her careful copy editing. Jane Isay enriched the final work with her imaginative editing, astute intellectual criticism, and warm personal presence. For typing of different drafts of the manuscript we are grateful to Carole D'Amico; to Martha Hoaglund, who assisted in other ways as well; and to Lily B. Finn, who helped coordinate so many facets of the work.

NOTE ON NAMES AND HISTORICAL PERIODS

In keeping with East Asian tradition we generally place the surname before the given name—for example, Kawakami Hajime. We usually refer to individuals in their youth by given name (Hajime) and then in adulthood by surname (Kawakami). When the given name changed several times (Nogi for example, used several different names before settling on Maresuke at the age of twenty-two), we selected the best known. Before the Meiji period, changing one's given name was common and caused substantial confusion even among Japanese. An individual had both an official or "true" name (*ji-tsumyō*) that remained unaltered and a common or popular name (*tsūshō*) that could be changed at different points in life. In addition, educated people, especially writers and artists, often adopted a pen name (*gō*) that might be changed several times. After a national census registration was established in the Meiji period it became more difficult to change one's given name and the practice declined. Even today, however, some Japanese change their given names after the occurrence of a disaster or its prediction by a fortune-teller. Because the situation differs with each individual in our study, we explain our use of names toward the beginning of each chapter.

In calculating ages throughout the book, we use the Western method, rather than the traditional Japanese method in which the day of birth is counted as one year, the next New Year's Day as two years, and so on.

The lives of the six Japanese men discussed in this book span the Tokugawa era, named for the family of ruling shoguns, and the Meiji, Taishō, and Shōwa historical periods, each named for reigning emperors. The Tokugawa era, from 1600 to 1868, is a time of strict national isolation and semicentralized feudalism. The Meiji period, from 1868 to 1912, is the time of Japan's emergence as a modern power. The Taishō period, from 1912, to 1926, includes important experimentation with democratic froms. The Shōwa period, from 1926 through today, includes Japan's interval of ultranationalism, militarism, and war, as well as the post–Second World War era.

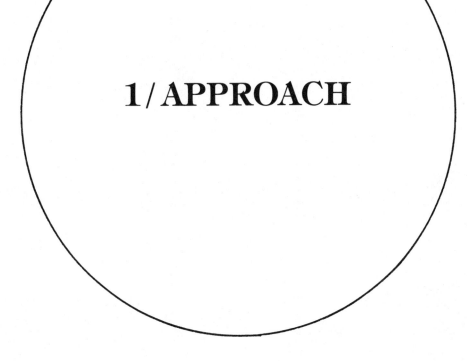

1/ APPROACH

O ur study of six Japanese men examines in some detail the way in which each experienced dying. We consider each man's approach to death not as an end in itself so much as a way of understanding the pattern of his life and the relationship of that pattern to the larger historical currents around him. This chapter provides the background for that examination. First we introduce Lifton's paradigm of death and the continuity of life, particularly in the context of Japanese culture and history. Then we present Katō's analysis of differences and similarities in elite and mass world views in Japan and how they have influenced attitudes toward death. These two approaches, which might be broadly termed psychohistorical and sociohistorical, structure our investigation and discussions throughout this book.

Until recently death has been mostly ignored as a conceptual issue in psychology. In part, this blind spot arose from Freud's famous dictum that "it is indeed impossible to imagine our death" and his view that death, as a negation of life rather than an entity in itself, can have no psychic representation. These observations, while not without their wisdom, ignore the abiding importance of human awareness that one was born and will die and the universal psychological struggle around imagining the end of the self. Paradoxically, Freud's cosmic projection of "the death instincts" as the great antagonists to "the life instincts" discouraged subsequent clinicians and theorists from approaching death as a psychological issue. The metaphysical distance of death became the rationale for ignoring it entirely. Yet Freud, contradictory figure that he was, recognized the cost of that human tendency to deny death and spoke of its causing us to live psychologically "beyond our means," a recognition in accord with a vast philosophical tradition that culminates in modern existentialism. Ultimately, however, Freud remained conceptually bound by the assumptions of his own psychological system; libido theory required that fear of death be viewed essentially as fear of castration.

A somewhat separate conception of death began with another psychoanalytic pioneer, Otto Rank. Rank stressed man's need for "an assurance of eternal survival for his self," suggesting further that "man creates culture by changing natural conditions in order to maintain his spiritual self." Rank equated fear of life with fear of death. He referred to the neurotic's "constant restriction of life," because "he refuses the

3

loan (life) in order to avoid the payment of the debt (death)." More recently, Ernest Becker explored various Rankian themes in two brilliant volumes, written not long before his own death in 1974, _The Denial of Death_ and _Escape from Evil_.

Indeed, American intellectual life has been experiencing something of a reawakening toward death and issues surrounding it—not only in various expressions of medical, psychological, and social thought, but also in philosophy, art, and literature. Of course, death has never ceased to be a central theme for poets, novelists, and painters. A related phenomenon has been the renditions of death by the mass media, sometimes thoughtful and illuminating, but more often melodramatic and exploitative, in what Geoffrey Gorer called "pornographic" expressions of violence.

In Japan as well, although there has been less denial to overcome, the issues surrounding death have increasingly come to the surface during the last ten years. We strongly suspect that this heightened concern about death, in Japan and the United States and in fact everywhere, has much to do with the actual and potential holocausts of our century—the nuclear bombings, death camps, mass killings, extreme environmental pollution, diminishing food and energy resources, and various forms of torture and terrorism.

Despite these general trends, death continues to be conceptually neglected in psychological thought. Part of the difficulty lies in the either-or approach death seems to evoke in theorists. They either almost totally disregard death or focus it so exclusively that it becomes the definitive explanation of virtually all human behavior. There exists the constant danger, present for instance in Becker's work, of replacing a dogma of sex with a dogma of death or death-denial. One may construct a brilliant thanatology, but still lack a psychology of life. What is needed, we believe, is a more integrated view of death and continuity.

In this book we examine both continuities and discontinuities associated with each death, asking what was perceived as coming to an end as well as what a particular person sought to perpetuate in dying (and in living). We explore how different ways of dying relate to larger principles and influence subsequent generations. We seek to give death its due relationship to life—both within a particular culture at a certain time in history as well as in more universal terms. And within this paradigm of death and continuity, we stress a principle of symbolization as the fundamental process of the adult human mind that links death and individual and collective life. We try to be dialectical rather than dualistic—that is, concerned with natural (and unnatural) life-death rhythms rather than artificially constructed dichotomies.

Our approach is fundamentally psychohistorical, an adjective as abused as it is important. In its noun form, we use "psychohistory" to mean the application of psychological methods to the study of historical issues. Our particular development of psychohistory stems originally from Freud, who evolved the first psychology worthy of being applied to history. But at the same time, we reject much of Freud's specific approach to history, especially his tendency to view history simply as the individual psyche writ large. Our framework includes two post-Freudian models. One of these, developed in the pioneering work of Erik H. Erikson, is that of the great man or woman *in* history. In his already classic psychobiographies of Luther and Gandhi, Erikson charts ways in which the great historical figure, in struggling toward solutions for overwhelming personal dilemmas, becomes a symbol for large numbers of men and women of that era, thereby achieving a breakthrough in human consciousness. Although the six men we have chosen probably do not qualify for that level of greatness, each struggled with cultural and historical currents crucial for modern Japanese and in the process had a considerable effect on the consciousness of his countrymen and on broader human consciousness as well. In this sense we may speak of them as significant historical figures and exemplars of important kinds of psychohistorical experience.

Shared psychohistorical themes, the second post-Freudian model we rely on, is developed primarily in Lifton's work. Unlike the usual application of this model—a psychological investigation of a group of individuals who commonly experience an important historical event—we explore six seperate lives and deaths in terms of their special significance. But we also seek to understand what these six men share—as Japanese, as men of modern, mostly transitional eras, as significant historical figures confronting issues of importance for their society, as human beings facing death. In other words, we are concerned not only with their significance as separate individuals, but also with common themes in their lives and historical connections. To study both aspects, we combine an Eriksonian approach to a significant figure in history with a shared-themes approach.

This shared-themes approach implies that each person is not only a special individual with a particular psychological life, but also is linked to collective experience and behavior at three levels: *specific historical currents* flowing through the individual's lifetime, particularly such major upheavals as the Meiji Restoration and the Japanese defeat in the Second World War; *cultural emphases and patterns*, such as the Japanese stress on continuity with the dead and on mother-child mutual dependency; and *universal psychobiological elements*, including struggles around death and dying and life processes of nurturing and growth. One of our major objectives is to elucidate how these three levels of collective historical, cultural, and universal experience are interwoven in the lives and deaths of six Japanese men.

Any attempt to connect individual and collective levels of experience raises questions about method. Again we stress that we do not view any of these men as totally representative of Japanese culture or history. Instead, we claim that they reflect particularly intense individual versions of historical and cultural conflicts and achievements in relationship to universal themes. In this sense our choice of men greatly structures our study and determines many emphases. Our goal, thus, is not to be comprehensive, but rather to evoke, in these six individual portraits, some of the major themes and human dilemmas of modern Japanese history. We work outward from empirical investigation of primary and secondary sources, to comparison of each of the six men with others in Japan and elsewhere, to informed speculation about more general psychological and historical significance. Though each case study is related as a unified story, we seek to connect direct psychological data about individual lives with a body of recognized social and cultural observations. All this would seem logical enough, even obvious. And yet it is rarely done, because both psychologist and historian hold so tenaciously to their respective safe havens of the single individual and the suprapersonal collective. In our collaboration we leave these safe havens. We do so with commitment to whatever psychohistorical rigor we can muster and with awareness of the inevitable vulnerability of our effort.

The paradigm of death and continuity we use in this book stresses motivation around life (form) and death (formlessness). The struggle to evoke and preserve the sense of the self as alive and avoid the sense of the self as dead is central to human experience. All living beings share the struggle to remain alive. But the urge to retain and enlarge the *feeling* of being alive—of vitality—is specifically human, indicating that an evolutionary trait of symbolizing mentation marks the border of biology and culture. These basic aspirations—remaining alive and retaining the "feeling of life"—are closely connected to the stress on the symbolization of human continuity in formative theory.[1] According to this paradigm, struggles for vitality and continuity take place at both a *proximate* level, which involves the immediate psychological experience of life, and an *ultimate* level, which expresses the links of the self to groups and principles beyond the individual.

These two dimensions are actually experienced simultaneously, and only our analytic cast of mind renders them separate. The ultimate dimension, which we call symbolic immortality, has been largely disregarded in psychological thought, more or less left to theologians and philosophers. We believe it to be part of man's evolutionary heritage, a corollary of the knowledge of death itself. A *sense* of immortality, then, is not simply a denial of death. Rather it reflects a compelling and universal inner quest for a continuous symbolic relationship between our finite individual lives and what has gone before and what will come after. It is a search for symbolizing continuities, despite the discontinuities of death. That quest is central to a human's special status as a cultural and historical animal. Understood in this way, the sense of immortality is in itself neither compensatory nor irrational, but an appropriate symbolization of our biological and historical connectedness.

The sense of immortality may be expressed in five general modes: biological, theological, creative, natural, and the special mode of experiential transcendence. One's awareness of involvement in these modes can vary enormously and cannot necessarily be equated with the power a particular mode, or combination of modes, holds for him. Another task of this book is to identify the tensions in each person's struggles to symbolize his immortality and to relate those struggles to

1. The formative-symbolizing approach focuses on the fundamental process of creation and recreation of images and forms that characterizes the human mental function. In this approach Lifton draws on the principles evolved by Ernst Cassirer and Susanne Langer, as well as on the formative and unitary emphasis of L. L. Whyte. Each inner image and more elaborated form is understood both as a configuration in itself and as a part of a larger configuration. Only by creating, maintaining, and breaking down and recreating viable form are we capable of experiencing vitality. In that sense, we may say that form equals life.

cultural patterns in modern Japan. The five modes of symbolic immortality thus provide a framework within which we can compare the relative differences between Japanese and other approaches to death. By studying the patterns of immortalization that are especially strong in modern Japan, we can explore a uniquely important expression of the interplay of the particular and the universal.

The (biological mode) of immortality is epitomized by family continuity, living on through one's sons and daughters and their sons and daughters, with imagery of an endless chain of biological attachment. This has been the most fundamental and universal of all modes. Its classic expression is found in premodern East Asian cultures, especially in the traditional Chinese family system, and in somewhat lesser and modified form in the Japanese family system as well. It was philosophically elaborated in Confucianism, with its intense focus on filial piety, and its related ancestor cult. Thus Mencius, Confucius's great disciple, could say: "There are three unfilial acts, and of these, lack of posterity is the greatest."

In Japan, even today, many homes retain in the *butsudan*, or Buddhist household shrine, the *ihai*, or mortuary tablets for deceased family members. This practice is a remnant of the longstanding Japanese combination of original Shintō reverence toward nature and ancestors and later Buddhist influence. Although such rituals undoubtedly have lost much of their psychological force in postwar Japan, they remain important to the Japanese cultural experience and can be revived, especially in crises. Many Hiroshima survivors, for instance, describe the special solace they feel when they literally talk to family members killed by the bomb and enshrined in their household altars. What they convey is much less a sense of religiosity than of ritualized effort to hold on to at least some part of those relationships and to maintain an unbroken sense of family continuity. Such sentiments are in no way unique to Japan. Related practices are found in Western cultures, although usually in somewhat less concrete form.

Because man is the cultural animal, the biological mode can never remain purely biological. The family itself is always at least partly symbolized in social terms. A concrete example is the Japanese family practice, still active, of adopting adult male heirs where none (or in some cases, none with adequate talent) are available in that biological generation. Another example is the stress on family honor. In Japan, "clearing one's name"—wiping out stains on one's reputation, repaying social and economic debts, avenging insults—has never been purely individual but has always been subsumed to the "family name." For the family is the most immediate group that defines so much of the individual's moral as well as biological existence.

The biosocial mode of immortality, however, can be extended outward from family to tribe, organization, subculture, people, nation, or even species. We might call this a process of "biologizing" the social group. That extension can be associated with numerous ethical principles. The Meiji Restoration of 1868, for example, was followed by a revitalization of the emperor system that combined its mythology of unbroken descent from the sun goddess with more modern expressions of nationalism. The Second World War was thus fought around a sacred constellation of family, feudal past, emperor, and nation. Though the Japanese experience has unique features, some such constellation always characterizes modern nationalism. The individual is energized by merging with an "immortal biocultural substance" for which he may willingly give his life and even more willingly take the lives of others.

It is precisely because of the psychic force of the biosocial mode that there is such a fine line between love of country and people and hate-filled, violent nationalism. A number of philosophical and evolutionary theorists, including eighteenth-century rationalists, Julian Huxley, and others, have advocated extending the mode beyond the immortal biocultural substance usually associated with nations. Unfortunately, however, we are still a long way from realizing this goal. We seem mired within the parochial boundaries of nationalism. But we still have hope, at least faint glimmerings, of a more encompassing vision of biosocial immortality that would provide each individual anticipating death with the image "I live on in humankind."

The second—and the most familiar—expression of symbolic immortality—is the theological or religious mode. It may include a specific concept of a life after death, not only as a form of survival but even as a release from the profane burdens of life into a higher plane of existence. A related concept is that of the "immortal soul," which Freud saw as man's characteristic way of expressing the denial of death.

But the theological mode need not rely on a literal vision of an immortal soul or afterlife. No such vision occurs in most Jewish and early Buddhist belief. And even in Christianity it is probably less fun-

damental than the quality of spiritual achievement symbolized by the
Christ story. The common thread in all great religions is the spiritual
quest and realization of the hero-founder, which enables him to confront and transcend death and to provide a model for generations of
believers. Thus the lives of Buddha, Moses, Christ, and Mohammed
encompass various combinations of spirituality, revelation, and ultimate ethical principles that could, for themselves and their followers,
divest death of its sting of annihilation.

The basic spiritual principle, with or without a concept of afterlife
or immortal soul, is the ancient mythological theme of death and rebirth. One is offered the opportunity to be reborn into a timeless
realm of ultimate, death-transcending truths. In that realm one can
share the immortality of the deity, obtain membership in a sacred
community, or make a covenant with God. Or that ultimate realm
might take on the more concrete imagery of a heaven or of the negative
immortality of unending suffering in hell.

Whatever the imagery, a sense of spiritual *power* is at the heart of
religion. That power may be understood in a number of ways—
dedication, capacity to love, moral energy—but its final symbolic
meaning is life-power and power over death. In Japan, that power is
suggested by the word *kami*. Though often translated as "god,"
"gods," or "spirit," the eighteenth-century Shintō scholar Motoori
Norinaga, defined *kami* more precisely as "a thing or person . . . felt
to possess some superior quality or power." Many premodern societies
have similar words that convey a quality of spiritual power derived
from a supranatural source, such as the Polynesian *mana*. Possessing
or living under the protection of this power, rather than the concrete
idea of an afterlife, is the more universal aspect of religious experience.

Claims by priests to possess this power, and their political in-
stitutionalization of it, converts theology to theocracy. Monarchies in
particular, both Western and Eastern, tend to derive from such theocratic routes. The Japanese emperor system has been a particularly
striking modern theocratic phenomenon. By stressing the absolute di-
vinity of the emperor—his mythical descent from the sun
goddess—Meiji reformers managed to build institutions around the
emperor based not only on the imagery of biosocial immortality but
also on compelling theological patterns. Those governing in his name
could quite readily take on the totalist claim to the dispensation of
truth and of existence itself. To serve and revere the emperor-

centered state could then permit Japanese to share in an especially vivid sense of immortality derived from experiencing the entire nation as a "sacred community" with unlimited spiritual power.

The third mode of symbolic immortality is achieved through creative works and personal impact on others—whether through great works of art, literature, science, or more humble influences. The artist has long been recognized as participating in this mode of immortality through his prophetic function. Malraux especially emphasized the continuity of artistic creation as the means by which man reveals himself. And he concluded that "more than any other activity, art escapes death."

Similarly, in scientific work, one becomes part of an enterprise larger than oneself, limitless in its past and future continuity. In the Japanese cultural experience the sense of immortality through works tends to be collectively experienced; that is, immortality related more to one's group—whether scientific, artistic, literary, familial, or national—than to oneself as an individual.

The great historical transition from religion to science refers to a major shift in the imagery through which large numbers of people in general (not just scientists or theologians) experience their sense of the continuity of human existence. In terms of our psychological relationship to these two world views, the question lies not so much in their comparative virtues as in the extent to which the vitality of each gives way to a dogmatic literalism that limits feeling and suppresses imagination. These are critical issues for modern Japan, especially since its embrace of Western science beginning in the late nineteenth century.

The fourth mode of symbolic immortality is associated with nature itself: the perception that the natural environment around us—limitless in space and time—will remain, and that something of oneself remains part of it. This mode has been especially vivid in Japanese culture, steeped as it is in nature symbolism. George Sansom locates the earliest and most persistent object of Japanese religious feelings in "the forces of nature in their devine embodiments as gods of mountain and valley, field and stream, fire and water, rain and wind." In early Shintō belief, as in much animistic religion, supernatural gods emerge from and eventually retire to the trees, mountains, and rivers—the natural cosmos—where they are joined by immortal human souls. Survivors of Hiroshima, for example, struggling to absorb their holocaust and to reestablish their own sense of continuity, often quote the popular saying: "The state may collapse but the mountains and rivers remain." Indeed, immediately after the bomb fell, the most terrifying rumor that swept the city about the mysterious "poison" (radiation effects) was that trees, grass, and flowers would never again grow in Hiroshima. Its image of nature drying up altogether, life being extinguished at its source, represented an ultimate form of desolation that not only encompassed but went beyond human death.

The Japanese give their special cultural stamp to a pattern that is, of course, universal. A Western expression of the natural mode of immortality is the ideology of nineteenth-century European romanticism, which was carried over into such twentieth-century ideologies as the "return-to-nature" German youth movements (some of which blended all too readily with the murderous romanticism of Hitlerism). The American cult of the great outdoors has its roots both in Europe and in transcendent perceptions of the natural dimensions of the New World and the American Frontier. This mode of immortality is also articulated in the longstanding Anglo-Saxon preoccupation with vigorously confronting the infinite dimensions of nature and with more narrowly cultivating one's garden.

The assaults on nature by advanced industrial society—especially in Japan and the United States—both threaten our relationship to nature and awaken image-hungers within us. During the 1960s and 1970s, these hungers have been expressed in America in widespread return-to-nature impulses, both organized and informal, and in America and Japan in the surge of local, national, and international movements to protect the natural environment from further destruction. Even as our perceptions of nature change—to include outer space, the moon, other planets—we continue to seek in those perceptions an ultimate aspect of our existence.

The fifth mode differs from the others in that it depends solely on a psychic state. This mode of "experiential transcendence" is a state so intense that in it time and death disappear. When one achieves ecstasy or rapture, the restrictions of the senses—including the sense of mortality—no longer exist. Poetically and religiously this state has been described as "losing oneself," not only in religious or secular mysticism but also in song, dance, battle, sexual love, childbirth, athletic effort, mechanical flight, or in response to artistic or intellectual creations. The experience is characterized by extraordinary psychic unity and perceptual intensity. But there also occurs, as described in some drug experiences, a process of symbolic reordering: one feels oneself to be different after returning from the "high state." Experiential transcendence and its aftermath epitomize the death-and-rebirth experience. It is central to change or transformation and has great significance for psychotherapy. Experiential transcendence includes a feeling of what Mircea Eliade has called the "continuous present" that can be equated with eternity or with "mythical time" (p. 17). This continuous present is perceived not only as here-and-now but as inseparable from past and future.

Japanese culture has emphasized relatively quiet forms of experiential transcendence in a number of spiritual and physical disciplines. Zen, as well as martial arts *kendō* (Japanese fencing) and *kyūdō* (Japanese archery), stresses freeing the mind of extraneous thoughts so that it can achieve a pure state. That state permits one to achieve a quality of effortless concentration—an "alert passivity"—which can then be applied to a particular skill.

This form of quiet transcendence has been evoked over decades and centuries in Japanese art, literature, film, and psychological and cultural life in general. The acceptance of, and even pleasure in, sadness—the sadness of change, loss, and death—has to do with one's sense of being part of the cosmic and the eternal. This feeling has been expressed in different historical periods by various terms, such as *aware* ("beauty in sadness"), *hakanai* ("fragile" and "ephemeral"), and *akirame* ("resignation"). Death-tinged sadness—lovers parting, life ending, cherry blossoms falling—is inseparable from and actually evokes the larger life process as manifested by beauty.

In postulating such a grand-scale theory of symbolic immortality, we must also account for the everyday idea of death, expressing the senses of *mortality* that develops over the course of a lifetime. Although Freud's concept of the death instinct is confusing and perhaps even a contradiction in terms, it does contain a valuable insight: the suggestion of a unitary vision in which death is inseparable from the life process. That is, death is anticipated, and therefore influential, from the beginning of life. But an individual's representation of death evolves only gradually from dim and vague articulation in the inchoate imagery of the infant to sophisticated symbolization in maturity. Lifton proposes a theory of evolving imagery around three subparadigms or polarities to represent the elaboration of the inner idea of death from earliest childhood: connection-separation, integrity-disintegration, and movement-stasis.[2] *alienation   lack of integrity/wholeness*

— Very early images of separation, disintegration, and stasis are "death equivalents" that anticipate the actual idea of death. By the second or third year, death begins to achieve some kind of conscious meaning. By the age of three, four, and five, children are thinking and talking, however confusedly, about death and dying. During the next few years those thoughts consolidate, so that the idea of death is more fundamentally learned and understood. At every developmental level conflicts exacerbate, and are exacerbated by, the struggles around disintegration, stasis, or separation. These death-linked conflicts reach a climax during adolescence. At each stage, the quest is for images and forms more malleable and inwardly acceptable at the particular historical moment than those available from the past. As a young adult, one moves more fully into the realm of historical action and then connects with the modes of symbolic immortality.

In middle adulthood, one becomes more impressed with the fact that one will indeed die. It becomes apparent that the limitations of physiology and life span will not permit the full accomplishment of all one's projects. Old people approaching death look back nostalgically over their whole lives, in what is in part a process of self-judgment sometimes called the "life review." They examine their lives around issues of integrity, connection, and movement and search for evidence of relationship to modes of symbolic immortality. The dying person may ask, "Has my life been connected? Has my life had some significance? Has it had some ethical meaning that I can assert as I die?

---

2. The theoretical basis of the first polarity around connection and separation can serve as an example. The inchoate imagery in this case is expressed in a seeking of connection, what John Bowlby (1969) has described as "attachment behavior" around sucking, clinging, smiling, crying, and following. The organism actively seeks connection with the nurturing or mothering person. Initially this quest is mainly physiological. Later it is internalized in pictorial image formation, and finally it becomes highly symbolized. The organism's evolution is from simple movement toward the mother to a nurturing relationship with her and eventually toward connection with other people, with groups, with ideas, and with historical forces. Where this striving for connection fails, as it always must in some degree, the alternative image is of separation, of being cut off. This image of separation forms one precursor for the idea of death. In a similar way, the fear of annihilation or disintegration and the absence of movement become symbolic representations of death. Lifton (1976) develops these ideas of death imagery in more detail.

Has my life had movement or progress?" These issues concern all people, but they have special intensity particularly for those who have been leaders or leading thinkers in times of rapid social change, like the men we study in this volume.

The struggle to reassert oneself just before dying occurs not only on the immediate level of one's life, but also on the ultimate level of symbolic immortality: "Do I live on in my family through what I have been to them, or in my works, or in nature, even though I now die?" Someone who has an inner sense of larger connectedness, of symbolic immortality, tends to have a relatively greater capacity to accept death and comparatively less death anxiety.

The life-review process, the struggle to assert connectedness, and symbolic immortality are all related to self-completion. In dying one seeks to round off—to give a final form to—one's life. As we see in the case studies, these struggles for self-completion and symbolic immortality are critically bound to the way of dying.

One extreme way of giving form to one's death and one's life is through suicide. The classical Japanese way of ritual suicide or seppuku, a prescribed form of self-disembowelment for samurai, was performed in order to perpetuate individual and group honor and avoid disgrace. However "illogical" or unacceptable such ritual suicides appear to us now, their logic within the samurai cultural milieu of Tokugawa Japan was clear enough. Such actions by samurai reasserted symbolic coherence for generations of followers, thereby extending imagery of self and world beyond individual death. Japanese attitudes toward suicide, thus, have much to teach us about universal psychological principles around taking one's own life and about approaching death in general.

The emphasis in Japanese culture given to death as an event, at least for the elite, illustrates the connection between death and group as well as individual completion. A particular way of dying becomes a means of perpetuating important cultural principles, thereby contributing to survivors' sense of immortality through the biosocial and creative modes. The intensity of a death scene may also, in itself, convey powerful images of experiential transcendence. The process is less paradoxical than it seems, because it is again the survivors who are affected, often indelibly, by such imagery.

All forms of death, including suicide, have powerful psychological impact on survivors. The survivor may be defined as one who has come into contact with death in some bodily or psychic fashion but who remains alive. Our study emphasizes the psychology of the survivor and its intense significance for Japanese culture. But the survivor ethos is felt beyond Japan. It has been thrust into special prominence by the holocausts of the twentieth century, imposing on all of us a series of immersions into death that mark our existence.

In another sense, not only holocausts (whether actual or feared) but rapid social change, with its "deaths" of old ways of living, makes survivors of us all. The paradigm of death and continuity, especially the theory of symbolic immortality, thus can contribute to a concept of historical change. If historical shifts are understood as alterations in the cultural stress given to one mode or a combination of modes, the general flow of history can be understood as the struggle of various collectivities to achieve, maintain, and reaffirm a sense of immortality under changing conditions. The Darwinian revolution of the nineteenth century, for example, entailed a shift from a predominantly theological mode to a more natural and biological one. The continuous transformation in China over the last few decades has involved a shift from a family-centered biological mode to a revolutionary mode that emphasizes human works but also includes elements of other modes and a periodic resurgence of experiential transcendence.

Two Japanese historical moments of dislocation and change are of special concern to us. The first is the Meiji period (1868–1912), when Japan moved from a relatively limited biological and biosocial (family and clan) mode to a much more inclusive focus on Japanese nation and culture, while radically extending its scope to encompass various Western influences. The other historical moment is the post–Second World War confusion, with its undermining or at least weakening of virtually all forms of symbolic immortality among the Japanese, especially emperor-centered cultural chauvinism and deification of various political-national institutions. In these two areas of transition, we direct considerable attention to diverging responses to cultural confrontation between Japan and the outside world. We chose our six subjects with these transitions in mind. We believe that their inner experiences have importance for other historical transitions, especially those of non-Western nations struggling to cope with the West.

In addition to the broader psychological patterns that influence Japanese attitudes toward death, we must also consider more particular social and historical factors. The six men we study in this book all belonged to the elite of modern Japan. Before examining them individually, we need some understanding of the differences and similarities in the elite and common Japanese world views. These characteristics can then be related to the major traits of modern Japanese attitudes toward death. This approach will help us locate the life and death struggles of the six men within larger social and cultural patterns, guiding us in our larger task to unravel the ways their struggles are both universal and Japanese.

Elite attitudes toward life and death differ from those of the the common people in two ways. First, the elite formulate their attitudes more consciously and usually more intellectually, which suggests that they generally place more stress on self-control and make greater use of a general framework based on an ideological or religious system. For example, in early Meiji, the relationship of former samurai with *bushidō*, the Tokugawa warrior ideology, was significantly different from that of the rest of society. Of the 400,000 members of the old samurai class (under 10 percent of the national population), less than 1 percent retained elite status in Meiji Japan. This segment of the elite felt the most intense personal identification with samurai culture. And this intensity made them special.

Similarly, only a small segment of the Japanese elite has maintained a deep and steadfast commitment to universalistic ideological systems. In a group-oriented society like Japan's, an individual who adheres to an ideological system that differs from the group's values is subjected to both explicit and subtle pressures in daily life. In extreme cases, the individual may be expelled from the group. Under such conditions, the elite most often possesses the luxury of rejecting compromises with the group, committing itself to an ideology, and living on the margin of society. Most intellectuals, however, accept the dominant ideological positions of society. For example, only a few intellectuals in Japan—mostly Christians and socialists—opposed the Russo-Japanese War and only a few protested the rise in ultranationalism from the late 1920s on and the Pacific War that followed—and they were primarily Christians and Communists who retained their beliefs in prison. They resemble those Americans who did not yield to McCarthyism in the late 1950s. Thus, at the end of the nineteenth century and beginning of the twentieth century, Protestantism and Marxism in Japan were almost exclusively espoused by the intellectuals and ignored by the common people. Even today the number of Japanese Christians, including both Protestants and Catholics, is less than 1 percent of the population.

The second difference between the elite and the mass world views arises from contrasting relationships to history. The elite, by definition, occupy positions of leadership and can directly influence at least some groups in society. As a result, the elite may feel a strong sense of responsibility for society, but they also can abuse the power of their social positions. Compared with the common people, the elite are more polarized in their relationship to political power. They tend either to be closely associated with or diametrically opposed to the government.

In the early Meiji era, for example, most Japanese were not committed either to the new government or the ancien régime. The elite, mostly former samurai, by contrast tended to take a stand for or against the Meiji oligarchy—hence the host of intellectuals in the imperial government on one hand and the promoters of "freedom and people's rights" in a formidable opposition to the Meiji state on the other. The attitude toward power profoundly affected each individual's life. In our study of these six men, we consider their different distances from the center of power as a decisive factor in their value orientations: whether and to what degree they were an insider or outsider of the political, economic, and cultural establishment. To be or not to be a "watchdog," as Paul Nizan remarked, is important not only for history but also for the individual psychologically.

Despite these differences, the elite share a set of values with the rest of society. In modern Japan, the world view held by the elite and common people was received from the secularized Tokugawa culture and might be described as a collectivity-oriented this-worldliness. This world view fundamentally distinguishes modern Japanese culture from individualistic monotheistic Western culture, especially the modern individualistic Protestant bourgeois culture of Europe and North America.

This shared framework between the elite and the masses has been supported by a number of factors in Japan's historical development during the last hundred years. First, the elite tend to have nonelite family origins, creating large areas of shared cultural patterns. This tendency clearly depends on the degree to which institutions of higher learning have been directed at and open to the common people. In this respect, Meiji Japan's educational system was more successful than prewar Britain's. As a result, leading figures in Japan's political, business, and cultural elite came from various social classes.

Japan's handling of foreign cultures has also helped control a divisive element. In general, when the elite are educated abroad, the cultural distance between them and the common people living in traditional culture widens, even with the literacy rate is high. Like colonial India, Japan in the early Meiji period experienced a widening of the cultural gap between elite and common people. But in Japan, the differences between the westernized elite and the traditional common people were reduced by the relatively high educational level of the people even before the Meiji period and by the rapid decrease in the relative importance of studies abroad for the elite.

Another factor accounting for the shared culture has been the degree to which elite values have been imposed on and accepted by the common people. In modern Japan, this ideological education was carried out by the efficient universal education system and the obligatory prewar military service for men. Since the elimination of the army, this function has been taken over by the powerful mass media. In addition to increasing the educational level of the common people, these systems have also become means for effectively manipulating Japan's homogeneous and group-oriented society. Although the values of the Tokugawa samurai class, such as self-control, were never completely internalized, the common people more or less accepted these values as moral goals. The rapid disappearance of Edo *chōnin* or townspeople's culture in Meiji resulted not only from the expansion of social mobility and the influence of Western culture but more important, from the imposition of cultural heritage from the samurai class.[3] At the end of the Tokugawa period samurai were increasingly influenced by chōnin; whereas in the Meiji period, the urban middle-class was educated with values inherited from the samurai class. The distance between the two necessarily decreased.

Finally, some members of the elite actively sought to reduce the distance between themselves and the common people. Some intellectu-

3. Edo was the city of the shogunate, or military government, during the Tokugawa period, and the political center of Japan. After the Meiji Restoration in 1868, it was renamed Tokyo (literally, "eastern capital").

als, for example, sought to strengthen the connections between the two groups through intellectual or artistic efforts or more directly through joint political or social activities. Such intellectuals have existed throughout world history, ranging from Michelet to Zola, from Dickens to Bernard Shaw, from Dostoyevsky to the Russian *v narod* ("to the people") movement in the 1870s. In Japan as well, a similar group of intellectuals arose from the late nineteenth to the mid-twentieth centuries. Among the six men studied here, Nakae Chōmin exemplifies this pattern.

In modern Japanese society, the characteristics of the elite and common people overlap significantly. The traits shared with the common people shaped important themes in the lives of each of these six men. Within the ways they approached life and death, we can discern different arrangements of elite and mass views. These factors help us grasp how "representative," and of what, these six men are.

In the shared world view, collectivity-orientation and this-worldliness are closely interrelated. Indeed, the direct group to which the individual in Japan belongs concretely expresses the ultimate reality of this-worldliness. The individual is usually highly integrated into such groups, which are often defined by territorial or employment boundaries. Although members of the group intensely compete for advancement, group harmony ultimately takes precedence over individual beliefs and goals. The boundaries of the group are usually quite strict, separating members from nonmembers and contributing to acute intergroup competition. Psychologically, the group provides the individual with a sense of security but also creates a sense of oppression that can lead to a desire to escape.

The emphasis on group orientation in Japan also tends to impede the individual's adoption of values that transcend the group. Thus, the belief in abstract and holistic religious and nonreligious ideological systems has not been widespread in Japan. We can see this tension between identification with a particular group and belief in group-transcending principles in our case studies. Three men held no religious beliefs and supported no metaphysical system, thereby sharing with their contemporary society a strong sense of this-worldliness. The other three struggled in various ways with religious or metaphysical systems.

The relative weakness in Japan of a commitment to values that transcend the group may explain difficulties in creating utopian ideas and producing fundamental social transformations. Defining an ideal future society requires values that go beyond the existing society. Although this-worldliness is not necessarily equivalent to supporting the status quo, the paucity of utopian literature and the weakness of revolutionary ideas in modern Japan are certainly related to the dominant trend of this-worldliness. In sum, within a secular culture, the custom of not thinking of a future world after an individual's death and the pattern of not considering a future utopian society originate from the same root.

By stressing the present, the Japanese world view emphasizes concrete daily events and experiences. The past no longer exists and the future has yet to come. A sense of virtue is felt in the saying "The past is the past" (*Kako o mizu ni nagasu*), and a sense of plausibility in "Tomorrow blows tomorrow's wind" (*Asu wa asu no kaze ga fuku*). Time is not felt to possess a beginning and an end, but to be merely a succession of events extending from the present.

These perceptions of time are clearly reflected in the differences between Western and traditional Japanese art. Japanese short poems, for example, depend on catching the impressions of a single moment. Similarly, kabuki theater, which is composed of acts with independent meanings that are only weakly related to each other, relies on immediate impressions and sensitivities. And, as composer Takemitsu Tōru has pointed out, Japanese music is not constructed as a single continuous work but arises from each separate moment and the relationship between tones and pauses. This artistic sensibility, which depends on the relationship between semiautonomous moments, arises from a Japanese conception of time that still persists today.

The artistic perception of time closely resembles the Japanese approach to history. Maruyama Masao, the eminent postwar political theorist, has identified the tendency to perceive events as occurring one after the other as a characteristic of "the Japanese historical consciousness." This suggests that the concept of continuity in Japan may have a different meaning from the modern Western idea of continuity as the experience of structured time. For Japanese, the continuity of the group is a given condition that is to be accepted and not a goal that one seeks to achieve. For modern, and especially urban, Westerners, the symbolic continuity of one's personal existence is not a given condition but is consciously recognized as a central goal that must be achieved through personal efforts. This contrast is similar to

Maruyama's distinction between history as "man-made" (*tsukurubeki rekishi*) and history as a "flow of events beyond individual influence" (*nariyuku rekishi*).

Modern Japanese attitudes toward death and life are thus embodied in a world view that stresses an orientation toward the collectivity and toward this-worldliness. That world view has continued almost unchanged since the Tokugawa period in rural areas and is probably shared by most of the urban population as well.

Two characteristics of approaching death in Japan relate to its world view and social patterns—the importance of "dying well," especially as defined by one's membership in a particular group, and the Japanese notion of the cosmos and how it influences attitudes toward death. We suggest that death in Japan is less an individual event than an occurrence within the group or community, and that death and dead people have a certain familiarity in daily life. Death thus appears as a very human process, into which a transcendental, absolute agent does not intervene. These aspects are related to a general awareness of being part of both the group and the cosmos at the time of death.

Initially, these approaches to death seem strikingly different, at least from modern Western society. But this difference is not necessarily caused by conditions unique to Japan. Indeed, discounting certain minor differences, Japanese attitudes reflect traditional Chinese feelings about death. Moreover, both characteristics—death as an occurrence in the community and its familiarity—could be applied directly to Philippe Ariès's description of European society during the Middle Ages.

The existence of these general patterns in other societies, however, by no means implies that they are expressed in similar cultural forms. For example, one phenomenon that is almost nonexistent in Western as well as Chinese culture is the Japanese "family suicide" (*ikka shinjū*). This style of dying still occurs frequently in Japan, illustrating how closely Japanese relate the image of death to the small group, especially the family. Thus, similar underlying approaches to death can give rise to radically different cultural forms of dying.

In Japan, death as an occurrence within the group or community is related to a particular kind of collectivity-orientation. Death signifies a change in status from one position to another within such Japanese communities as the family or village but not an expulsion from the group. In this sense, because one remains within the security of the community, death might be considered less severe than ostracism.

The high integration of the individual into the group also influences attitudes toward death. In societies that stress the priority of the group over the individual—such as most military groups and modern Japanese society (at least in comparison with modern Western society)—people tend to have less resistance to death than in more individualistic societies.

Such community orientation, however, places restrictions on dying. One must "die well," in a way that does not harm the interests of the community or violate its rules. Since the Tokugawa period, the ritual rules for death have mostly been derived from Buddhism. Except for unusual circumstances and special groups, according to these rituals, "dying well" has generally meant dying quietly and not dramatically.

The most important special group with its own rules for dying is the Tokugawa samurai. Like groups of warriors in all societies and cultures, samurai had to be prepared for death. But during the peaceful Tokugawa period, samurai readiness to die a warrior's death on the battlefield was transformed into a way of assuming responsibility for one's offenses to the community, as preparedness to commit suicide. In short, suicide became a sophisticated instrument of social control.

The most ritualistic form of samurai suicide, which demanded extreme self-control, was seppuku. This extraordinarily complex ritual system used what was often coerced suicide to ensure a high degree of socialization and to reintegrate the dying person into the group. From the samurai's perspective, seppuku symbolized the ultimate level of individual self-control, rather than the breakdown of the individual. By taking hold of death through ritual suicide, the samurai also took hold of life. But because seppuku fulfilled one's responsibilities as defined by the group, it strengthened both the structure and the rules of the community.

In general, ruling groups seek to impose parts of their values and behavior patterns on those they rule. The concept of dying well, for example, was spread through the common people during the Tokugawa period. And after the Meiji Restoration, the mass educational and military systems contributed to its further spread. We must stress, however, that it was not the *form* of seppuku that was popularly accepted, but rather the motivation for and the consequences of suicide for the group. Indeed, seppuku has been an extremely rare form of suicide in modern Japan. Although a tiny number of soldiers committed seppuku in 1945, in the ensuing thirty-three years Mishima's death in 1970 is the only generally known case. What has persisted into modern Japanese culture are the customs of "apologizing by dying" and of committing suicide to resolve what is perceived as an otherwise unresolvable situation, as we discuss further in chapter 8. Even today suicide is used to maintain order within a small group. This type of suicide is an example of taking hold of death without following a carefully articulated, prescribed ritual like seppuku.

Suicide in Japan today thus seems more plausible than in the West, although the vast majority of suicides in Japan as elsewhere probably results from serious psychological disturbance. Yet suicide in present-day Japan is not usually considered "bad," and rarely "evil" as it has been in the West. Japanese society retains an evaluation of suicide as "good," or at least acceptable, especially when used to take social responsibility for one's acts.

Quantitatively, Japan's suicide rate is not that different from other advanced industrial nations. According to the latest World Health Organization statistics, Japan belonged to the middle range of developed countries, with a suicide rate of 18.0 per 100,000 persons, close to the French rate of 15.6 but lower than Denmark's (26.0) and Germany's and higher than America's (12.1).[4] The Japanese patterns of a gradually increasing incidence of suicide with age, and of differences between male and female and married and unmarried, resemble the patterns of other countries. But the rate of suicide for those between twenty and twenty-five is higher in Japan, and there is a relatively narrower difference in rates between the sexes.

For many Japanese, the sense of belonging to the group at death is accompanied by a feeling of dying into the cosmos. This "cosmos" encompasses not only the physical world but all living things as well as the souls of the dead (kami). Although not personalized, the cosmos is harmonious; and although not always a place of happiness, it at least is not a place of tragedy. For it does not distinguish between righteous and unrighteous, between moral rights and wrongs, or between classes. The Japanese conception of the cosmos resembles what eighteenth-century Shintōist Motoori Norinaga called "the way of the gods," but not as anthropocentric (see Earl, pp. 68–72); or what Westerners think of as Mother Earth, but not as concrete; or what the Chinese call "heavenly nature," but not as rational.

4. The Japanese statistic is for 1975, all others are 1974.

The dominant Japanese image of what happens at death is that one "enters" the "cosmos," stays there for a time, and then gradually fades away and disappears. For example, the Japanese have long celebrated the annual Festival of the Dead (*bon*) within a Buddhist ritualistic vocabulary to express their respect for ancestors. When a family member dies, the soul remains nearby in an unspecified place, and once a year, at the Festival of the Dead, returns to the family butsudan or home shrine. Thus, both before birth and after death the human soul belongs to the same group, in this case the family. But after a set period that relationship weakens. Thirty-two years after death, the dead soul (*shisha*) merges with the community of spirits and becomes a kind of ancestor god (*kami*). Thus the systematized close relationship between the living and the dead usually lasts less than two generations. Although the bon certainly expresses a popular desire for some sense of continuity after death (or symbolic immortality in the biological, natural, and religious mode), that continuity is neither eternal nor absolute as in Christianity and in certain Buddhist sects.

The sense of living in the cosmos thus becomes a sense of dying into the cosmos. If the space in which the soul of the dead person momentarily rests may be called the cosmos, then it can be seen as representing an idealized reflection of the actual small group. The cosmos is created by preserving the harmony and security of the small group but eliminating the competition, class struggle, and confinement with its desire to escape. And because the cosmos eliminates individual differences and includes no transcendental agent, there can be no last judgment after death. No one goes to heaven just as no one goes to hell. Most of the elite share with the common people this sense of the cosmos and its associated disinterest in religion. And when both approach religion, they often alter the contents and style of the religion of alien origin, such as Buddhism, to fit the more deeply ingrained sentiments about the cosmos.

True, the Buddhist notion of a cause and effect concept of reward and punishment (*inga ōhō*) provides a kind of last judgment, performed by the Great King of Hell Emma. But in Japan (at least since the end of the Heian period in the late twelfth century), people believed that if the dying person is enough of a believer, then Amida, the Buddha of the Pure Land, and Jizō, the Bodhisattva patron of children, could relativize the sentence and save anyone. Then, during the Tokugawa period, the secularization of popular culture largely removed the remaining images of judgment and hell from the popular Buddhist world view, enforcing the belief that Amida could save anyone. In other words, Amida become nothing more than one form of the personification of the cosmos. As a result, only the "cause and effect" remained from the cause and effect concept of reward and punishment, and even that gradually became equivalent to a vague sense of "destiny." Because destiny is an uncontrollable factor in human life, this concept contributed to a tendency among the common people to accept the situation in the world and especially the concrete structure of groups. Thus in the Buddhist world of the Tokugawa period, the acceptance of the social structure and the acceptance of death, both based on a sense of resignation (*akirame*), existed together as mutually reinforcing.

Buddhism also provided the Japanese common people with another concept about death—impermanence (*mujō*). The Buddhist notion of impermanence is not simply that human life is short, an idea that has been expressed in nearly every human society since the time of Gilgamesh, but functioned in two particular ways. By saying that not only man but all objects in nature and culture are constantly changing, the concept relativized human death and attenuated its impact. And because impermanence can exist only by denying permanence, it required accepting the premise of the permanence of the cosmos. Though highly scholastic speculative Buddhist philosophy does not necessarily accept this premise, it does hold at least for the popularized concept of impermanence.

The cosmos, also, however, symbolizes the experiences of the community. The continuity of the cosmos, while all things within it change, thus represents the continuity of the community, despite the death (and resulting changes) of an individual member. Thus, while in Western modern societies the death of the individual is paramount, in Japan the perceived immortality of the group is dominant and symbolically relativizes the death of the individual.

During the Tokugawa period the elite were influenced by the Neo-Confucian world view, which consciously rationalized the sense of the cosmos contained in the preexisting Shintōist world view. Neo-Confucianism also gave ancestor worship a central position and completely lacked a concept of a last judgment. The differences between the elite and popular views of death and life appeared mainly as differences between the vocabularies of Neo-Confucianism and popular Buddhism—both systems of thought shared a fundamental sense of the cosmos that has persisted basically unchanged into modern Japan.

Thus, one important characteristic of modern Japanese people is a relatively weak consciousness of symbolic immortality for the individual and a generally less conscious sense of permanence or endless life. In fact, we can identify all the various modes of symbolic immortality within Japanese culture. The relative weakness of individually centered symbolic immortality compared with Western culture is mainly a difference in degree. But this difference in degree, in our view, derives from fundamental contrasts between Japanese and Western cultures, as reflected in their art and sense of history.

Another general aspect of the Japanese attitude toward death is its resigned acceptance of the cosmic order at the emotional level and of the natural order at the intellectual level. This attitude emerges from a culture that did not stress the separation between death and daily life, or the cruelty of death, or the dramatic, extraordinary aspects of death. The final result of this acceptance with resignation is manifested as a calm self-control or a carefully arranged plan. But that interpretation is not correct for the vast majority of Japanese deaths. In most cases, death looms suddenly before the individual's eyes. As a ninth-century poet wrote, "I knew I had to go this way, but I did not think it was so soon." What is gradually produced is not preparation for death, but a sense of resignation. And it is not self-control that makes resignation possible, but the sense of resignation that makes self-control possible.

The elite, however, generally seek to take hold of death with their own hands to ensure the meaning and purpose of their life. Elite deaths thus tend to be highly individualized. Reasons for the tendency to individualization are undoubtedly complex, but in general derive from a need to overcome conflicts resulting from internalized social changes and to achieve a sense of personal integrity. At the same time, in a way similar to the samurai elite, the self-control they show toward their individualized deaths depends on a sense of resignation. In other words, the resignation that is transformed into passivity among the common people is the basis for the self-control and activity among the elite.

Since the Second World War and the occupation, however, Japanese society has been permeated by Western images, while the social structure has changed as a result of a concentration of population in urban areas, the atomization of city life, and the diminishing integrative power of traditional small groups, especially the family. These factors have not changed the importance of the sense of belonging within the Japanese value orientation, but they have changed attitudes toward the death of a member of nonfamilial groups. The community now takes less care of the dying person, and the fear of death has increased. Death for Japanese has become increasingly traumatic and more separated from daily life.

Most Japanese today thus seem to have moved in their personal approach to death from an existence within a particular group (especially the family) to a reliance on the cosmos. This assessment is based on materials we do not use directly in this book—the wills, diaries, interviews, and conversations with Japanese of various social classes both during and after the Second World War. For example, when someone says, "I don't believe in religion, but I have a religious feeling," "religion" refers to the teachings of a particular religion, while the "religious feeling" refers to what we call the sense of belonging to the cosmos.

The six men we have studied are in ways very modern. Though they achieved much, it is achievement at a cost, midst dislocation, accompanied by pain. We believe there is much to learn from them about certain elusive questions having to do with the way individual men die and live, with their continual struggle to maintain and extend essential connections beyond the self. Their lives instruct us in the special duress we all experience during times of change and in the paradoxical conflicts that never cease to define the human condition.

2 / NOGI MARESUKE (1849–1912)

The Emperor's Samurai

Nogi Maresuke

FROM THE WRITINGS OF NOGI MARESUKE

Death Poems

The light of god shines no longer,
The Great Lord's memory is revered all the more.
— Nogi Maresuke

The god departs from this world,
The Great Lord's memory I know and follow.
— Nogi Maresuke

Departing there is no day of return,
Hearing the ceremonial promenade there is no meeting.
— Nogi Shizuko, the wife of Maresuke

(Ohama, *Nogi Maresuke*, p. 192)

Complete Testament of Nogi Maresuke

1. On this occasion of the passing of Emperor Meiji, I am filled with remorse and have decided to commit suicide. I am aware of the gravity of this crime. Nonetheless, since I lost the regimental colors in the battle of 1877, I have searched in vain for an opportunity to die. To this day I have been treated with unmerited kindness, receiving abundant imperial favors. Gradually I have become old and weak; my time has disappeared and I can no longer serve my lord. Feeling extremely distressed by his death, I have resolved to end my life.

2. After my two sons died in battle, my seniors and friends constantly urged that I adopt an heir. Since ancient times, however, the difficulties of adopted heirs have been discussed, and there are many examples, in addition to the case of Nogi Taiken. If I still had a child of my own, the honor of having received a noble title would force me to name him my successor, but to avoid leaving behind a possible disgrace I think it is best not to defy heaven's order by adopting a son. The tombs of my ancestors should be cared for by relatives, as long as they are related by blood. I request that the Shinsaka residence be donated either to the ward or to the city.

3. I have written separately about the distribution of my property. My wife, Shizuko, will manage all matters I have not mentioned.

4. I ask Captain Tsukada to choose appropriate military articles from my belongings—such as my watch, tapemeasure, telescope, riding equipment, and sabers—and distribute them in my memory to my staff in the army. The captain's efforts in two consecutive wars were monumental. Shizuko is already in-

31

formed of this distribution so please discuss it with her. I leave my other posses-sions open to negotiation.

5. Gifts from the emperor (and from other members of the imperial family), as well as various articles with the imperial family crest, should be collected and presented to the Peers School. I ask Mr. Matsui and Mr. Igaya to deal with this matter.

6. Present the Peers School those of my books which it can use and give the rest to the Library of Chōfu. Those which are useless may be disposed of in any fashion.

7. The writings of my father, grandfather, and great-grandfather should be considered part of the history of the Nogi family. They should be strictly col-lected, excluding any truly unnecessary works, and placed for eternity either in the hands of Marquis Sasaki or in the Sasaki Shrine.

8. I bequeath the exhibit of my belongings in their present condition to the Army Exhibition Hall.[1] This, I believe, is the best way to preserve it in com-memoration of the Nogi family.

9. As Shizuko gradually enters old age and encounters episodes of illness, the house of Ishibayashi, in addition to being inconvenient, will be very depressing. Therefore, this house should be be given to Shūsaku and Shizuko has agreed that she should live in the Nakano house.[2] I leave the house and land in Nakano entirely in Shizuko's hands.

10. I requested that Baron Ishiguro attend to matters related to my corpse. The body should be donated to an appropriate medical school. It is enough to place my hair and teeth (false teeth included) beneath the gravestone. (Shizuko take note.) I requested that my gold watch with the imperial gift inscription be presented to Tamaki Masayuki. I forbid him to carry this watch when not wearing military uniform.

All the detailed matters not mentioned above are to be taken care of by Shizuko. During the lifetime of Shizuko the name of the house of Count Nogi shall be honored; and when her life is finished, the goal of extinction of the Nogi line shall be accomplished.

to Yuji Sadamoto   Taishō First Year
   Odate Shūsaku   September 12, Evening
   Tamaki Masayuki   Maresuke
   Shizuko

Ohama, *Nogi Maresuke*, pp. 193–94

1. The exhibit included the sword, lance, and armor that Nogi had received from Lord Mōri of Chōshū.
2. Odate Shūsaku (1866–1927) was Nogi's younger brother.

On the evening of September 12, 1912, General Nogi Maresuke, the popular hero of the Russo-Japanese War, wrote his last will and testament. The next day was important in Japanese history—the imperial funeral cermony for Emperor Meiji, the nation's first sovereign of the modern era. Nogi dressed that morning in full military uniform and posed for a formal photograph with his wife Shizuko. The general then visited the Imperial Palace to pay his last respects and returned home to lunch with his wife and her elderly sister. It was already late in the afternoon when Nogi and Shizuko retired to their living quarters, two traditional tatami-mat rooms on the second floor of their home in the well-to-do Akasaka section of Tokyo.

In a room downstairs, Shizuko's sister sat waiting. It seemed odd to her that the general was not attending the funeral proceedings. He was still upstairs with his wife at eight o'clock, just after sundown, when the first cannon shot signaled the departure of the imperial hearse and the final passage of Emperor Meiji through the palace gates. Soon after, the sister heard a strange noise from the second floor. The maid ran to check on her master, but the door to the living quarters was locked. From within came a pained but incomprehensible voice. The elderly sister immediately telephoned the local police station, but its line was busy. The neighborhood doctor was also unreachable. Finally, by chance, a passing policeman from Nagano prefecture, specially assigned to Tokyo for the imperial funeral, responded to the maid's agitated calls and entered the Nogi compound to investigate. Minutes later he forced open the fastened door and inside discovered General Nogi lying on his side in a pool of blood and Shizuko kneeling with her forehead on the floor. They had been dead for less than an hour. By nine o'clock, Dr. Iwata Bonpei of the Metropolitan Police Headquarters had arrived and was exhaustively recording the details of the room and the corpses. He confirmed that the deaths were suicide by sword.

Nogi and his wife had committed *junshi*, suicide in which a vassal follows his lord into death, according to the formal samurai ritual of self-immolation known as *seppuku*, literally "slitting the abdomen." The general scrupulously prepared and carried out his suicide plans. As an extra precaution, he apparently dismissed for the day a stable boy and a young male servant, both part of the Nogi household. Nogi and Shizuko, once in their rooms, gathered photographs of the emperor, their two deceased sons, and Nogi's parents. The general wore

33

his imperial army dress uniform and Shizuko donned a formal traditional kimono. The death toll of the funeral cannon ended Nogi's
wait. Kneeling, he removed his jacket and unsheathed his sword. The
general then unbuttoned his military trousers, lifted his undershirt,
and sliced his abdomen three times with the razor-sharp blade. After
carefully rebuttoning his trousers, Nogi placed the long military
sword between his knees, point up. In a final death lunge, he threw
himself on the sword's tip, jabbing it through his neck and severing his
left carotid artery. Nogi died instantly as his red blood spurted over
the tatami mats. At some time in this process, Shizuko drew her short
dagger, a weapon traditionally carried for self-protection by the wife
of a samurai, and stabbed herself several times above the heart, probably dying in agony.[3]

Even before the imperial funeral ceremonies were finished, rumors
began to spread that Nogi and his wife had committed junshi. Newspaper headlines the following morning substantiated the reports. The
front page of the *Asahi shinbun* declared in bold characters: "General
Nogi and Wife Commit Suicide Together; As Imperial Cannons
Explode They Commit Junshi." Because the government did not
make public all the details of Nogi's suicide, newspaper stories were
partially contradictory. But even without a full official disclosure, the
public reacted to the junshi with enormous emotion and controversy.
Some considered the act an anachronism because junshi had been out-
lawed for more than two and a half centuries.[4] But the majority of the
Japanese people and most of the press praised Nogi's ritual death as
the supreme glorification of his absolute loyalty to the emperor. This
day of junshi began the new myth of Nogi Maresuke, one of the key
folk heroes of pre-1945 imperial Japan.

Nogi's death marked the end of a transitional era for Japan. During
the Meiji period, Japanese leaders renounced Tokugawa isolationism
and set out systematically to establish the foundations of a modern
state. They abandoned old customs and adopted new systems, producing waves of social upheaval. The imperial institution played a key
role in this process. Nearly all members of the elite shifted their loy-

3. When Nogi composed his testament he evidently was unaware of his wife's intention to commit sucide with him.

4. The Tokugawa regime made junshi illegal in the mid-seventeenth century as
part of its efforts to curb samurai loyalty to the local lord and strengthen central control, especially over outlying domains.

alty from feudal lords to the emperor, and many identified with the sovereign as a person. Although some samurai violently opposed the Meiji government, claiming that it was not following the emperor's true will their opposition was either suppressed or institutionalized and absorbed. Thus by the early twentieth century, toward the end of the Meiji period, the general public and the elite had come to regard Emperor Meiji as the symbol of the nation's emergence as a military and industrial power.

Nogi personified both the pride and the pain of Meiji Japan. Publicly, he represented the nation's triumphant chauvinism and military expansionism resulting from a combination of Japanese spirit and Western technology (*wakon yōsai*). Privately, he typified the often bitter individual struggles of adjusting to rapid changes in social values. His personal drama arose largely from difficulties in playing the roles expected of him by his family, his clan, and his state. He was pressed first to become a samurai, against his own inclinations, then to become an imperial army officer, against his samurai ideals. Parts of that drama are still being reenacted by individuals struggling against the overwhelming forces of group integration in Japanese society.

The event of Nogi's death—his way of resolving his personal conflicts—took on a mythic dimension in Japanese society. His suicide merged personal and historical dimensions. Yet Nogi was the exceptional case. In the death of Emperor Meiji on July 30, 1912, most Japanese saw the end of an era; Nogi saw the end of his life.

In 1849, during the late Tokugawa period, Nogi Maresuke was born as the eldest son of a samurai family.[5] His father, Nogi Maretsugu, was a samurai official serving the long-established and powerful Mōri clan from Chōshū, a feudal domain (*han*) at the western tip of the main island of Honshū. Chōshū, in turn, was subordinate to the Tokugawa shogunate (central feudal authorities) which had ruled Japan since the early seventeenth century, when the great military leader Tokugawa Ieyasu subdued the numerous clans and established a hegemony centered in the capital city of Edo. Ieyasu's authority as shogun was legiti-

5. Nogi used other given names in his youth and adopted Maresuke in 1871 at the age of twenty-two. For simplicity we refer to him in youth as Maresuke and in adulthood as Nogi. After the Russo-Japanese War, the general achieved the status of a living folk hero and was popularly called Nogi-san, ("Mr. Nogi"), which is more intimate than Nogi or General Nogi.

mated by the emperor. He instituted the double-layered Tokugawa
baku-han political system that survived for two hundred and fifty
years. It was a semicentralized feudal structure that effectively bound
the domain to the shogunate through political, military, and economic
measures and by splitting the samurai's loyalty between his immediate
group in the domain and the greater group under the shogun. Chōshū,
nonetheless, managed to maintain some autonomy from the shogunate's control because of its distance from Edo, its relative economic
strength in both farming and trade, and its traditional enmity toward
the Tokugawa clan. This autonomy was crucial in the mid-nineteenth
century in allowing Chōshū, supported by other outlying domains, to
play a central role in upsetting the balance of the Tokugawa system
and ultimately in contributing to its destruction.

As a child Maresuke was immersed in the elite environment of the
samurai, those who ruled the three other classes of Tokugawa
society—the farmers, the artisans, and the merchants. One of the
primary symbols of his samurai childhood, with both real and mystical meanings, was the sword. These powerful instruments of death
against others and against self were characterized by superb
craftsmanship, highly developed technology, and legendary strength.
The same sword was often used for centuries, passed down through
generations of warriors in a samurai family, thus symbolizing the continuity of tradition and of family. In the Tokugawa period in particular, the sword distinguished the samurai class from all others. In the
late sixteenth century, just after the brilliant general Toyotomi
Hideyoshi unified Japan's warring clans, he conducted a "sword hunt"
and confiscated all peasants' weapons. Thereafter only samurai were
permitted to own and carry swords.

In addition to enhancing the samurai's power and authority, the
sword also symbolized the boy's passage into manhood. Between the
ages of thirteen and fifteen, the son of a samurai, who had previously
been allowed to wear only the medium-sized *wakizashi*, was presented
with his *katana*, a long sword. From then on he would display both
weapons. Maresuke, who was born just before the end of the Tokugawa period, was in the last generation of Japanese samurai children
fully imbued with the mystical symbol of the samurai sword.

It is important to remember that the samurai concept instilled in
Nogi was that of the Tokugawa period, of warriors in peacetime. During the two hundred and fifty years of Tokugawa rule, the social role
of samurai had changed radically from warrior to bureaucrats. Their

qualifications were expressed in the word coined and popularized in the Tokugawa period to designate the "way of the samurai": *bushidō*. This highly moralistic system of thought embodying the samurai ideal stressed absolute loyalty to the feudal lord and demanded the cultivation of such virtues as will power, courage, and honor. The samurai's ultimate act of self-discipline and duty to his lord was idealized in the ritual suicide of seppuku. By slitting open his abdomen and exposing his intestines, the warrior proved his sincerity and purity.

Tokugawa bushidō, however, supplied no practical instructions on how to win battles and no detailed prescriptions of strategy or tactics in war. This differed markedly from the teachings for sixteenth-century samurai, who spent much of their time fighting in civil wars. Indeed, the books and papers written on bushido during the Tokugawa period were increasingly designed for administration and not for battle. The martial arts were practiced to cultivate personal values rather than to win an individual duel by sword. Even battles were considered occasions to prove absolute loyalty to the lord rather than opportunities to destroy the enemy. In this framework, the samurai sword became almost exclusively a ritual object, since most samurai were simply armed bureaucrats. As a semireligious symbol of status in Tokugawa society, the samurai's sword required proper treatment— its cleaning, when and where and how it could be worn, who could touch it, were all strictly regulated.

Tokugawa bushidō permeated Nogi's childhood surroundings. From adolescence on, he strove to prove the strength and sincerity of his samurai convictions. In adulthood, he fervently preached samurai values, emphasizing the moralistic aspects of a soldier's life. When a general in the imperial army, he recalled the principles of bushidō as the basis of his childhood education and as a personal religion replacing Buddhism or Christianity. Adherence to bushidō values provided Nogi and many other samurai in the Meiji period with a sense of cultural continuity and integrity that helped counter the threat of disintegration posed by the impact of Western ideas. But Nogi came to advocate the samurai ideal of Tokugawa bushidō as a type of ideological totalism (see Lifton, 1961, especially chapter 22). His total commitment to it, and his rigid insistence on a complete return to a "pure" Japanese spirit, blocked the pragmatic use of Western technology. And his disregard for military strategy in modern warfare had disastrous consequences.

As a young boy, however, Maresuke resisted efforts by society in general and by his father in particular to mold him into a samurai. He was physically weak and shy, in sharp contrast to his younger brother, Makoto, who was much larger and more aggressive. Maresuke often played with his sisters and preferred reading books to fighting. His father, an expert in the martial arts, was disgusted by the literary interests and passivity of his first son and heir. With the full support of his wife, Maretsugu imposed especially harsh discipline to correct the boy's intolerable weaknesses and turn him into a true samurai. To inculcate the proper samurai spirit, Maretsugu undoubtedly related the famous story of the *Akō Gishi*, a tale of forty-seven "righteous samurai" in the early eighteenth century who avenged the death of their lord, Asano Naganori of Akō, by killing the samurai official responsible after decades of dedicated preparation, hardship, and dissimulation.[6] The forty-seven *rōnin*, or masterless samurai, then committed mass seppuku. This story could have produced an especially lasting imprint on Nogi, since ten of the Akō samurai had committed seppuku in the Edo residence of the Mōri clan, Maresuke's home during the first nine years of his life.

Maresuke's formal education from the age of six, in accordance with his status as the son of a Tokugawa samurai-bureaucrat, covered both literary and military arts. His training gained further importance and rigor because he was the first son of a Chōshū official. Maresuke began studying the Chinese classics and poetry, horsemanship, archery, riflery, and military history. By the time he was in his early teens, he could occasionally substitute for his father in the performance of official domain business. Yet, against the wishes of his parents, Maresuke continued to prefer studying literature to practicing the samurai martial arts. At school, his relatively slow physical development was a source of embarrassment, and he was ridiculed by his schoolmates, who nicknamed him "crybaby" (*nakito*).

At the age of fourteen, Maresuke approached his father and requested permission to become a scholar instead of a samurai-bureaucrat. Perhaps his appeal might have been granted if he had been the second son, but it was inconceivable for the first son of a samurai family in To-

6. In reality, only forty-six rōnin fought Kira and then committed mass seppuku. The kabuki theater adaptation of the tale, however, includes one additional samurai who initially signed the oath to avenge the death of his master but later withdrew from the plot.

kugawa society, particularly for the heir of Nogi Maretsugu. Confronted with his father's categorical refusal, Maresuke secretly left and sought refuge at the residence of Tamaki Bunnoshin, a relative living in nearby Hagi. He begged the famous teacher-scholar to receive him as a student and disciple.[7] At first Tamaki rejected his pleas, because the young man would have been forsaking his samurai background and training. Later he was persuaded to change his mind by his wife, who warmly welcomed Maresuke into the Tamaki household in a way he had never experienced in his own family.

During the day, Maresuke worked hard in the fields, gradually building a sense of physical self-confidence. At night, he studied the teachings of Tamaki's disciple and nephew, Yoshida Shōin, one of the most influential ideological leaders of the period, who combined emperor-centered nationalism and samurai self-discipline with a pragmatic awareness of the superiority of Western technology.[8]

In 1865, Maresuke began to commute from Tamaki's to Meirinkan, the official school of Chōshū. As before, the seventeen-year-old explicitly opposed the wishes of his father and chose to study literature instead of military science. Tamaki, however, persuaded the youth to train simultaneously in the martial arts at Meirinkan. This time, with his new strength developed from farmwork, Maresuke excelled and became well known at the school for both his physical and mental abilities. He was on his way to becoming a samurai.

Japan was on its way to becoming a modern state. The country had been forcibly opened in 1853 through the "gunboat diplomacy" of U.S. Commodore Matthew C. Perry which created complex diplomatic and domestic political problems. Various conflicting political factions appeared: those in favor of opening the country (*kaikoku*); those who totally opposed the foreigners (*jōi*); supporters of the emperor

7. Tamaki was an advocate of the "loyalist" credo of *sonnō-jōi* (literally, "Respect the emperor, expel the foreigners").

8. Through his school, writings and actions, Shōin inspired many young samurai activists—particularly in his home domain of Chōshū—to revolt against the rule of the Edo shogunate. But at the age of twenty-nine, in 1858, he was executed by the Tokugawa government for plotting to enact his political beliefs. Maresuke learned by heart Shōin's "Seven Rules for Samurai" ("Shiki shichi soku"). This short treatise, characteristic of Shōin's thought, called for a total commitment of self to a larger moral purpose and an absolute requirement of loyalty. Shōin was part of the first wave of nationalistic energy in the mid-nineteenth century that focused on the symbol of the emperor and was propelled by the external and internal pressures on Japan. More waves were to follow.

(sonnō); advocates of a unification of imperial Kyoto and Tokugawa Edo (kōbu gattai); and opponents of the shogunate (tōbaku). Some domains, particularly traditionally closed domains associated with the Tokugawa clan, supported the shogunate's negotiations with the foreigners; others, especially the more distant and powerful domains, were more independent and opposed the Edo regime's policies.[9]

In the late 1850s, Nogi's domain of Chōshū was the base for a militant anti-Western and proemperor faction (sonnō-jōi) centered around Yoshida Shōin. The xenophobic character of this movement, however, gradually diminished. Several times in 1863 Chōshū bombarded Western ships passing through the straits of Shimonoseki (between the islands of Honshū and Kyūshū) to protest trade treaties signed by the shogunate with the foreign countries. The British, French, American, and Dutch responded in August 1864 by sending an allied fleet to Shimonoseki which easily destroyed Chōshū's feeble coastal defenses. The defeat by Western military techniques dramatically demonstrated the ineffectiveness of traditional samurai military techniques against the overwhelming military power of the Western nations. Chōshū leaders began adopting the superior Western military technology and eventually even advocated opening the country. At the same time, support for the emperor grew more militant and antishogunate.

In August 1864, the same month that the four Western powers attacked Chōshū, the shogunate ordered a massive military expedition of 150,000 men to punish the rebellious domain. The Tokugawa forces, joined by troops from many domains, were met by two major military groups from Chōshū—first the regular army composed solely of samurai which was basically conservative in military thinking; and second numerous auxiliary militia, patterned after the kiheitai, literally "shock troops." Organized in 1863 by samurai Takasugi Shinsaku, a student of Yoshida Shōin, to support the regular army, the kiheitai was a revolutionary military style because it followed the Western military practice of recruiting soldiers not only from samurai but also from commoners. In September 1864, the Tokugawa and Chōshū

9. Opposition to foreigners did not necessarily coincide with opposition to the shogunate. For example, the imperial court, as well as several influential domains, and to some extent the shogunate itself, preached a collaboration between Kyoto and Edo to repel the foreign powers. Part of the aristocracy, however, and some samurai activists, especially in the outlying western domains, were radical pro-emperor supporters against the shogunate as well as violently antiforeigner.

forces were poised for battle. Although victory was almost certain for the shogunate, neither side attacked. Through the mediation of Saigō Takamori, a leader from the domain of Satsuma in southern Kyūshū, a deal was worked out in which the conservative faction came to power in Chōshū, surrendering to the Tokugawa forces in return for a guarantee of safety for the domain's lord and a promise to purge the leaders of the various proemperor groups.

Three months after the withdrawal of Tokugawa forces, civil war erupted in Chōshū, spurred on by the rise of many new radical proemperor military bands. One of them, the *hōkokutai* ("patriots' battalion"), was formed in February 1865 by Nogi and his childhood companions, who pledged to "devote ourselves totally to doing all that is necessary. He who changes his mind will commit seppuku" (Ohama, p. 18). Antishogunate samurai recaptured domain leadership and once again Chōshū assumed an arrogantly rebellious stand. This time, however, opposition was directed away from the Western powers and exclusively toward the Tokugawa regime. The antishogunate movement was developing a supradomain basis; in January 1866 Satsuma and Chōshū overcame their traditional rivalries to join in military alliance. Thus, when the shogunate ordered its second punitory expedition against Chōshū that June, it was without Satsuma support.

Most important, Chōshū was able to arm its forces with 7,000 rifles purchased with Satsuma's help from a British merchant in the port city of Nagasaki. Chōshū mobilized and strictly disciplined all available forces against the shogunate army. The hōkokutai of which Nogi was a member was merged into a mixed army under the command of Yamagata Kyōsuke (later, Yamagata Aritomo), a Chōshū samurai who became one of Japan's foremost military and political leaders. During the late summer and fall of 1866, these Chōshū forces, with soldiers recruited from outside the samurai class and armed largely with Western guns, soundly trounced the shogunate expedition. The unequivocal defeat by a single domain seriously undermined Tokugawa power and pushed the Edo regime one step closer to ultimate demise.

For Nogi, as well as for Japan, the late 1860s were years of turbulence and critical choice. Nogi participated in Chōshū's military defeat of the shogunate in 1866, but much to his chagrin he missed many of the subsequent battles which led to the Meiji Restoration. In his first direct battlefield experience, a bullet struck his left foot and seriously disabled him. Soon after Chōshū authorities ordered him to return to the domain school, Meirinkan, where once again he studied literature. For a twenty-year-old samurai, separation from his fighting companions and from the action at a crucial historical turning point must have been difficult. He was aware of the events occurring in central Honshū during 1867 and recognized their historical importance.

In February the Emperor Komei died and was succeeded by a young sovereign known as Emperor Meiji. Several months later, various antishogunate domains, including Chōshū, moved troops into Kyoto to "protect" the new sovereign. The threat to Tokugawa stability finally pushed the regime to its breaking point, and in October the shogun resigned his post. Two months later, while the Tokugawa regime and the court were groping for a new form of government, domain troops occupied the emperor's palace in Kyoto and proclaimed a restoration of imperial power. In January 1868, proemperor troops decisively defeated shogunate military forces at the battles of Toba and Fushimi, and in April they captured the Tokugawa castle at Edo. The 250-year Tokugawa hegemony collapsed and a coalition of antishogunate samurai declared itself the new government. This relatively bloodless coup, enacted in the name of the emperor, is known as the Meiji Restoration.

Throughout 1868 sporadic fighting continued between troops of the new Meiji government and supporters of the Tokugawa regime, particularly in regions north of the capital. Nogi was determined to rejoin his Chōshū compatriots in the hōkokutai fighting for the emperor. In May 1868 he attempted to leave Chōshū without official permission but was caught, arrested, and sent back to Meirinkan. Two months later, on the pretext of a relapse of his foot injury, Nogi withdrew from the school. When he finally rejoined his militia unit with the approval of domain authorities, it was as a scholar, an assistant instructor of Chinese classics. Nogi's former comrades, however, did not fully accept him back into their group and his feelings of alienation intensified. He felt isolated in their midst and sought an escape.

The young scholar-soldier's alienation from his Chōshū peers was temporarily resolved in late 1869 when domain authorities transferred him to Kyoto to learn French military techniques and to serve in the imperial guard. This move not only separated Nogi from his fellow militiamen but placed him on a different path, one that eventually led him to oppose them in principle and in battle. In early 1870, he was ordered to return to his own domain as part of a national military force dispatched to quell the disruptions of local militia bands, some of which included Nogi's childhood schoolmates. Nogi obeyed orders. Although he was acting against the interests of his friends and his clan, he was fulfilling goals and expectations set by his father—he had become a military man.

Soon after the formation of the Japanese Imperial Army, Nogi was appointed to the rank of major.[10] He was twenty-two years old. During 1872 and 1873, he was transferred to army bases in several cities, and from September 1874 until December of the following year was stationed in Tokyo, where he worked for the central army command. The period in Tokyo is regarded by Nogi's biographers as one of his happier times. He seems to have maintained good personal relations with those close to him—family, friends, superiors, women—while enjoying the freedom and status of a young single elite military officer. He drank almost nightly with acquaintances from the military, visiting bars and geisha houses until early hours of the morning. He often spent evenings with Yamagata, his commander from Chōshū, who had become Japan's top military officer after the Restoration.

In the early 1880s, Japan's new government implemented a series of radical social transformations, often with far-reaching and turbulent effects. The samurai coalition that assumed power had adopted a position that might be called enlightened authoritarianism. Its pre-Restoration support of the emperor and resistance to foreigners (sonnō-jōi) had become a post-Restoration governmental policy of supporting both the emperor and an open country (sonnō-kaikoku). The Meiji oligarchs began to reorganize society, promote modernization, and destroy the structure of the Tokugawa samurai hierarchy.

Although many samurai had collaborated in bringing the new government to power, the Meiji leaders proceeded to dissolve the samurai class, stripping the old elite of their identities, privileges, and stipends, a matter of great importance. In 1871, the feudal domains were converted into local administrative units (prefectures) directly controlled by the central government, and the samurai lost their exclusive badges of nobility—their rights to carry two swords and to wear their hair in topknots. Many samurai felt more than disoriented; they felt as if they were losing their souls. These revolutionary social

10. After this appointment, Nogi changed his given name to Maresuke, using the first character from his father's name of Maretsugu. This symbolically affirmed his connection with his father, especially in becoming a military man.

transformations on the heels of the imperial restoration fueled existing samurai resentment against the Meiji government which arose in part from residual loyalty to the Tokugawa shogunate or to a particular clan, and in part from residual anti-Western sentiments.

A turning point in opposition to the new government was reached in 1873 when a dispute over whether to invade Korea split the Meiji leadership. Those who remained in the government increased their control over national power. Those who left, including Saigō Takamori, became the nucleus of a violent, diehard samurai opposition. Among the samurai extremists were Nogi's friends, his brother, and his mentor, Tamaki. During the next four years, thousands of former samurai protested the government's policies, claiming that the Meiji oligarchy had betrayed the samurai class and was destroying Japanese traditions. They virulently opposed the symbolic death of the elite cultural class to which they belonged.

In December 1875, Nogi was appointed commander of the Fourteenth Regiment stationed in Kokura, in the north of Kyūshū, a position crucial to the defense of the Meiji government. Rebel samurai groups were actively organizing opposition to the central authorities and sporadic revolts had begun to erupt the year before. Nogi replaced a commander considered unreliable because he was the younger brother of Maebara Issei, a Chōshū samurai who quit the Meiji government in 1870 to become a leader of the opposition. Nogi soon found himself in a similar position. His brother, who had become the adopted heir of Tamaki, Maresuke's mentor, was the major spokesman for the same Maebara. Officially, Nogi's brother and mentor were his enemies in battle; from their point of view, he was a traitor and a disgrace as a samurai. From February through October 1876, the two brothers met and corresponded often as the main negotiators for the disaffected samurai and the national government. During this period, Nogi on numerous occasions assured his military superior Yamagata that his true loyalties lay with the imperial army, the emperor, and the state. But he was in some sense betraying his only brother, whom he loved deeply, and his first mentor, whom he loved and respected as a spiritual second father. Nogi thus violated his duties to both his actual family and his surrogate family.

At the end of October, in Kumamoto in southern Kyūshū, a group of rebellious samurai known as the League of the Divine Wind attacked the imperial garrison and prefectural office. This violent outburst was followed several days later by similar riots in Akizuki and Hagi. Government troops advanced to quell the revolts and, in the battle at Hagi, Nogi's brother was killed. Tamaki, when he realized that the cause had failed, committed seppuku. Although Nogi never ordered his regiment into battle against the samurai, neither did he desert the military to join his brother and mentor. His guilt at these two deaths was accompanied by professional humiliation. His military superior, a former leader from the hōkokutai, sharply criticized Nogi's failure to lead his soldiers into battle and formally issued a biting reprimand, demanding to know why Nogi, who commanded a large army, had not fought and had only pleaded for reinforcements. By resisting military action, Nogi avoided a face-to-face confrontation with his brother and his mentor. It also began a pattern of withdrawal he was to repeat in later crises. In this one episode the young officer suffered a double dishonor for his inaction: he fulfilled his obligations neither to his family and mentor, nor to his army and state.

In February 1877, Nogi was offered a chance to redeem himself and restore his tarnished reputation as a soldier and a samurai. Under the leadership of Saigō Takamori, samurai troops in Kumamoto had revolted against the Meiji government in an attempt to secede and precipitate civil war. Nogi's regiment from Kokura in northern Kyūshū was summoned to join in a huge governmental force organized to suppress the insurrection. Engaged fully in fighting, he might be able to put aside his guilt over the deaths of his brother and mentor. But Nogi was overzealous and reckless. Arriving on February 22, he immediately led his regiment forward to attack Kumamoto Castle from the front. In the ensuing struggle, the regiment's flag carrier was killed and the flag—presented by the emperor as symbol of the state, and considered a more or less sacred object—was lost to the enemy. Nogi's first impulse was to search for the flag personally, although in the height of the battle it would have meant certain death. He had to be physically restrained from doing it. Later, as commander of the regiment, he accepted full responsibility for the disgrace and requested appropriate punishment. Yamagata advocated "extreme punishment" for Nogi, but Major General Nozu, commander-in-chief of the First Brigade in Kyūshū, defended the young officer for his valor and endorsed a more lenient reprimand. Nogi was pardoned because of his battlefield successes and was never punished.

Nogi thus embodied conflicts created by the great social upheavals following the Meiji Restoration—in particular those generated by the enforced shift of samurai loyalty from the shogun to the emperor and his new government, and from traditional local communities to the more abstract new state. The government needed samurai loyalty in support of the new regime but also was obliged to transform it. The object of loyalty had to be canalized from the feudal domain and its lord to the nation-state and its emperor. When Nogi joined the imperial army as an officer, he pledged his loyalty to the emperor. In the 1860s, Nogi fought alongside Chōshū samurai in the pro-emperor cause; but in the 1870s he fought against them. The principles of bushidō demanded that Nogi side with his family and the samurai from Chōshū, while his new role as a national supraclan military officer clearly prescribed contrary loyalties.

The loss of the regimental flag at Kumamoto was indelibly etched on Nogi's conscience. Both his formal notice accepting responsibility and requesting punishment and the official order absolving him were beside his last will and testament the day he committed junshi. His testament states that since that day in Kumamoto, when he was twenty-nine years old, he had been seeking an opportunity to die. Nogi's mood after his failure in Kumamoto is expressed in a poem he wrote on New Year's Day, 1878:

> Last Year was a time of many battles,
> All things from today are of the new year.
> Leisurely, the year's first calligraphy portrays a war chronicle,
> My self is nothing but a person spared death.

> (Ohama, p. 57)

This was Nogi's first year of intensive death encounters. In late 1876, his brother and his mentor died. In the following February, he suffered the spiritual death of losing the regimental flag, as well as the battlefield deaths of many men under his command. Then, in October, his father died. Nogi referred to himself in the New Year's poem as "*shiyo no tami*," a person spared death. Nogi was a survivor, and he found it difficult to justify.

According to Nogi's published diary, he responded to his burden of guilt by drinking heavily during 1878 and 1879. Although partly resulting from the demands of military social life in Tokyo, his relentless and melancholic drinking, approaching alcoholism, was his way of at-

tenuating or avoiding the immobilizing guilt and shame of the year of
death encounters. At the same time he completely abandoned his
loyalties to his domain, sometimes refusing to drink with other
Chōshū samurai, to serve the emperor with a total commitment—
even in drinking partners. Service to the emperor was all he had left.

Nogi's nighttime entertainment was not limited to liquor. He also
frequented restaurants and geisha houses. Even outside the military,
his incessant carousing came to be known as "Nogi's wild merrymak-
ing" (*Nogi nō goyū*). His widowed mother, who managed his Tokyo
home, sought repeatedly to arrange an appropriate marriage for her
son, perhaps hoping that marriage plus her influence might halt her
son's disintegration in alcoholism. Nogi, however, stubbornly refused
all Chōshū women—another rejection of domain loyalties—and demanded a wife from Kagoshima in Kyūshū. He and his mother finally
compromised, and in August 1878, Nogi received a twenty-year-old
bride from Kagoshima. Immediately after the wedding ceremony, the
groom departed with his soldier cronies to celebrate the occasion with
drink. Although his marriage interfered little with Nogi's social en-
gagements, his wife Shizuko now bore the abuse in the family, from
both Nogi and his mother. Bitterness between mother and wife less-
ened somewhat after the birth of the first child, a boy, but the truce
between the two women only contributed to his further estrangement
from them and to his more resolute embrace of Tokyo's world of entertainment.

In 1885, at thirty-seven, Nogi was promoted to the rank of major
general and transferred to Kumamoto for a year. He continued his
nightlife there, although at a slower pace than in Tokyo, until late
1886, when he was assigned to Germany to study military techniques.

That assignment reflected another major transformation of Japanese
military technique and organization. First came the samurai ideal;
next, as young men were integrated into the nascent imperial army,
French military advisers were used; third, the Prussian military
machine became the model. As Japan shifted from a samurai to a
Western model in pre-Restoration days, French and British military
models competed for prominence. Satsuma, after defeat by the British
fleet in Kagoshima Bay in 1863, adopted largely a British model, while
Chōshū, after several losses to French and other Western ships in the
Shimonoseki Straits, modernized its forces according to a French

model. The shogunate, after its defeat by Chōshū in 1866 also realized the power of Western military technology and training and belatedly sought to modernize its forces with French help under the guidance of the French consul general. At this time, the British did not intervene in the internal political and military struggles as actively as the French; and imperial Germany, more of a land than a naval power in Europe, was not yet present in the Far East. Thus, the French military model was dominant for both sides in pre-Restoration Japan, and in the early years of the Meiji regime.

As the Meiji oligarchs were annihilating and converting the last supporters of the Tokugawa regime, they began to reevaluate the modernization program and chose the most efficient and appropriate Western models. They selected the British model for the navy, and, after the Prussian victory over France in 1870, adopted the German model for the army. Nogi's study tour in Germany was not only an integral part of his training as an elite military officer, but also of the plan to transform the Japanese army.

Nogi spent his year in Germany primarily observing military field maneuvers and listening to daily lectures delivered in French by a German officer. Although he apparently had learned some French during his earlier training in Kyoto, the language barrier placed Nogi very much outside German society. He wrote in his diary for only eighteen days during the first two months after his arrival in Germany, recording the visits of his lecturer and the military maneuvers. During the entire year abroad, Nogi never described German landscapes, towns, food, or people. Alienated by German society, he was not interested in the environment, the culture, or the people, with whom he had almost no serious communication. Nogi's experience contrasted with those of a young military doctor he met and befriended in Berlin, Mori Ogai. While Mori immersed himself in European culture, Nogi dealt with a threatening environment by plunging back into his sense of traditional Japaneseness. The doors of Japan had opened to the West, but the mind of this former samurai remained closed.

Nogi returned to Japan at the age of forty and presented his superiors with a long report on the Prussian army that emphasized two conclusions: first, officers should serve as examples of military discipline; and second, the military uniform should be worn at all times with pride and austerity. Yet the year in Germany was a turning point for Nogi. It transformed him into a traditionalist. German military discipline had revitalized his relationship to the samurai ideal, now in terms of character traits rather than group loyalties. Exchanging his evening clothes for a military uniform and abandoning his evening habits, Nogi became a proper military man embodying the traditional samurai ethics.

Even so, Nogi was suspended three times from the military. The first suspension occurred in February 1892, about three years after his return from Europe, when Nogi was stationed in Nagoya as the commanding officer of the Fifth Infantry Brigade. Although the suspension was ostensibly for reasons of health, it was in fact self-imposed—Nogi's way of protesting the appointment of Lieutenant General Katsura Tarō as his immediate superior. Katsura, several years younger than Nogi, was one of his old Tokyo drinking partners. While Nogi was abroad, Katsura had remained in the central military administration and had risen rapidly in the hierarchy. The humiliation of being ruled by a former subordinate, one who represented his former way of life, was more than Nogi could endure. True to his newly self-imposed military ethics, Nogi requested a leave of absence. For the next nine months, he farmed a plot of land he had purchased in Tochigi. His withdrawal to an agricultural life followed two Japanese cultural principles: avoiding direct confrontation within the group through passive rather than active protest, and assuming the role of the wise hermit.

In December 1892, Nogi was promoted to commanding officer of the First Infantry Brigade in Tokyo and resumed military duty. In 1894 when fighting broke out between Japan and China he was sent to the mainland. He was successful in many battles, particularly at Port Arthur, which he took in one day, and he was promoted to the rank of lieutenant general. In late 1895, Nogi's division proceeded to Taiwan, where it assisted in the island's "liberation" by fighting local guerrilla forces. After a six-month rest in Japan, Nogi was appointed governor of Taiwan and returned to the colonized island with his family. Although aware of a malaria epidemic raging in Taiwan, Nogi's aged mother, in the stoic manner of a samurai's wife, refused to remain alone in Tokyo. Already weak when she arrived in Taiwan, she contracted the disease and died one month later—another family death in connection with Nogi's service to the emperor.

Nogi's utter inability to govern Taiwan eventually led to his second suspension from duty. He knew almost nothing about the political aspects of the military and was ignorant of the practical rules of international diplomacy. In governing Taiwan, Nogi relied on Tokugawa samurai moralism and exhorted his subordinates to behave "correctly" toward the indigenous population. Unfortunately, Nogi as governor encountered serious difficulties in transforming his moralistic political theories into concrete programs. Moreover, he had no notion of how to stabilize the economic situation. Frustrated by his inability to implement effective policies, Nogi resorted to seizing British interests in Taiwan, throwing a blockade around Britain's consulate. His timing, however, was inopportune. Japan's Matsukata cabinet was already squabbling with Germany over rights to Kiao Chow Bay and desired no further conflicts with England. Nogi's rash action was not officially supported and drew criticism from members of his own staff. In November 1897, Nogi resigned the governorship after serving only one year. The government, unable to locate an appropriate position for him, temporarily suspended him from duty. Nogi resumed his agricultural life in Tochigi.

Nogi's third suspension from duty was also related to rigidity and failure. In 1898, he was reinstated as commander of a new division based in Kagawa prefecture. This post gave him an opportunity to implement his personal theory of military education that he had formulated in Germany. Nogi devoted all his energies to the program, even participating in training exercises with the recruits. It was a practical test of his theory that samurai training, with its emphasis on discipline and self-control, could produce an effective modern soldier.

In 1900, at the outbreak of the Boxer Rebellion in China, Japan sent thousands of troops to protect its interests. Among those regiments dispatched was a special group from Nogi's Eleventh Division in Kagawa. The following year, many high-ranking officers, including the major in command of troops from the Eleventh Division, were accused of having stolen silver during the Japanese occupation of T'ienchin Castle. The army punished only one officer, suspending a lieutenant general held responsible for the incident. Nogi however, was deeply angered and injured at his major's betrayal of loyalty. Particularly painful, we suspect, was Nogi's feeling that the theft made a mockery of his military education program and its principle of samurai moralism. Nogi decided to retire once more to his agricultural retreat, although he continued to make frequent visits to Tokyo. This time, his "peasant life" lasted nearly three years, which he spent writing poetry and reading about bushidō and military and general history.

The declaration of war against Russia in February 1904 resulted in Nogi's recall to active duty. It also marked the beginning of his second "year of death." In May he was made commanding officer of the Third Army and was charged with capturing Port Arthur, a repeat of his feat in the Sino-Japanese War in 1894. His two sons, Katsusuke and Yasusuke, were already on the battlefield when their father assumed command. Just before leaving Japan, however, Nogi was informed of the death of his eldest son at Port Arthur. The next day he wrote a letter to his wife informing her of the death. He had earlier told her that for the duration of the war he would not write to her and she was not to write to him, as if he did not exist. Nogi seems to have expected and perhaps hoped that he would not return alive.

The Japanese people anticipated a quick victory at Port Arthur, the strategically crucial base for the Russian Far Eastern Fleet. Many towns, in optimistic expectation, prepared banners for the victory celebration. But the Japanese seige of Port Arthur in 1904 against the Russians was quite different from that of 1894 against the Chinese. In August, the Third Army launched its first all-out frontal attack against the Russians, hoping to seize the fortress. Nogi's strategy ended in massacre. Russian machine guns plowed down Japanese infantrymen, killing more than 15,000 men, nearly one-third of the 50,700 soldiers and officers under Nogi's command. Port Arthur did not fall with the second major frontal attack ordered by Nogi in October, nor with the third in November. In Tokyo, Nogi was denounced as an inept, "no-policy" general who was senselessly murdering the nation's youth. Public outrage at the Port Arthur massacre occasionally erupted into violence directed personally against the general. Nogi's home was stoned, insulting letters were sent, and his wife publicly accosted. Nogi was treated as a national villain for being unable to end the bloody seige of Port Arthur.

Repeating failure after failure, Nogi turned his forces toward Hill Meter 203, which overlooked the Port Arthur harbor and fortress. This target, originally proposed by imperial headquarters, had been earlier rejected by an adamant Nogi in favor of frontal attack. In late November, when he finally began the assault on the strategically located hill, Japanese troops again were slaughtered: Nogi compensated for a shortage of weapons by using "human bullets" and a "determined spirit." Another 13,000 Japanese soldiers died in the battle of Hill 203.

One British journalist who witnessed and recorded the entire seige of Port Arthur wrote:

The horrors of the struggle seem to belong rather to a barbaric age than to the twentieth century. The miserable fate of thousands of wounded, who, had they been attended to, would have been saved, will ever form a dark page in warfare. The struggle was rendered intensely interesting by the fact that the Japanese endeavoured to combine modern weapons and methods of destruction with obsolete formations in attack. The result was unprecedented carnage; and we have probably witnessed these old-fashioned assaults on forts for the last time.

(Ashmead-Bartlett, pp. 470–71)

Unfortunately it was not the last time. The soldiers sacrificed at Port Arthur were the forerunners of those to be sacrificed in the Pacific War.[11] Nogi directly engineered the first carnage and symbolically oversaw the second. In life and in death Nogi represented the costs of imposing an outmoded rigid moral code on a modern industrial and technological world—the costs of the violence inflicted on the Japanese people and of the violence they inflicted on others.

Nogi's ultimate humiliation at Port Arthur was that he was not in command of the final military operation at Hill 203 that resulted in victory. The commanding officer of the Manchurian forces, Field Marshal Oyama Iwao, had expected the defeat of Port Arthur in November. When Nogi was unable to capture the Russian fort by the end of that month, Oyama sent his top military strategist, General Kodama Gentarō, to replace Nogi as director of the Port Arthur seige. In deference to Nogi's reputation, this change in command was not publicly announced until later. On November 30, General Kodama assumed de facto control of the Japanese forces at Port Arthur. The next day, Nogi's second son died in the assault of Hill 203. On December 6, the critical high point was captured, and Japanese artillery began a deadly shelling of Russian ships in the Port Arthur harbor. On New Year's Day, the Russian commander, General A. M. Stessel, surrendered to Nogi.

Victory at Port Arthur was hailed as proof of Japan's prowess against the outside world, particularly against the West. It was also

11. And before, in the First World War—at Verdun, for example—there was a similar combination of modern weapons and obsolete formation, with even greater carnage. But Japan played a minor role in that war.

taken as vindicating Nogi's spartan samurai philosophy. But the "proof" had been obtained only through enormous sacrifice. The 240 days of the Port Arthur seige produced nearly 58,000 killed and wounded. Although Nogi was responsible for these losses, the Japanese "victory" at the Port Arthur bloodbath made Nogi a still more celebrated military hero. Once Hill 203 was captured and the battle terminated, the Japanese people seemed to forget Nogi's murderous role. He was idolized for ending the long struggle and for suffering the loss of his only two sons. In particular, the press publicized Nogi's attitude to his personal sacrifice as the perfect stoic example for the people to follow. To Nogi the actual experience was one of humiliation and loss—military disgrace and the deaths of others.

Nogi's sense of death guilt and his search for a survivor mission were reflected in his public behavior following the Russo-Japanese War. In contrast to other military leaders, such as Tōgō and Kodama, Nogi demonstrated great concern for war invalids and for the families of dead soldiers. He argued persistently for the presentation of "honorable titles" to all dead soldiers and personally contributed to the government's Institute for Invalid Soldiers. Nogi visited families of dead soldiers to express his sympathy and, indeed, empathy at their losses. Nogi, more than other leaders, was personally affected by the inherently contradictory sides of the military officer as both victimizer and victim—that in victimizing his own soldiers, as well as the other side's, the officer becomes his own victim. Nogi responded to the burden of responsibility for mass murder by attempting to assuage his feelings of guilt. Even then, or particularly then, Nogi adhered to his bushidō ideals.

The reality of humiliation behind Nogi's myth of victory was paralleled by the wider circumstances of the Russo-Japanese War. In March 1905, the Japanese army won the battle of Mukden, but practical limitations of financing a prolonged war against Russia made the prospects of continuing success exceedingly small. Japanese military and government leaders were clearly aware of this. The Japanese public, however, fueled by a chauvinistic press, was in near total ignorance. The myth of the unbeatable imperial army was publicly unchallengeable, even while the Japanese government, through the mediating initiative of President Theodore Roosevelt, was negotiating with the Russians. When the terms of the peace treaty were announced in September 1905, militant nationalists burst into the streets of Tokyo. Rioters rejected the treaty's lack of an indemnity from Russia and the restriction of Japanese rights to only half of Sakhalin Island. A rare press conference by General Yamagata, in which he explained directly to the public why it was necessary to accept the treaty, helped calm tempers. Still, rising Japanese nationalism, bloated at the first victory of an Asian nation over a major Western power, retained its dangerous myth of military invincibility. Japan's civilian and military leaders hid the final failure of war against Russia as they hid Nogi's final failures at Port Arthur.

Japan's triumph over Russia created an attitude of self-complacency while accelerating industrialization on a Western model. High-ranking military officers indulged themselves in *sake* and women. Political leaders were involved in scandals. And the young elite of the middle and upper classes became increasingly attracted to Western ideas and entertainments. Newspaper criticism of these tendencies became commonplace, while popular resentment rose, particularly among those who had lost relatives and friends in the war and among the invalids themselves. Economically, the government was promoting investments in heavy industry. The Southern Manchuria Railway Company, for example, which became Japan's largest industrial conglomerate in the 1930s, was founded in 1906 as a direct result of the Russo-Japanese War. But economic difficulties as a result of the enormous war expenses persisted. The government had ample reasons to restrict luxury expenses and glorify service to the state. Its moral campaign was intended to merge political and economic goals while consolidating the military success over Russia into the beginnings of a colonial empire.

In 1907, while still holding his military rank, Nogi was appointed director of the Peers School, established in 1887 for Japan's modern aristocracy. His new office was mostly honorific, without any real influence inside the oligarchy, because the government maintained popular respect for Nogi's image as hero of Port Arthur while excluding the failed general from the inner circles of power. Nogi became the leading educator of the aristocratic youth but also the symbolic educator of the entire nation. A rigid traditionalist and strict moralist since his return from Germany, he was a formidable propaganda tool of the government. Nogi rarely drank sake or associated with women, had no scandals in his private life, and lived in almost ostentatious modesty. He also continued to advocate and enjoy such traditional customs as the Japanese martial arts. In short, Nogi was the perfect symbol in the government's campaign against decadence.

Nogi attempted to suppress the growing cosmopolitan mood of Peers School students. He instituted a compulsory dormitory system and imposed strict regulations for every minute detail of school life. He lectured his students that all physically strong boys should become military or naval officers, that students should practice martial arts rather than Western sports, that they should wear modest and clean clothes, and so on. It was a revival of Nogi's Tokugawa samurai moralism.

But Japan was moving inexorably toward westernization. Students in general, and elite students in particular, considered Nogi's instructions nonsense. One group in the Peers School, a literary and artistic movement known as *Shirakaba* ("white birch"), which was started by such students as future novelists Shiga Naoya and Mushakōji Saneatsu, criticized Nogi's speeches as dull, anachronistic, and unconvincing. Nogi apparently could not understand the student's strong resistance to his ideas.[12] What is most striking in the texts of those speeches now is not their preaching of samurai ideals but their triviality, their primary concern with such things as clothing and facial expressions. Even when discussing such grand ideas as patriotism, the tone of Nogi's speeches lacks the power, the fire, and the freshness of conviction. In a curious way, the texts do not evoke the image of a samurai, stubborn but vigorous, anachronistic but dignified; but rather the image of a worn-out old man, dull, repetitious, and full of stereotyped phrases, a man seemingly neither enthusiastic about nor convinced of the message he preached. No wonder future novelists felt a lifeless artificiality about Nogi's performance.

But Port Arthur had established Nogi's reputation beyond Japan's national borders. Nogi was one of the few Japanese known abroad in the early twentieth century. Still confident of its own role in world history, Europe could afford to congratulate a small, distant non-Western country for its defeat of giant Russia in modern warfare. Many countries—Prussia, France, Chile, Rumania, Great Britain—

12. Nogi consulted Mori Ogai (see chapter 3) about the students' attitudes. Although Ogai's exact response is not known, his diary entry of April 24, 1912 ("Told General Nogi that arguments of Shirakaba should be carefully followed") suggests some sympathy for Nogi's critics.

presented Nogi with national decorations. And in 1911 he returned to Europe and visited various royal families as an official state representative. In this way Nogi was used by the Japanese government, and accepted by foreign nations, as a symbol of the Japanese hero.

Behind this public image was a man who during much of his life considered himself a failure and experienced despair. At the immediate psychological level he seemed to have felt himself, for many years prior to his junshi, to have no right to be alive. His death guilt was like that of many survivors of intense death encounters. They may be preoccupied with death, including a self-accusatory sense that they had no right to be alive while so many others died. These preoccupations, paradoxically, can replace any need to commit suicide, and in that sense can enhance life: by declaring and experiencing one's own death guilt one can inwardly "win" the right to remain alive.

Nogi's feelings may have served this function (at least until what he considered the right moment for suicide came along). He was enormously vulnerable to such death guilt, probably as a result of his intense psychological struggles earlier in life—struggles with the authorities of his family and clan, notably his father, his sustained personal struggle against becoming the military-minded, ultramasculine, ideal samurai they wished him to become. He eventually turned into just that—with a vengeance. He experienced enormous residual resentment; although he tended to suppress direct anger he revealed by his indirect, often petulant, resistance to immediate authority, how strong that anger really was (a pattern encouraged by many aspects of Japanese culture). Perhaps because he never really believed himself to be an adequate, much less ideal, samurai, it was all too easy for Nogi to expect to fail, to take actions that must result in failure, and then react to failure with strong inner feelings of disintegration and isolation and with static or numbed inner deadness. We see this pattern in its most extreme form in Nogi's first year of death encounters (1876–77), during and after which his death guilt must have been staggering, contributing considerably to his alcoholism, depression, and probably his deep sense of meaninglessness.

The pattern is repeated years later after his three suspensions from the military, especially in relationship to his second year of death (1904–05). Each suspension was part of a losing struggle with adult integrity—the sense, moral and psychological, of holding together around ethical principles. That form of disintegration—combined with survivor guilt of specific kind in response to the death of his two sons, and of a more general kind in response to the tens of thousands of men killed in his misguided, anachronistic military assaults—seemed to leave him in a state of extreme humiliation and despair. Hence his listless caricature of the samurai ideal during his last years as head of the Peers School. His only hope for revitalization lay in a good—a perfect—death.

He found that in his form of suicide. Nogi's life, his diary, and especially his testament suggest that he yearned to live and to die as a samurai. His lifelong belief in a moralistic conception of samurai ideals may, in part, have been an attempt to balance his weakness in military techniques. It also reflects Nogi's inability to become fully part of modern Japan. His inbred attachment to bushidō thus contributed to his consistent failure in the rational calculation of gains and losses required by military games. Nogi's ultimate scheme was to die through a definitive act designed to render manifest his virtues.

In reviewing Nogi's suicide, we should emphasize its distinguishing characteristics: as junshi, it was the suicide of a vassal for his lord; and as seppuku, it was the suicide of a samurai. Nogi's junshi was the culmination of his personalized relationship with the emperor. It was not the norm in Meiji Japan but an aberration. His total identification with the emperor was an absolute loyalty not to an institution but to a person who transcended his own family and clan. Nogi was a deeply torn man who required an absolute authority to legitimate, if not to justify, his personal history and counter his guilt for betraying his own people. Nogi had to die for the emperor because he did not die for or with his family and friends. Junshi validated his life. It proved that he really meant his service to the emperor in a way he could not serve Tamaki, his early mentor.

Perhaps Nogi waited many years for the death of Emperor Meiji, so that he could carry out his self-execution on the day of the imperial funeral. By committing seppuku, Nogi concretized his ideal self-image as a true samurai and absolved his feelings of failure, guilt, and inadequacy. He atoned for his reckless attack during the 1877 Satsuma Rebellion and loss of the regimental colors. He also atoned for the three bloody frontal attacks on Port Arthur, when men with bayonets were sent again and again to be slaughtered by Russian machine guns. (Nogi's stubborn and irrational adherence to the frontal

attack had been a shift from anachronism to madness: he was challeng-
ing the fire of machine guns with the spirit of the samurai.) Through
seppuku, Nogi terminated his private individual reality and immor-
talized his popular heroic myth. It transformed the melancholic old
general insulated from the real centers of Meiji power into the proud
and unbeatable samurai commander of Port Arthur. His two goals of
self-punishment and self-validation were mutually enforcing: in a
single act, Nogi expiated his guilt and substantiated his samurai
character.

For Nogi, death became an avenue to immortalization on several
counts—the further immortalization of ancient cultural forms, the
immortalization of an emperor system newly created out of very old
cultural materials, and of course of General Nogi himself who became
a folk hero and a rallying point for just about every national call to
purification and military valor. Moreover, his act came at a time of
faltering Meiji energies, when Japan was ripe for some form of national revitalization. Nogi probably did not understand all this, but he
found a way to connect his private psychological struggles with the
collective aspirations. The form of death he chose affirmed a sense of
"living on" in principles larger and more enduring then the body and
self he put an end to. In a more universal sense, Nogi's death suggests
how the act of suicide can be a means of affirmation or revitalization.
We can, through his death, begin to understand that suicide in Japan,
and the West as well, can aim at some form of affirmation and immortalization.

Although Nogi was a manifestly unsuccessful educator and general,
he became an immensely successful public symbol of virtue. One
popular storyteller in the melodramatic *naniwabushi* style of recital,
Kyōyama Shōen, produced a piece in his repertory entitled "General
Nogi." Written in 1912, the lyrics portrayed Nogi as the "personification of bushidō when he was alive, the divine protector of the country
when he was dead." And his junshi was "beautifully and bravely performed (*isagiyoshi*), representing the great righteousness." This kind of
popular mythology reflected the success of the government in promoting a national illusion of the absolute power and virtue of ancient cultural principles. This national illusion had important practical consequences: it provided a sense of unity and a source of energy in Meiji
Japan's rapid industrial and military growth.

The government welcomed Nogi's junshi for its impact in revitalizing the samurai spirit, but was troubled by two aspects. First, junshi
was a personalistic anachronism. A soldier's devotion to the throne
should survive the particular emperor's death. Second, Nogi's request
to abolish his family, which held an aristocratic title, contradicted the
state's hierarchical ideology. The government therefore emphasized in
its initial public statements and later official textbooks Nogi's loyalty
and devotion to the state and his honesty and modest life. His inclination and need to identify with the Emperor Meiji as a person was
largely disregarded.

The government also hid many details of the suicide from the public. A year after Nogi's death, Dr. Iwata privately printed some sixty
copies of his firsthand medical report to distribute to friends, but the
government seized the pamphlets and prevented disclosure of its contents for many years. By nature, an objective account of an event is
incompatible with mystification and mythification. The government
preferred that Nogi's seppuku be told in naniwabushi, not in scientific
reports. In fact, until 1934 the Japanese people, except for a few
bureaucrats, were completely unaware of what really happened in
Nogi's residence that September evening of 1912.

Nogi's testament states his motivations for suicide and what was to
be done after his death. In the first clause, Nogi referred to his death
as jisatsu (suicide) rather than seppuku or junshi and cited three reasons
for ending his life: "remorse" and "distress" at the death of Emperor
Meiji, the loss of the regimental colors at Kumamoto in 1877, and his
old age and increasing weakness. While clearly preforming the ritual
of seppuku and junshi Nogi also wished to stress his personal conflicts
and limitations, an emphasis quite opposite from the government's.
By killing himself, Nogi also may have been thanking the emperor for
the "unmerited kindness" he received.

The second clause requested that the noble Nogi family line be dis-
continued, "to avoid leaving behind a possible disgrace" and "not to
defy heaven's order to adopt a son." It also donated the Nogi compound to the city or ward government. In the text prepared for official
released on September 16 government officials deleted these two unprecedented last requests because they violated the Meiji state's policy
of enshrining the family system, especially the nobility, as sacred ex-
tensions of the emperor. The People's Newspaper (Kokumin shinbun),
however, managed to publish the entire original testament on the day

the official text was released, thereby exposing the manipulation and embarrassing the authorities. But the government did not give up. Three years later despite vehement public protests, the government restored the Nogi family line by appointing an heir descended from the Mōri clan lord—a clear violation of the general's last will and testament.

Death freed Nogi from his immediate problems but not from history. The Meiji regime as well as subsequent Japanese governments transformed Nogi Maresuke into a formidable instrument of militaristic and nationalistic propaganda. While still alive, after the Russo-Japanese War, Nogi's image united nationalistic fervor in support of the state and silently summoned the populace to endure personal losses and the grief of war. Death by junshi enshrined Nogi as a divine model for soldiers, as a sort of military god, whose devotion to Emperor Meiji was recast into a generalized devotion to all national causes, including those that were expansionist, xenophobic, atavistic, and collectively suicidal.

Although Nogi's junshi shocked Japan as an anachronism, his "loyalty to the emperor" and "honest and virtuous deeds" were praised and his suicide proclaimed a "warning to decadent society." Editorialists, writers, historians, and philosophers all joined the chorus of voices honoring Nogi. Among the most vocal was Tokutomi Soho, editorial writer of the *People's Newspaper,* who called Nogi's suicide the highest point ever reached by Japanese tradition.

Other opinions were markedly critical. Arahata Kanson, a Christian and one of Japan's early socialists, called the public's reaction "nothing more than sad dreams of inmates of a mental hospital." And Shiga Naoya, one of the Shirakaba group at the Peers School, wrote in his diary, "When I heard from Eiko that Mr. Nogi had committed suicide, I thought, 'What a stupid fool!' He seemed just like some maidservant acting without thinking." Christian leaders, such as Uemura Masahisa and Kashiwagi Gien, did not endorse Nogi's suicide, but did praise his personality. Both Uemura and Kashiwagi viewed Nogi as the personification of bushido, although the former bitterly criticized the "theatrical character" of bushido itself, while the latter condemned the "defects of bushido" that led to Nogi's self-sacrifice. Outspoken critics were rare, and almost no one published attacks of his junshi. But most intellectuals considered the act anachronistic and were aware of the government's manipulation. Although public criticism was limited in quantity, its influence, particularly among young intellectuals, was widespread and deep.

One person who sharply perceived the malaise and the resentment created by Nogi's final act was his friend from Berlin days, Mori Ogai. Ogai analyzed his own ambivalent sentiments as a confrontation between traditional and Western values. The conclusion of his inner conflict was to defend Nogi firmly—that is, the samurai style of life and death. Only Ogai defended Nogi's suicide in thoughtful, creative fashion in a series of samurai stories written immediately after Nogi's junshi. It is important to understand the difference between the popular praise and Ogai's defense. Praise, which served the propoganda purposes of the state, was the fashion. Defense was an individual action which articulated a definite personal attitude toward such a major cultural problem.

Ogai believed that if Japan did not preserve its old traditions, at least in spirit, then there would be no style, no form, no rule for contemporary Japanese in their daily life. He seemed to fear that the core of culture, the meaning of stylization itself, would disintegrate as the nation rapidly changed.[13] Although junshi was an anachronism in 1912, Ogai felt that bushidō embodied an important sense of continuity and order by prescribing human emotions, thoughts, and actions. And in the chaos of Meiji Japan's emergence into the modern world, the abstraction of principles of self-discipline and loyalty from bushidō and their application to all of society, not just samurai, had an important function in minimizing social disruptions and maximizing social cohesiveness. This seemed, in Ogai's mind, to justify Nogi's junshi.

One certainly unintended consequence of Nogi's junshi was to motivate Ogai to study the Tokugawa period, which proved to be extraordinarily productive in his literary work. Alive, Nogi destroyed the lives of many Japanese and Russians; dead, his legacy, as a sym-

13. The "theatrical character" of bushidō was pejorative for Christian leader Uemura Masahisa, but not for Mori Ogai. Theater is the style of actions. During the Tokugawa period, bushidō elaborated, codified, and defined a certain style of human behavior. Similarly, during the modern period in Japan, Western traditions interacted with existing practices to form another style. Different cultures, in contrast to barbarism, may be defined by different ways of stylization, not on stage but in social life.

bolic tool of Japanese militarism, helped to destroy the lives of many more Japanese, as well as Chinese and Americans. He created nothing, except perhaps one thing. He created, by inspiring Mori Ogai, the most perfect prose that has yet been written in modern Japan.

Nogi's testament portrays a totally this-worldly man. He believed neither in Buddha, nor in the Christian God, nor in an afterlife. Eight of the ten clauses in his testament were practical and detailed instructions about such daily matters as the distribution of his property and a place to live for his wife. He even requested that his corpse be made available for use by a medical school. This document creates an inescapable impression of Nogi's exclusive concern with this world, in a very realistic and pragmatic manner, and his disregard for all metaphysical thoughts about the mysteries of human death.

A great many Japanese both before and after the Restoration shared Nogi's focus on this world. The ultimate values, the purpose of man's life, and the meaning of history can be defined only by factors immanent in society, culture or daily life, which are all relative to circumstances. When circumstances become complex, the required responses become contradictory. When a man lives amidst clashes between different value systems, as Nogi did throughout his life, then he makes a desperate effort to maintain the identity of self by regarding an immanent factor as transcendent or by considering a historical authority (that is, an authority not over but in history) as absolute. Instead of a God in Heaven, Japanese have believed in a master on earth. And in the world where Nogi lived, the master of masters was the emperor.

Although very few people committed junshi for Emperor Meiji, a death for the emperor was certainly far more real to most people than a death for an ideological belief. The emperor was part of the community; an ideological belief was not. The basis for the meaning of life and death thus resided not in an absolute beyond the community, but in the community itself. In the secularized world of Meiji Japan, people died, if voluntarily at all, not for God, not for an abstract cause, but for lover, for family, for master, and eventually for the emperor. Death separated Nogi from the Japanese world, but death also brought him closer to it. This general emphasis on concrete community rather than abstract ideology remains true in present-day Japan. But Nogi's particular human combination—of achievement, confusion, folly, glory, anachronism, rigidity, despair, and determined self-completion—was that of the Meiji era.

COMMENTARY / R. J. Lifton

Anyone who examines a particular moment in history makes a judgment about its significance—by applying certain criteria, often unmentioned, about why that act or event is worthy of our attention. Those criteria include psychological as well as broadly historical assumptions. Nogi's suicide can be remembered and experienced as a historical turning point, as a shift in ultimate levels of involvement or in the predominant mode of symbolic immortality.

Thus a general flow of history can be seen as the struggle among various collectivities to achieve, maintain, and reaffirm a sense of immortality under constantly changing conditions. Those conditions— the overwhelming threat of Western military technology and the threat to Japanese cultural integrity posed by Western culture— changed over the course of Nogi's life. In response the Japanese struggled to modify and extend the predominant biological and biosocial mode of symbolic immortality that existed in family and clan. The Meiji Restoration thus sought to impart a sense of living on indefinitely in immortal emperor and nation, which required radically expanding the biosocial mode by making emperor and nation become one's eternal "clan." But other modes were also involved—the religious mode in the revival of Shintō and in the establishment of something like emperor worship, the creative mode or human "works" in the new institutions that had to be built (in relationship to emperor, government, education, or military), and even to a degree the special mode of experiential transcendence.

Concerning the last, the longstanding Japanese cultural pattern of cultivating something close to an ecstatic state around anticipating and staging a heroic form of death on behalf of a "higher purpose" now had to be carefully reorchestrated to relate specifically to the new emperor-nation constellation. That meant suppressing older versions of death-ecstasy, of junshi and seppuku, to create newer ones. The Tokugawa regime, in outlawing junshi, had taken a step toward a more inclusive biosocial mode of immortality (toward what we call nationalism); one could no longer express ultimate loyalty to one's clan or feudal lord, but one could still retain the samurai's privilege of an honorable self-inflicted death (*seppuku*) if one had run afoul of the shogunate and the regime wished to grant that privilege. The Meiji regime took a more radical step in suppressing the samurai sword culture, a step which many rebellious samurai groups perceived as a threat to *their* cultural integrity.

Now Japan was to take on the ultimate prerogative of the modern state, its exclusive control over the death sentence and human sacrifice, notably wars. The overall process of manipulation of death-centered experiential transcendence reached its zenith in the kamikaze deaths during the Second World War.

Nogi's seppuku was a way of looking backward to go forward, seizing on an already distant cultural memory as a way of establishing, and in a psychological sense legitimating, the new marriage of emperor and state as a mode of symbolic immortality for all Japanese. But is that not directly parallel to what Japan itself did? I know of no other nation in which something close to a revolution was labeled a restoration.

In my work with Japanese youth during the early sixties I was struck by three different categories in their images of time: the mode of transformation or image of making all things new; the mode of accommodation or image of strategic psychological compromise in combining what was, is, and might be (among a great majority of young Japanese); and the mode of restoration, or image of a golden age of the past in which perfect harmony prevailed (young rightists emphasizing the sacredness of the emperor).

In using these categories I was trying to find a level of discourse that was both individual and historical. I found that the modes of transformation and restoration, seeming opposites, tended to resemble each other more than either did the mode of accommodation, and that each had a striking paradox. The young transformationist, in his dreams and associations, revealed profound nostalgia (for such events as shrine festivals or traditional food) so that his images of transformation were partly energized by old utopias of both personal and historical kinds. The restorationist, similarly, tended to reveal a somewhat suppressed fascination with and attraction toward contemporary cultural elements (ideas of Marx and Freud and the achievements of science and technology) so that his images of a golden age served partly to ward off the seductions of modernity (Mishima Yukio [chapter 7] was a striking example of this tendency).

But the restorationist calls forth imagery of the past to ward off new influences as well as to come to terms with them and even to absorb and use them. Broadly speaking, that was the pattern of the

Meiji Restoration—and, individually speaking, of Nogi's ritual suicide. His act expressed a powerful imagery of a golden age in the service of radical new cultural forms—it harkened back to old and "simple" modes of symbolic immortality to usher in new and more complex modes and combinations of modes. The price proved to be very great indeed, but how many could realize that at the time?

COMMENTARY / S. Katō

War and revolution produce popular military heroes, but social changes that follow often discredit and destroy these public symbols. The popularity of heroes is thus related to the survival of particular regimes and ideologies.

Like Nogi after Port Arthur, Pétain after Verdun was a triumphant general who became a national hero through political manipulation. Both became national symbols associated with militaristic governments. But though Nogi through his suicide became a centerpiece of Japan's militaristic folklore, Pétain became head of the Vichy government after the French debacle of 1940 and collaborated with the Nazis. The downfall of these regimes brought about the downfall of their heroes, but with important differences. Demilitarization in Japan after 1945 gradually buried the memory of Nogi—but without any public criticism or discussion of his symbolic or actual wartime roles. Quietly Nogi's stories and even his name disappeared from postwar media and textbooks. By contrast, the Liberation in France brought Pétain to trial, found him guilty, and sentenced him to death. Yesterday's national hero became today's traitor. Pétain's sentence was commuted to life imprisonment only by de Gaulle's personal intervention, and he finally died in prison. The paths of these two military heroes suggest that while in France ideological issues are extremely important—sometimes even too important—in Japan they are secondary.

Sometimes during times of rapid change, heroes oppose the regime and bring about their own symbolic and real downfall. Power struggles within the oligarchy and an inability to adapt to new situations can drive some leaders to oppose those who were once in the same camp. Saigō Takamori, for example, a hero of the Meiji Restoration, waged an unsuccessful civil war against the new government. Similarly, Lin Piao, once hailed as a hero of the Chinese revolution, failed—at least according to official Chinese reports—in an attempted conspiracy against Chairman Mao and died in a plane crash. In this sense, Lin Piao's fate resembles Saigō's, but a striking difference exists between their public images after death. Saigō, after his death in Kagoshima, became popular among the people, which the Meiji government reluctantly tolerated. After Lin Piao's plane crash, however, the Chinese government launched the "criticism of Lin" movement, which was a kind of postmortem trial with ideological attacks on his ideas and deeds.

The ultimate fate of a hero is thus closely linked to the regime's emphasis on ideology. In French and Chinese societies, which tend to emphasize ideology, the hero's downfall must be ideologically justified through public accusations. In Japan, however, where ideology is not as important, ideological justifications are not necessary to discredit individuals, especially the symbol of a group, whether a company or the nation-state. Instead of ideology, the harmony of the group is stressed, particularly when the group as a whole shifts to a new ideological stance. Official public accusations of public figures are avoided because they are perceived as threatening group harmony. Thus while militaristic Japan made Nogi into a national hero, non-militaristic Japan has not judged him but has simply ignored him. Will the symbol of Nogi emerge again some day? That possibility certainly exists, especially if militarism in Japan is revived. But it seems unlikely, at least in the immediate future.

3 / MORI OGAI (1862–1922)

"Neither Fearing nor Yearning for Death"

Mori Ogai

FROM THE WRITINGS OF MORI OGAI

Testament

Here, upon my deathbed, I have asked my friend, Mr. Kako Tsurudo, the one person I have known without any secrets from my boyhood to this very moment of my death, to take the trouble of writing down my last wishes. Death is a very serious matter which ends all. However powerful the state may be, I believe that it cannot act against my will. I would like to die simply as Mori Rintarō of the province of Iwami. Though I may be associated with the Ministry of the Imperial Household and the army, I refuse all formalities from them on the verge of my death. I am going to die simply as Mori Rintarō. On my gravestone, not a single letter shall be inscribed other than "GRAVE OF MORI RINTARO." I place in Mr. Nakamura Fusetsu's hands the task of calligraphy and request that absolutely all honorary ceremonies sponsored by the ministry or the army be canceled. Necessary steps should be taken to assure the fulfillment of my last requests. These are the words I leave with my one and only friend, and no one shall interfere with them.

(Selected Works of Mori Ogai [Mori Ogai shu], vol. 7, p. 428)

"Reveries" ("Mōsō")

My thoughts about social relationships occur randomly one after the other, but eventually they are reduced into the individual self. The self is at the center of these relationships, tying them together like threads pulled from all directions. The ultimate disappearance of this self is death.

Since my childhood I've always liked novels, and after learning other languages I spent my free moments reading foreign novels. Every one that I read portrayed the disappearance of self as the most severe and most profound pain imaginable. Still, I cannot conceive of the dissolution of my self causing all that pain. If I were to die by sword, I would at that moment probably feel physical pain; or if I were to die by disease or poison, undoubtedly I would feel pain from the corresponding symptoms of suffocation or convulsions. But the passing of the self would produce no pain.

Westerners say that not to fear death is characteristic of savages. Perhaps I am one of those "savages." I can remember many times in my childhood when my parents admonished me that since I was born in the house of a samurai I had to be able to perform seppuku, to slit my abdomen. And I remember thinking that there would be physical agony and that it would have to be endured. Indeed, I may be one of those so-called savages. Nonetheless, I cannot accept the Westerners' view as right.

But neither can I remain indifferent to the disappearance of my self. Its departure without my having thought about or known what it really is would be terrible. It would be truly unfortunate—in the same way that leading what the Chinese scholars call a purposeless life is unfortunate. When I think how terrible and unfortunate it would be, I feel an acute emptiness in my heart and an inexpressible loneliness.

It is these feelings which cause me anguish and pain.

I used to experience this pain often on sleepless nights in my Berlin lodging house. At those times, everything I had done since birth seemed infinitely trivial. I felt I was nothing more than an actor performing on stage. My heart was flooded by all the fragmental concepts of Buddhism and Christianity, but they vanished immediately without leaving me even a moment of solace. I would then search the various facts and reasonings of natural science for something which might serve to console me. But that too was in vain.

One of these nights I decided to try reading some philosophy. After waiting for the break of day, I left to buy Hartmann's Philosophy of the Unconscious.[1] *I chose Hartmann for my first venture into the world of philosophy because his works were being debated as the most up-to-date system. They were even said to be, along with the railroad, among the greatest contributions of the nineteenth century.*

It was Hartmann's three stages of illusion which impressed upon me the value of philosophy. He proposed this scheme to demonstrate the impossibility of achieving happiness in the present world through youth, health, friendship, love, honor. Hartmann exposes all of them as illusions. Love, for example, is nothing more than pain; therefore, the root of sexual desire should be suppressed. Only by sacrificing these types of happiness can man contribute his small part to the progress of the world. The second stage is seeking happiness after death, which requires the assumption of individual immortality. But the individual's nervous system ceases to function with death and his consciousness is destroyed. In the third stage happiness is sought in the future of the world. For this, one must assume that the world will continue to develop and progress. But no matter how far the world advances, senility, disease, and the miseries of the human condition will never be eliminated. Man will become more sensitive with progress and he will feel these pains even more acutely. Thus, even if these three stages are experienced, happiness will not be achieved.

In Hartmann's metaphysics, this world could not have been created better.

1. The most famous work of Eduard von Hartmann (1842–1906), known as "the philosopher of the unconscious" for his efforts to reconcile rationalism and irrationalism by emphasizing the central role of the human unconscious.

Nonetheless, he answers the question of whether the world should exist in the negative. The basis for bringing the world into existence is what he calls the unconscious. But rejecting life is meaningless, since the world will continue to exist as always. Even if present-day man were to successfully decimate himself, somehow the next human species would emerge and repeat the same process. Therefore it is better that man affirm his life, resign himself to the ways of the world, submit to the pains and agonies that must occur, and wait for the world's salvation.

I looked at Hartmann's conclusion and shook my head in resistance. Still, I found myself quite attracted to his exposure of happiness as an illusion.

(*Selected Works*, vol. 7, pp. 290–91)

"How should one obtain knowledge of oneself? Reflection reveals nothing. But action might do. Try to fulfill your obligations. Then you will know your worth. What are your obligations? Only the day to day demands of life." These are the words of Goethe.

To consider life's daily demands as one's ultimate obligations and to strive for their fulfillment is precisely the opposite of ignoring the realities of life. Why am I unable to attain this goal?

To consider the fulfillment of life's daily demands as all one can do, one must know how to be satisfied with one's limitations. I am not capable, however, of being satisfied with my limitations. I am a man who is forever discontent. For some reason, I cannot see a gray bird as a blue bird. Lost on the road and dreaming, I am still searching for that blue bird. If you ask why, I cannot answer you. This is simply how my mind works.

It is in this state of mind that I descend the slope of life. And I know that at the bottom is death.

But death is not frightening. Although others speak of a fear of death which rises in old age, I do not feel it.

In my youth I felt keenly that I wanted to solve the puzzles confronting me before reaching the final destination of death. But that desire gradually dimmed. I still see the unsolved puzzles, and I still believe they must be solved. But I am no longer in such a hurry to solve them.

Recently, I heard of Philipp Mainländer and read his philosophy of salvation. Mainländer recognizes Hartmann's three stages of illusion but says that it is futile to try to affirm life by exposing the illusions. He disagrees with Hartmann's view that although everything is an illusion, we still should pursue the illusions since we are going to die anyway. People first watch death from a distance and then turn away in fear. Next, they draw a big circle around

death and continue to walk on, trembling. That circle gradually becomes smaller and smaller until finally they throw their tired arms around death's neck
and look at death eye to eye. _It is in the eye of death that one finally finds peace._
Saying this, at the age of thirty-five Mainländer commited suicide.

I have neither a fear of death nor Mainländer's longing for death.

 _Thus, neither fearing nor yearning for death, I walk down the descending
slope of life._

(Selected Works, vol. 7, p. 294)

Thus neither fearing nor yearning for death the old man dreamed unrealized
dreams and lived out his last days.

 On rare moments his memory would flash before him traces of decades past,
like a long chain. Then the old man's piercing eyes would open wide and stare
afar into the sea and the sky.

 It was at those times he wrote these worthless old scraps.

(Selected Works, vol. 7, pp. 296–97)

On his way home from the imperial funeral on the night of September 13, 1912, Mori Ogai, director of the Army Medical Corps and a leading literary figure in Meiji Japan, heard rumors that General Nogi had committed suicide.[2] Ogai, like many others, doubted the veracity of the stories and stated so in his diary that night. But it was true. And during the following days, the impact of Nogi's "heroic" death weighed heavily on the aroused public and on Ogai. The writer-doctor thought often of his personal relationship with the general. Six days after the emperor's funeral, Ogai attended another funeral—Nogi's. He then returned home to write in one sitting the first draft of "The Testament of Okitsu Yagoemon" ("Okitsu Yagoemon no isho"), a short story based on a case of junshi in the early Tokugawa period. This story, which defended the act of junshi, was Ogai's public response to Nogi's suicide. Ogai located Nogi's death in Japanese experience and extended its meaning by a creative act.

In the fictional testament of Okitsu Yagoemon, Ogai described why that samurai chose to commit junshi and follow his lord in death. The similarities to Nogi were clear: like Nogi, Okitsu placed absolute loyalty and obedience to his lord above all else; like Nogi, who sacrificed many soldiers at Port Arthur, Okitsu was forced to kill his colleague to complete the mission assigned to him by his lord; and like Nogi at Kumamoto, Okitsu had immediately planned to commit seppuku but postponed the act to continue serving his lord. Okitsu also bravely, and somewhat recklessly, fought at war, holding high his lord's banner. He, too, expected a battlefield death—but survived. And after his lord's death, Okitsu served the young heir while waiting for the proper occasion to die. Finally, on the thirteenth anniversary of his lord's death, Okitsu decided that the heir was firmly established and that the defunct lord's household was secure. "Tomorrow, having attained the desire which I have cherished for years, I will in good heart commit seppuku before the honored grave of Lord Myōgein" (Mori, 1971, p. 147).

"The Testament of Okitsu Yagoemon" had at least two levels of

2. In a sense his two identities were externalized in his names—his bureaucratic self was known as Mori Rintarō and his literary self as Mori Ogai, his pen name. We refer to him during childhood as Rintarō, and during adulthood both as Mori and as Ogai (which is how he is most popularly called even today). We usually use Mori when referring to his nonliterary side, and Ogai when referring to his literary self.

meaning for Ogai. On one level, it was his defense of his personal friend Nogi. Ogai had known the general for many years and their warm friendship became particularly intense when either of them was in crisis. But Ogai's story of Okitsu was by no means motivated only by friendship. Although Okitsu's testament reflected Nogi's position, Ogai did not identify totally with Okitsu or Nogi. Both belonged to the past, while Ogai belonged very much to the present, if not to the future. But Ogai's argument suggests that their suicides represented Meiji Japan's cultural roots in Edo society.

Thus, on a second level, Ogai defended the continuity of Japanese cultural traditions as symbolized by junshi. Okitsu's deeds (and thus Nogi's deeds) were not the result of madness, as some claimed (and as even Ogai might have wondered), but were the consequence of carefully thought-out decisions, of a deep commitment to samurai values, and ultimately of a particular cultural attitude toward death. The clear, objective, and subdued style in the story conveys the hero's detachment from his own fate, his calmness at facing death, his immutable self-control. Ogai undoubtedly regarded seppuku and junshi as outdated, but at the same time he believed in the importance of their underlying principles—of disciplined will power and personal loyalty. Indeed, Okitsu Yagoemon's absolute self-control in dying expressed the ideal that Ogai sought to live up to in his own life.

Even before Nogi's suicide, Ogai had articulated his own attitudes toward death in the autobiographical short story "Reveries" ("Mōsō"). Ogai, who was then forty-nine and relatively healthy, was reaching the peak of both his literary productivity and his army medical career. He wrote that he felt little anxiety at the thought of the ultimate disappearance of his self. In an often cited sentence, he stated: "Thus, neither fearing nor yearning for death, I walk down the descending slope of life" (*Selected Works*, vol. 7, p. 294). This view of death is one of the most detached and serene ever expressed by a modern Japanese writer. That serenity seemed to be reflected in the facial expression of his death mask.[3] But behind the mask was a life of enormous conflict and pain.

When Ogai began to recognize the imminence of his own death in 1921 and 1922, his composure partially denied the seriousness of his illness, while he transformed his awareness into literary creations. For

3. The custom of having a death mask made was imported from Europe in the late nineteenth century and continued through several decades of the next century.

many years Ogai had suffered from tuberculosis; by the time he turned sixty it reached an advanced stage and caused him great physical pain. Yet he told none of his friends, even keeping knowledge of his worsening state from his family. He did not even write about it in his diary, except for a single line noting a possible recurrence of the pleurisy he had contracted in youth. Ogai thus lived his last years attempting to ignore his fatal disease, refusing until the very end to submit to medical examination.

In a February 1920 letter addressed to Kako Tsurudo, his closest friend and also a doctor, Ogai in one line mentioned an attack of "acute nephritis after influenza." In the same letter, he quoted his brother-in-law, an anthropologist with medical training, who warned him of "kidney sclerosis." Thereafter, until May 13, 1922, less than two months before his death, Ogai never discussed his deteriorating health in his diary or in any of his letters. His behavior suggests that his psychological pattern of denial was, to an important degree, serving an obstinate commitment to continue building his literary legacy until the last possible moment.

Ogai suspected his impending death for some time. From October 1920 to November 1921, he was writing the last of his Tokugawa Confucianist biographies, *The Last Year of Katei's Life* (*Katei shogai no sue ichinen*), in which he discussed the nineteenth-century scholar's fatal disease. Ogai postulated two possible causes of death: heart failure in the case of beriberi, and uremia in the case of nephrosclerosis. He concluded that the more probable cause was uremia,

because heart failure usually does not occur very early in the course of the disease, while uremia develops suddenly. Apparently Katei was not aware of his approaching death. A sudden death that surprises the unprepared patient could be due to heart failure at a late stage of beriberi, or to uremia at any point in the disease of nephrosclerosis.

(*Ogai zenshū*, vol. 18, p. 573)

Ogai's clinical style, detailed in its description of symptoms and rigorous in its diagnostic reasoning, was explicitly a discussion of Katei's disease. But it also seems to have been an indirect reference to Ogai's own illness. When he wrote these lines, Ogai was certainly contemplating, if not already convinced of, his own self-diagnosis of renal failure.

Ogai thus masked both his concern and his knowledge about the seriousness of his condition. He acted as if nothing were happening, maintaining his usual attitude toward his children, continuing his regular administrative duties at the Imperial Library and National Museum, and nearly finishing his last major work (*Gengōkō*), a historical survey of the etymology of the names of the Japanese-Chinese years.

In May 1922, he wrote three letters to his friend Kako in which he only gradually revealed the truth about his fatal illness. In the first letter, dated May 3, Ogai noted vaguely that he had some physical ailments, adding that he was at the first step of old age, which was drawing near not gradually but in quantum jumps (*"sprungweise"*). In the second letter on May 24, he wrote that he felt better but that his problems caused by a "pathological process" in a particular region, perhaps renal failure or lung emphysema, which was developing sprungweise. In the third and last letter written May 26, Ogai for the first time stated clearly that something was wrong in his left lung and kidney, something that would lead to his death.

He explained in detail his reasons for not consulting a doctor: if he knew by medical examination exactly what was going on in his body, then it would be difficult for him to avoid thinking of that process, which would in turn disturb his state of mind. He might also be required to abstain from working. Even if he could live a year longer by ceasing all work on *Gengōkō*, he preferred to continue writing and risk an earlier death.

On June 15, Ogai stopped going to his office. Nine days later, he dictated a letter to his first son, a physician then in Germany, describing his deteriorating condition. On June 29, Ogai finally submitted to medical treatment by Nukada Susumu, who confirmed the diagnosis of nephrosclerosis and tuberculosis. Nukada, however, abided by Ogai's wish to keep secret the diagnosis of advanced tuberculosis to avoid possible harm to the family's social relationships. On July 6, Ogai dictated to Kako his short testament, and three days later, he drifted quietly from coma into death. Ogai's very controlled death reflected precisely the life he had lived. Its conflicts were never permitted to interrupt his basic life projects.

Mori Ogai was a man of extraordinary intellectual range and versatility. He combined scientific and literary achievement in a way equaled by no other modern Japanese figure, and probably by few anywhere. He is one of the few people in the Meiji period who might be called a genius. Ogai was a modern physician who played a leading role in Japan's development of the Western scientific method, a high military bureaucrat committed to a hierarchical system that he sometimes found suffocating, and a writer of exceptional prose which blended an exquisite aesthetic sensibility with a cool, clinical logic.

His writings encompassed a broad scope of cultural and social problems within Japan's rapidly changing society: they went beyond science and literature as such, to the national language, food, housing, sex and morality, aesthetics, and even socialism. Like most Meiji thinkers, Ogai chose the conflict between Western and Japanese cultural traditions as his central theme. Yet he was one of few Meiji intellectuals who was deeply grounded in both the European and traditional Japanese world. The achievement stimulated by this conflict of cultures is truly staggering.

Ogai's success, however, was accompanied by sharp (internal conflict) between Mori the bureaucrat and Ogai the author. Both the imperial army and his family demanded Ogai's integration into the conventions and rituals of Meiji society. Only through his life as a writer was he able to preserve the integrity of his individual self as creator and builder. In many ways, Ogai's life was delicately balanced between accommodating to various external pressures and controlling his emotional and intellectual conflicts. But at the last moment, in the testament he dictated just before his death, Ogai suddenly and forcibly asserted what he felt to be his true self, defying the public authorities with whom he had compromised for about forty years: he refused the conventional funeral ceremonies and rejected the official titles on his gravestone: "I will die simply as Mori Rintarō."

In 1862, six years before the Meiji Restoration, Mori Rintarō was born as the first son to a family that had served for more than ten generations as doctors for the feudal lord of the Tsuwano domain. The combination of these two traditional elements—the eldest son, a medical family—placed Rintarō into a pattern from which it was nearly impossible to deviate. His immersion from birth in familial and social traditions predetermined his future: he was to become the next family head and he was to be a doctor.

Because the two previous Mori generations had no male heirs, the line and its profession could be continued only if Mori women married doctors who could be adopted into the family. Rintarō, then, was not only the firstborn and eldest son of his generation, but also the first natural male heir in three generations. He was, inevitably, the focus of extraordinary family attention, hope, and ambition. He was to be responsible for upholding family tradition and bringing honor to the family name, as well as for supporting his parents in old age and guiding his siblings in youth. Rintarō represented the family's continuity; the family's symbolic immortality, so to speak, had to be carried on his shoulders.

The eldest son succeeded the father, alone inheriting all family assets, and exerted near-total authority over other family members in such matters of education, marriage, and choice of profession. This preeminent status of the eldest son, rigorously respected in Tokugawa samurai society, was legalized after the Meiji Restoration by Japan's first civil code and was particularly stressed in middle-class families.[4]

The Mori family was in this sense typical: Rintarō was treated and educated altogether differently from his two younger brothers and sister, who were taught to respect their eldest brother's opinions only next to their father's. And whenever Rintarō encountered difficulties, the entire family—grandmother, mother, brothers, sister, and brother-in-law—came to his aid.

His mother, Mineko, exerted a pervasive influence on Rintaro's development—partly because his father, Shizuo, was an "adopted" heir, which gave Mineko much of the responsibility for maintaining the family line, and partly because of Shizuo's passivity. When Rintarō began learning the Chinese classics at the age of seven, for example, Mineko struggled long hours to overcome her lack of formal education and taught herself the difficult Chinese texts so she could supervise her son's studies. This close emotional and intellectual relationship between mother and son persisted until 1916, when Mineko died at seventy, only six years before her son's death. She was thus one of the most powerful, and at times restrictive, forces molding Rintarō's life.

In Tokugawa society, especially from the eighteenth century on,

4. As part of the postwar democratic reconstruction of Japan by occupation forces, a family law enacted in 1947 sought to abolish the family system by equalizing both the husband-wife relationship and the rights and duties of children. Needless to say, legal reforms alone could not uproot the tradition of primogeniture deeply embedded in Japanese cultural and social patterns, although important attitudinal and behavioral changes have occurred in the last three decades.

Confucian teacher-scholars, doctors, and Buddhist priests were the three major intellectual professions. Teaching and medicine had several common traits. First, any samurai, farmer, or merchant regardless of family background, could theoretically become a teacher or a doctor. Although in fact many entered the professions by succeeding their fathers, this theoretical mobility differed from samurai, whose status was strictly hereditary.[5] Buddhist priests and monks were similarly recruited from all social classes. Second, in contrast to Buddhist priests, some teachers and doctors were employed by domain governments—and eventually by the shogunate—and were treated as middle-rank samurai in terms of salary (tens or hundreds of *koku*) and status.[6] Although most teachers and doctors were self-employed, those serving feudal lords were almost totally integrated into samurai society and often into the hierarchical structure of samurai administration. And third, Confucian teacher-scholars and doctors received similar traditional training. Their education overlapped because medical knowledge was part of the comprehensive Confucian system based on Chinese classics. Without knowledge of those classics, medical skills were inaccessible, and even Japanese medical texts were written in Chinese. For the same reason, a Confucian scholar well versed in the Chinese classics could easily read all available medical texts and function as a medical doctor.

The two professions were essentially interchangeable. In fact, a great number of eminent Confucian scholars, such as Ogyū Sorai, came from medical families. Some, when not employed by the government, supported their scholarly and literary activities by practicing medicine privately.[7]

The Mori family held a highly respected position within Tokugawa

5. In the last years of the Tokugawa period, however, many samurai and many domain governments became indebted to rich and increasingly powerful merchants. One method for settling accounts was to allow merchants to purchase samurai status—the right to wear two swords.

6. A koku was a unit of volume, approximately 5.2 U.S. bushels, used primarily for measuring rice and rice paddy yields. During the Tokugawa period, the koku was the basis of a system for taxing farmers and for distributing stipends to samurai according to their rank.

7. The Confucian physician-scholar tradition provided something of a cultural model for Ogai's combination of medical and literary worlds. We might consider this a Japanese parallel to the Western Renaissance man. But whereas the Renaissance ideal was embodied in exceptional individuals, the Confucian tradition in the Tokugawa period was completely institutionalized.

society. The family head, as personal doctor for the domain lord, occupied a position equivalent to an eminent professor in an elite medical school today. His prestige spanned the two intellectual professions
of medical doctor and Confucian scholar. Although the samurai's
status was based on his location in the hierarchy and the level of his
stipend, the official domain doctor was respected regardless of salary.
He was thus within but separate from the samurai administrative
hierarchy and samurai culture. The Mori family, therefore, exemplified many samurai values: the family's reputation, patriarchal
lineage, samurai spirit, courage to commit seppuku, and loyalty to the
lord.

The role of Tokugawa doctors differed in one important respect
from that of Confucian scholars: among Tokugawa intellectuals doctors tended to be the most receptive to Western technology, while
Confucian scholars tended to be the most resistant. In the early
eighteenth century, books dealing with three areas of scientific study
were translated from Dutch into Chinese—astronomy and the calen-
dar, geography, and medicine—making the information available to
Confucian scholars in Japan. In the mid-1700s, Dutch doctors in
Nagasaki demonstrated startling therapeutic results, based on principles of anatomy and surgery, that were almost nonexistent in Sino-
Japanese medicine. Proof of the new science's practical benefits impressed Japanese medical specialists. Even before Western medicine
was fully accepted, many Japanese in the Tokugawa period, including
Rintarō's father traveled to the city of Nagasaki to be trained in
"Dutch medicine."[8] And many major feudal lords, including the shogun, employed Dutch-trained doctors side-by-side with Confucian
doctors. Until the Meiji period, Dutch medicine continued as the elite
and major form of Western medicine practiced in Japan.

A striking characteristic of Japan's westernization is that a non-
colonized nation on its own initiative assessed and then chose diverse
Western models. Other Asian countries which were colonized or
half-colonized experienced the West only through the colonizing
power. This pattern somewhat resembles the earlier situation in Japan

8. Nagasaki was a semi-open city from the early seventeenth century on. The Tokugawa regime at that time expelled all Portuguese missionaries and traders from
Japan but allowed Dutch and Chinese merchants to continue operating under close
control in Nagasaki, making that city Japan's link to the outside world during the Tokugawa era.

during the Tokugawa period, except that it was the inward-looking shogunate, not a foreign colonial government, which designated and maintained strict control over the sole source of information about Western technology, the port city of Nagasaki. The shogunate chose the Dutch as Japan's intermediaries to the West because it viewed them as the most militarily and religiously benign of the imperialistic powers.

The shrewd and pragmatic Meiji leaders abolished this single-source, restricted policy and used well-informed Japanese and European advisers to select the most advanced and "appropriate" Western models in each field. Just as they picked and chose among British, French, and Prussian military models, they shifted from a Dutch to a German medical model soon after the Restoration. In the early 1870s, the core of the Tokyo Medical School's staff was made up of German doctors. Mori and other medical students in his class no longer learned Dutch language or methods, but were trained completely according to the German medical system.[9]

Mori's childhood education set the foundations of his intellectual patterns for life. Rintarō was immersed from an early age in samurai values of duty, discipline, and preparedness for death. As the future successor to the family's profession, he received a tricultural education—the Chinese classics, indigenous Japanese learning, and early exposure to the Dutch language. At seven, Rintarō entered Yōrōkan, the domain school, where he received a classical education, and after two years was awarded a prize for his scholastic abilities. His father began to teach him Dutch at the age of eight. Young Rintarō was considered something of a child prodigy in the domain and when Yōrōkan closed its doors in November 1871, a year after the dissolution of the feudal domains, the Tsuwano lord recommended that Mori continue his studies in Tokyo. The following year, the Mori family moved to the new nation's capital.

As a result of reforms following the Meiji Restoration, educational

9. This pattern of superimposing more "advanced" foreign medical systems on previously adopted foreign practices was continued in the post–Second World War transition period, when the American system of medical education gradually replaced German textbooks and terminology. Because many of today's Japanese doctors were trained in the pre-1945 German-based system, however, the present situation is very much a technical and cultural mixture, parallel to what must have occurred during the Meiji transition. Clinical charts and records today are still an often confusing jumble of Japanese, English, and German.

and employment opportunities increased sharply for ambitious young elite and commoners from all over Japan. The new egalitarian system was radically different from the Tokugawa method of selecting students for important educational institutions on the basis of the political power of the candidate's domain and the hierarchical rank of his family. Fukuzawa Yukichi, founder of Keiō University, observed in his autobiography that under the Tokugawa regime, stupid boys from influential domains had more opportunities than intelligent boys from powerless domains. This change benefited Rintarō, since Tsuwano was a relatively uninfluential domain.

In Meiji Japan, as is still true today, the city with the most diverse and numerous possibilities for advancement was Tokyo. Not surprisingly, the capital city's population, over 1 million during most of the Tokugawa period and until the early nineteenth century the largest in the world, grew explosively in the Meiji period.

Rintarō advanced quickly in Tokyo. In 1872, only four years after the Restoration, he was, at age ten, learning German. Two years later he began attending preparatory courses for medical school. Meanwhile, in the fall of 1872, because his parent's new home was too far from the school for commuting, Rintarō took up lodging in the residence of Nishi Amane. His landlord was from a family that had traditionally served Tsuwano lords as doctors and thus was close to the Mori family. Moreover, Nishi was one of the leading intellectuals promoting modernization in the early Meiji. Six years before the Restoration Nishi and others were sent by the shogunate to Holland as the first Japanese students abroad. On returning to Japan, Nishi became a member of the brain trust of the decaying shogunate. After the Restoration, the Meiji government invited Nishi, with his highly-valued talents and knowledge, to participate in its efforts to establish new political, military, and cultural institutions. From 1872 to 1876, when Mori Rintarō lodged in his home, Nishi held a high rank in the imperial army. He also taught Western subjects to the emperor at the court and to students from Tsuwano at his private school. In 1873, with Fukuzawa Yukichi, Nishi founded the elite club of modernization proponents, the *Meirokusha*, to accelerate the introduction of Western culture into Japan.

Nishi apparently cared little about the adolescent from Tsuwano staying in his residence, although he must have been aware of Rintarō's unusual brightness. It is also difficult to say with certainty how much Nishi influenced Mori. Although he wrote a biography of Nishi after the statesman's death in 1897 at the family's request, the book was thoroughly objective and factual and included no personal impressions. Yet when Nishi's wife published a book of her short poems, Ogai wrote a preface, stating that as a child he had admired her household and was grateful for her warmth to him.

Because Mori was always conscious of his homeland, declaring in his testament that he wanted to die "as a man of Iwami," we can reasonably surmise that the bright and ambitious boy viewed Nishi, possibly then the most successful man from Tsuwano, both as a role model and as a rival. Given the paucity and precariousness of modernizer role models and the general role-consciousness of Japanese culture, Nishi is likely to have been especially important to Mori. Social change in all cultures intensifies the need for a model that can provide a reference point of stability.

In 1874, Rintarō became the youngest student to enter the Tokyo Medical Preparatory School. Three years later, when Tokyo University was established, he became a scholarship student in the medical department. Characteristically, Rintarō was well organized in his studies and received good marks with little effort, which gave him free time to read literature. Just before graduation, however, he suffered a mild bout of pleurisy, possibly tubercular, at which time his grandmother moved into the dormitory with him to prepare his meals and care for the family's prized child. A fire at Rintarō's lodging house during final examinations destroyed many important study notes, adding to his worries. In 1881, at the age of nineteen, he graduated from medical school, eighth in a class of twenty-four.

After medical school, Rintarō wanted to continue his studies in other fields, particularly in literature and journalism. Considering the force of the family medical tradition, this desire was a remarkable manifestation of self-assertion and interest in writing. The year of his graduation, he published his first newspaper article in the *Yomiuri shinbun*, hoping to join the exciting and burgeoning newspaper business. His parents, however, vetoed the idea of a literary career and prevailed on him to follow his father's medical career for economic reasons and, above all, for the sake of the family.

He attempted to obtain a scholarship from the Ministry of Education to study medicine abroad, but was denied a grant because of his relatively undistinguished graduation rank. Rintarō then began to consider a military career. One of his classmates, who had joined the military, recommended him strongly to the Army Medical Corps, and Nishi also promoted Rintarō's appointment.

Rintarō's decision to become a military doctor in 1881 was unquestionably a compromise reached under pressure from his parents and friends. But it was also pragmatic: the army would pay for his books, provide him with economic security, and satisfy his family's demands for social status. Most important for Mori the army offered him a chance to study abroad. But the compromise required various accommodations with established authorities, including his parents, Nishi, and General Yamagata, the powerful protector in Mori's later military career. Becoming a military doctor also demanded an internal accommodation, a painful sacrifice for the poet and the dreamer in Ogai.

The decision started Mori on his double existence in life as bureaucrat and creative writer. He was forever torn between two sets of values, between identifying with such groups as his family, the Tsuwano domain, the army, and the Meiji state, and an inner core that could only exist beyond the reality of his daily life in the imaginative world of his literary works.

Nearly three years after entering the army, which was then reorganizing on a German model, Mori was selected to investigate the Prussian system of hygenics. In August 1884, he boarded a ship in Yokohama bound for France, and by October he had reached Berlin. Mori then traveled to Leipzig University, where he began studying the nutrition of the Japanese military diet. He also stayed in Munich and studied with Max von Pettenkofer, founder of the science of hygienics. In 1887, Mori returned to Berlin to study with Robert Koch, the great bacteriologist who discovered the tubercle bacillus. In logical and direct fashion, Mori sought out Germany's, and indeed the world's, leading scholars in the field of public health, attended their lectures, and studied in their laboratories. Because he was sponsored by the Japanese army, the German authorities gave him wide freedom in choosing where and with whom to study. In the 1880s, neither Prussia nor other countries in Western Europe felt threatened militarily or culturally by the recently emerged Japanese nation. Europeans generally welcomed the inquisitive Japanese bureaucrats, students, scholars, and military leaders and supplied them with advice and models on how to modernize as rapidly and effectively as possible.

Germany at this time was a new and aggressive nation-state. Recently unified after the Napoleonic War under the kaiser and Prussian bureaucracy, it combined advanced sciences in national institutes with aristocratic traditions, especially among military officers. Nineteenth-century Europe viewed Germany as a success story, especially for having caught up with the more advanced countries, such as England and France. Japan aimed to achieve the same success. Japanese scholarship students in civil and military matters considered Germany as the model not only for medicine and military organization, but also for the basic project of modernization itself.

Germany was a more attractive model to the Japanese elite than other Western countries because of its success as a latecomer in the modernizing process. Germany combined modernity in some sectors with tradition in others. The "catching-up" processes in Germany during the late eighteenth and nineteenth centuries and in Japan after the late nineteenth century were both characterized by rapid centralization of government with limited provisions for democracy, and by a series of contrasts (see Katō, 1970): modernized heavy industries alongside many premodern elements in agriculture; new science and technology, contrasted with traditional arts and literature; and an advanced system of school education parallel to unchanged human relations and values, especially in private life. Indeed, in any catching-up process, it is probably impossible for a nation to develop all sectors with equal speed.

In choosing areas for modernization, both Germany and Japan tended to focus on the rational in public life and on the emotional in private life. In nineteenth-century Germany, for example, we can observe a thoroughly rational and systematic approach to sciences and the romantic temper in art and literature which culminated in Wagnerian ecstasy. In Meiji Japan, Köbel, a German professor of philosophy at Tokyo University, noted a similar dichotomy in the Japanese mind—reading Kant at the university, while indulging in sentimental traditional *shamisen* songs at parties.

The German bureaucratic system was highly structured, a sign of modernity according to Max Weber, while capitalistic production remained underdeveloped in comparison with England, as Marx observed in his preface to *Das Kapital*. In Japan, capitalism was guided and advanced by the government, which in turn was scarcely controlled either by the elected Parliament or by public opinion. The builders of Meiji Japan probably felt an affinity with imperial Germany in their plan for a future bureaucratic state and perhaps in their anticipation of the implications of the catching-up process.

Mori approached Germany in search of models that could strengthen the Japanese state. His experiences were structured and in part restricted by German and Japanese bureaucracies. The small but close colony of Japanese students in Berlin limited Mori's freedom of action; each kept informed of the others' lives. The group was tied by bonds of friendship but also by competition and antagonistic factionalism. Still, Mori's life in Germany was relatively free. He responded to Germany with youthful energy and considerable sensitivity and he developed a good command of the language. A sense of liberation fills his *German Diary (Doitsu nikki)* and even the recollections of his German years written much later in "Reveries." Mori was exceptional among the Japanese sent to Germany at that time. Few others could communicate in German as well as he, and some, such as Nogi, not at all. Mori Ogai was fascinated by the Western environment and actively associated with many Germans.

In Germany, Mori first cemented his identification with the Japanese bureaucracy. As part of his studies, he trained for several months with the Prussian infantry and learned the Bismark regime's political and military methods of social control. This intimate knowledge of Germany helped him rise within the Japanese military medical administration. Second, he acquired an immutable belief in the universal validity of a single system of scientific knowledge that transcended all differences in national culture and history. He studied at laboratories leading the world in experimental research. Even the word *Forschung* ("research") fascinated Mori, carrying a unique weight and a brilliance since, as he later recalled, an equivalent Japanese word had not yet been created. In Germany he learned a lasting dedication to research, sensitivity to method, and respect for facts.

He also gained a strong foundation in European cultural traditions. He read widely in literature as well as philosophy, including major German classics and such late nineteenth-century authors as Schopenhauer, Hartmann, Nietzsche, and Hauptmann. This firsthand knowledge of German literature made Ogai, after his return to Tokyo, the best qualified translator of Western literature in Meiji Japan. His early translations exposed Western nineteenth-century literature to most Meiji writers for the first time, and his presentation of Western literary concepts initiated a significant departure in Meiji literature from Tokugawa literary traditions. Four years of living with a Western language also influenced Ogai's style of Japanese prose, rendering it unusually explicit and logical.

Mori participated in the social and cultural life of the German military elite, joining his Prussian military colleagues at the theater, dances, and parties at coffeehouses and beer halls. These experiences helped liberate him from the restrictions on his senses imposed by his samurai upbringing and Confucian education. .

Mori lived in four German cities during a period of three and a half years, but traveled very little outside Germany, staying only briefly in Vienna to participate in international conferences and then in London and Paris on his way back to Japan. Because his experiences beyond German borders were extremely limited, Mori's intense encounter with German culture probably caused him to equate it with European culture in general. His later tendency to sprinkle his literary works with French words and expressions reflected the habits of German writers and even military officers. Perhaps in the late nineteenth century the contrasts between any West European country and Japan were so striking in practically all respects that subtle differences among European societies seemed almost negligible to the eyes of a young Japanese visitor. His major concern must have been not Prussia or Germany in a specific sense, but the West in general.

While in Germany, Mori's most dramatic confrontation with the Western world occurred in 1886 and 1887 in a public newspaper debate in Munich with Edmund Naumann, a German geologist who had spent ten years in Japan (1875–86). The controversy originated in an article written by Naumann on the Japanese land and people and published in June 1886 in a widely read Munich newspaper, *Allgemeine Zeitung* (June 26 and 29, 1886). A few days later, the same paper published a resume of a lecture given by Naumann at the *Anthropologische Gesellschaft* in Munich (*A.Z.*, June 30, 1886). Mori felt that he could not allow the arguments of Naumann to pass uncriticized. On December 30, 1887, he published his response, "The Reality of Japan." The debate continued one more round: Naumann replied to Mori's criticisms in January 1887, and Mori wrote his last article on February 1. Mori's decision to challenge publicly Naumann reflected a strong impulse to defend his country but also a will to examine some of its complexities and contradictions.

Naumann began by emphasizing the backwardness of Japanese so-

88 / MORI OGAI

ciety, pointing to such aspects as poor food and dirty clothes, and a great number of cases of contagious diseases and blindness. The geologist wrote that married women in the country commonly dyed their teeth black and that nakedness in public was popular in certain regions. He vehemently criticized Japan's westernization, claiming that the Japanese indiscriminately imported Western customs and institutions with no specific goals in view, merely as part of a national fashion. Naumann contended that importing just the fruits of Western civilization would weaken Japan and separate it from its own cultural essence. Naumann thus decried the dilution of Japanese traditional culture. He expressed a kind of imposed cultural relativism, which valued the traditions of Japan because of their differences from those of the West and condemned those Japanese who imitated the West and did not respect their own past.

Mori attacked Naumann's first point by demonstrating that his opponent's description of Japan's "backwardness" was a collection of extreme exaggerations, false generalizations, and simple ignorance. Mori cited facts that the Japanese people were sufficiently nourished, that their underwear was no dirtier than that of Germans, and that acute epidemic diseases were largely controlled, giving Japan a relatively low mortality rate. Blind persons were often visible on the streets, Mori explained, because of their professional activities in Japan as masseurs. And in the 1880s, very few women had black teeth and no Japanese was walking around naked in public. Against these stereotypes, which reflected prevalent European racial prejudices against Orientals at the time, Mori had no difficulty defending his country.

Naumann's criticisms of Japan's pattern of westernization, however, were more difficult to refute. On one hand, Mori certainly recognized that at least in part Naumann was right. (Later, in Japan, he echoed Naumann's statement in warning his countrymen that importing the fruits of scientific knowledge did not transplant the seeds of scientific development.) On the other hand, Mori could not accept the proposition that westernization would weaken Japan, as he himself was one of the young elite responsible for promoting it.

Mori responded by insisting that Japan's policy of importing Western institutions was highly selective, choosing only those institutions demonstrably useful for the country's present and future; and that despite faults in the Japanese experience, the country would overcome problems in the course of development, as an inexperienced child learns and grows through errors and shortcomings. Retrospectively, Mori was generally correct in his anticipation of how westernization would proceed in Japan. But at that time, he, as well as Japan, had little choice other than to promote westernization with as much wisdom as they could call forth and to believe in its ultimate positive value.

Naumann's final point challenged the very basis of Mori's cultural identity. Here the Western observer went beyond criticism of the state of westernization in Japan, to judge Japanese attitudes toward Japanese traditions. So far as westernization was concerned, the relationship between Germany and Japan was that of teacher and disciple. Naumann, representing Germany, naturally had some right to comment on Japanese attitudes toward westernization. But with regard to Japanese traditions, a German observer as teacher was perceived as threatening Japanese cultural identity. Yet Mori's rebuttal to Naumann conceded that some forms of westernization led certain people to abandon elements of Japanese culture. And in speaking of traditional culture, Mori was unsure how to evaluate or place Japan's experience in the context of world and modern Japanese history.

Mori certainly knew much more than Naumann about Japanese traditional culture, but the problem also required an understanding of Japanese traditions as cultural entities and of their role in the far-reaching social transformations based on Western models and technology. As a young man living at an early phase of the process, Mori inevitably lacked this broad cultural-historical sensitivity, which tended to weaken his arguments. For example, on the subject of Japanese and Western traditions of painting, he argued for oil painting with Japanese subject matter, which Naumann could have easily countered to underline his general thesis of the importance of indigenous traditions.

For our purposes, the most important aspect of the Mori-Naumann debates is not the polemical exchange as such or its outcome in the German press, but its effect on Mori. The young doctor, still in his mid-twenties, learned much from his encounter with Naumann, especially about his own weaknesses and his need to reevaluate Japanese traditional culture. That task became a central theme in Mori Ogai's intellectual and literary life. Indeed, the story he wrote a quarter of a century later defending General Nogi and his subsequent historical writings may be considered as part of a continuing response.

Toward the end of Mori's European years, Dr. Ishiguro Tadanori, his superior in the Army Medical Corps, came to Berlin. Mori acted as his guide and interpreter, especially in the International Red Cross Conference in Karlsruhe in 1887, and then joined Ishiguro in the long journey back to Japan. To Mori, Ishiguro represented the restrictive cobweb of Japanese society in general and of the army in particular. Although Ishiguro was pleased with having the younger physician's assistance, Mori felt tense and depressed by the constant presence of his superior. In one of his short stories written in 1889, he reflected: "When I first came to Germany I thought I understood my own destiny. I swore that I would never again become a machinelike person. But it was only a temporary freedom, like that freedom a bird with bound legs feels in flapping its wings. The bonds around the legs cannot be untied" (*Selected Works*, vol. 7, p. 164).

Ishiguro symbolized Mori's reintegration into the Japanese social hierarchy and his separation from European culture, medical science, and German friends. Another example of Mori's mood of sad resignation is a classical Chinese poem he sent from Paris to Ozaki Yukio, a strongly individualistic liberal and member of Japan's early parliament, whom he had met in London.[10]

> If one doesn't touch poisonous snakes one can avoid
> venomous anger
> Waiting for a good opportunity and keeping silent for
> a moment is the best strategy
> Many thoughts in the night of a lonely figure
> in the sea isles
> Men in exile meet together to speak of
> common worries
>
> (Kobori, p. 685)

Although meant to reflect Ozaki's exile, the poem expressed Mori's own inner feelings about leaving the individual freedom of Europe and returning to his responsibilities and inevitable conflicts in Japan.

While in Germany, Mori became intimate with a young German

10. Ozaki had been banned from Tokyo in 1887 under the Peace Preservation Act because of his antigovernment activities in the freedom and popular rights movement (see chapter 4), and he chose to study in London rather than live in another area of Japan.

woman.[11] Mori must have known quite well the affair's implications for his military career. Yet "Ellis" is never mentioned in his long and detailed *German Diary*. We know about her only through accounts of the relationship's tragic conclusion in Japan. Immediately after Mori's departure from Marseilles, "Ellis" boarded a boat for Japan, arriving at Yokohama two weeks after him. Mori, however, neither met her boat nor visited her at the hotel in Tokyo where she was staying. Instead, he informed his family—his mother, brother, sister, and brother-in-law—and on the day of her arrival, they discussed how to bury the affair as silently as possible.

His relationship with "Ellis" threatened the family's future projection of itself in the person of Mori and his career: marriage to a German could eliminate any chance of success in the military. Officers had to obtain formal permission from their superiors to marry, and although marriage to a non-Japanese woman was not explicitly forbidden by law, in practice, it occurred only once in the seventy-five years before 1945. Marriage to a foreigner also threatened the family line carried on in Mori—any offspring, including the family heir, would be considered impure.

The Mori family acted immediately. For three weeks Mori's brother and brother-in-law, a professor at Tokyo University's faculty of medicine, gently but firmly tried to persuade "Ellis" to return to Europe. During this period, they were in constant contact with Ishiguro, Mori's superior, who apparently also pressured Mori to resolve the affair. Ishiguro's diary briefly records separate visits to his home by Mori, his family, and his closest friend, Kako Tsurudo (Hasegawa, 1971, pp. 235–36).

Mori's personal and family affairs were thus inseparable from the army's concerns. The Mori family and the military bureaucracy cooperated in their determined efforts to reintegrate the eldest son into Japanese society. To rejoin his family and his army, Mori thus had to betray a love relationship—betray himself—and cruelly reject a helpless German woman who had the extraordinary courage to travel halfway around the world to a strange country.

11. According to Hasegawa Izumi, the real name of Ogai's German woman friend is unknown. In his short story "Ballerina" ("Maihime"), she is called "Ellis." While this spelling seems strange for a German name, the most common guess is that Ogai borrowed the name from the German translation of a novel of Turgenev which misspelled the English name Alice as "Ellis."

When "Ellis" finally agreed to leave Japan the Mori family prepared her return ticket, provided her travel expenses, and booked a cabin in a French liner leaving Yokohama. On October 17, about three weeks after her arrival, the family, and at last Mori, escorted her from her hotel to the ship. On the same day, Mori visited Ishiguro, according to the diary of the latter, to report that "Ellis" had departed. Years later, his sister recalled the event in her memoirs: "Everything thus went smoothly without inflicting any damage to our precious eldest brother. Nothing was more important than that" (Hasegawa, 1962, p. 197).

But the conflict between Mori's emotional attachment to "Ellis" and his obligations to family and army did not disappear when she left Japan. He channeled his internal tensions in a direction that became second nature to him, into literary creation. "Ballerina," his first short story about his life in Germany, was published in January 1890. Its subject matter was so personal that he consulted his family before publishing it. The story describes the love affair between a dancer, who was romantically called a ballerina, and a Japanese bureaucrat-student studying in Germany, and his agonized decision of whether to stay with her or return to Japan. Its main character is persuaded by a friend to return to Japan for the sake of the army, the nation, and his future career. But in the last line of the story, the saddened lover expresses a lingering sense of regret for his decision: "Even today I have in my heart a feeling of hatred for that friend."

Writing and publishing "Ballerina" was Mori's protest against the restrictions of society and against the rule of his mother. It set a pattern, which persisted, of compromising in real life while protesting in the world of fiction. He accepted the conservative values of his family and the army while subscribing in his literary works to individualism. He was integrated into his social milieu but maintained a stubborn independence of mind. Mori Ogai began to live this dual existence, at the latest, during his years in Germany. With extraordinary control of his passions and perfectly disciplined behavior in private and public, Mori succeeded in balancing the two sides of his self, though never without pain, throughout his life.

At the end of 1888, with "Ellis" gone, Mori resumed his career in the military and assumed his responsibilities as head of the family. The affair was perhaps excused as an impetuous youthful mistake. But

Mori knew that if he were to be successful in the Meiji bureaucracy, he could afford no further indiscretions.

Soon after his return to Japan, Mori was officially appointed as an instructor at the Military Medical School. He subsequently published several articles based on his public health studies in Germany, starting with his investigations of Japanese nutritional habits. At the same time, he engaged in laboratory experiments on such topics as the military diet, portable army rations, and the hygienics of brick construction methods. In 1889, Mori founded Japan's first medical journal, the *Hygienics Journal*, to promote the Western scientific rationalism he had learned in Germany and to attack the emphasis on personal connections, authoritarianism, and irrationalism which he believed to govern the Japanese medical world. The following year, he began publishing a second journal, *New Medical Journal*, to advance the concept of experimental science in the field of medicine and to argue the unity of medicine against those who differentiated Eastern from Western medicine.

Mori's crusade challenged enormous vested interests. Many doctors, who maintained prosperous practices in Sino-Japanese medicine, adamantly resisted the spread of Western medicine. Whatever his general awareness of the diversity of cultural values, Mori was uncompromising in his emphasis on the universal validity of the experimental science he had learned in German laboratories: "Medicine is neither European nor Japanese; it is international" (*Ogai zenshū*, vol. 29, p. 458). Mori saw himself as enlightening Japan about "true" science. Although he would never again be as aggressive in the debate of East versus West in medicine, these polemics were necessary for him to make sense of his studies in Germany, and for Meiji Japan to promote the modernization of medicine.

During the same period, Ogai became active in literary affairs. He published several translations in 1889 and used the manuscript fees to found a literary journal later that year. Its title, *The Weir Papers* (*Shigarami sōshi*), was chosen to signify that the journal, like a weir or low dam in a rushing river, would employ literary criticism to give direction to the new style of Western-influenced literature. He enlisted the support of other leading Meiji authors and the journal rapidly gained fame. In 1890, Ogai wrote two additional short stories about his life in Germany: "Notes on Bubbles" ("Utakata no ki"), and "Messenger with a Letter" ("Fumi zukai"). Like "Ballerina" they deal with the central theme of self-discovery in a highly evolved literary style. They helped establish Ogai's reputation in the Meiji literary world as an innovative and capable author who introduced new themes in Japanese writing.

Mori's personal life after returning to Japan underwent rapid changes. His mother, who had absolutely insisted that "Ellis" leave Japan, did not wait long to consolidate her victory. In February 1889, she arranged Mori's marriage to the eldest daughter of Vice-Admiral Akamatsu Noriyoshi. Nishi Amane, who had known Akamatsu since 1862 when they traveled together to Holland, acted as the go-between for the marriage. Considering Nishi's immense prestige in the army, we might say that the marriage symbolically joined navy and army elites. Personally, however, Mori felt no affection for his bride. He considered the marriage to be a pragmatic arrangement for enhancing family status. And this it accomplished—at least for a time.

"Ballerina," a major literary accomplishment for Ogai, was not an auspicious beginning for his marriage. Although he received his family's approval to publish "Ballerina" and make known his affair with "Ellis," his new wife was unaware of the story until it appeared in print. In this concern for his family's feelings and utter disregard for his wife's, Ogai was behaving all too conventionally. His wife became enraged when she read the story and the incident contributed to the breakdown of their eighteen-month marriage. Shortly after the birth of their first son, Ogai abruptly divorced his wife, simply sending her home.[12]

The reasons for the divorce are not entirely clear. Some biographers stress Mori's dislike of her character and his near-physical revulsion toward her. Others interpret the divorce as the result of conflicts between the wife and Mori's mother, who first promoted the marriage and then virtually imposed the divorce on him. Mori was supported by his family in pressing for the divorce, although it obviously ran against the interests of Admiral Akamatsu and Nishi Amane. And it is quite possible that the divorce created some difficulties for his army career. After the divorce, Mori's attitude toward marriage became de-

12. Under the one-sided Japanese legal code at the time, the husband retained this prerogative.

cidedly negative and for the next ten years he remained single—but not alone. Again, at his mother's urging and choice, he adopted a "secret" mistress who lived in a nearby house. Such arrangements were not unusual in the society of prewar Japan, particularly for the elite class to which Mori belonged.

Mori's parallel dedication to his career as a medical administrator and to his work as an author became increasingly difficult in the mid-1890s. He was promoted in 1893 to director of the Military Medical School, which curtailed his outside literary activities for reasons of time as well as status. The outbreak of the Sino-Japanese War in August 1894 resulted in his assignment to Korea. With his departure, both his literary and medical journals halted publication. During the war and its aftermath, he published very little. Back in Tokyo in October 1895, Mori resumed the directorship of the Military Medical School, but was unable to regain his earlier creativity. The literary journal he founded to replace *The Weir Papers* lacked the wide-ranging impact of its predecessor, and the medical journal he established in 1897 was less vibrant and certainly less militant about modernizing medicine than Mori's publications just after his return from Germany. Mori fulfilled his administrative duties, gradually advancing in the Army Medical Corps hierarchy. Outside of his bureaucratic responsibilities, he continued translating Western works, wrote an objective biography of Nishi Amane at the request of the Nishi family, and taught aesthetics at Keiō University and anatomy to students at the Tokyo Art School, as he had before the war with China.

In June 1899, as part of an internal bureaucratic power struggle, Mori was demoted. His superiors, who resented his earlier attacks on the Japanese medical establishment and claimed his literary activities detracted from his administrative responsibilities, downgraded him to chief of the Twelfth Brigade's Medical Corps in Kokura in northern Kyūshū. Mori's way of dealing with the humiliation demonstrated his creative flexibility. He briefly considered resigning from the military, but his friend from medical school days, Kako Tsurudo, advised him to accept and endure the demotion. Mori characteristically settled for a rational compromise, accommodating himself to the situation, rather than temporarily withdrawing as the proud Nogi often did, or taking a decisive stand by resigning in protest as the rebellious Nakae Chōmin chose to do (see chapter 4).

In fact, the tour of duty that Mori spent in Kokura was neither as painful nor demeaning as he had expected. He overcame his sense of humiliation and began to enjoy the slower tempo and abundance of free time, the most he had known since Germany. He learned French, lectured to the division's military school on the military tactics of Karl von Clausewitz (1780–1831), studied history and the doctrines of Wang Yang-ming, and was instructed in Zen Buddhism by a local priest. Mori gradually acquired a new circle of friends, gained the personal confidence of the division commander, and grew increasingly comfortable with his version of life in the provinces.

One of Mori's new friends, the editor-in-chief of the local *Fukuoka nichinichi shinbun*, asked him to write a critique of the literary world for the special New Year's Day issue on the first day of 1890. The somewhat rambling but bitterly satirical essay that he produced, "Who is Ogai Gyoshi?" ("Ogai Gyoshi wa tare zo"), articulates Mori's internal and external struggles with his literary self.[13] He complains that his reputation as a novelist, which he argues was logically unjustifiable since he had written only a few short stories, had caused him innumerable troubles: medical doctors and government bureaucrats said they could not discuss technical issues or entrust important matters to a "novelist." The reputation was "truly impossible to adjust to and brought me little happiness."

Mori explains that Ogai Gyoshi was born when he first addressed his writings to the public in the magazine *The Nation's Friend (Kokumin no tomo)*. But the fame that he gained later, particularly through his own publication, *The Weir Papers*, marked the beginning of distrust from the medical and bureaucratic worlds. After tracing the origins of Ogai Gyoshi, the essay declared that as a result of recent battles with the new literary establishment, Ogai Gyoshi had died. At the same time Mori bitingly attacked the new writers, suggesting they were unskillful and uneducated, and referred to them as "what the Greeks call 'epigones.'"[14] In a climactic burst of emotion, Mori proclaimed, "Ogai has been killed, but I have not died." From his Kokura retreat, Mori expressed his defiance and declared his rebirth.

In the last few months of 1901, Mori's mother selected a new prospective wife for him and dispatched her to Kokura. The trial relation-

---

13. Ogai Gyoshi is a pen name that Mori used.
14. Meaning untalented imitators of genuine creators.

ship in northern Kyūshū was apparently successful: in January 1902, the forty-year-old Mori remarried. His wife Shige, who also had been previously married, was twenty-three, attractive, and the eldest daughter of a judge. But once they moved their household to Tokyo, following Mori's transfer there, relations between wife and mother-in-law gradually deteriorated.

Soon after his return to Tokyo, Mori rejoined its literary activities. For two years, he published various works on art and aesthetics, founded two literary journals, and translated books on anatomy for artists, the philosophy of race, and military strategy. In February 1904, war was declared between Japan and Russia, and in March Mori was sent to Manchuria.

Mori's attitude toward the war was extremely aggressive, even for a soldier. He viewed the conflict in clear racial terms: yellow versus white. This reflected the wild nationalism then raging in Japan, but it was also related to his personal experience of racial discrimination in Europe. During the nearly two years of fighting, Ogai wrote mainly poetry, including a number of long poems. Some of his poems were narrowly patriotic and quite conventional in language, image, and ideas. After the peace treaty was signed at Portsmouth in September 1905, he returned to his post as director of the Military Medical School in Tokyo.

Now his literary interests turned toward *waka*, the traditional Japanese poetry, and in mid-1906 he became manager-secretary with his friend Kako of a poetry group called Tokiwakai. A central figure in the club was Field Marshal Yamagata Aritomo, one of Japan's most powerful military and political figures; he and Mori became increasingly friendly. In 1907 Yamagata intervened in the bureaucracy on Mori's behalf to counter those who still opposed his advancement. He was then promoted to army medical commissioner, the highest rank attainable by a military medical officer, and appointed Chief of the Bureau of Medical Affairs in the Ministry of War.

Having achieved the pinnacle of his career in the military medical bureaucracy, Ogai, now in his late forties, entered his most productive literary period. He wrote several important works in 1907 and 1908, but his first year of truly prolific writing was 1909, when he published nine short stories and several plays, nearly one major work a month. Ogai continued this explosive phase of writing: in 1910 he wrote fourteen novellas and stories and several plays, and in 1911 he wrote seven short stories. He also began to translate Goethe's *Faust*, and the first part was published in 1913. Ogai's writings were not only voluminous, but spanned many topics: aesthetics, social problems, and philosophy. Certain themes stand out: his continued emphasis on traditional forms, his strong sense of self, and his persistent pattern of living through his literature.

Ogai and Nagai Kafū founded *Mitabungaku*, a literary monthly in which Ogai published many of his short stories. As an individualist, aesthete, and prose writer, Kafū largely shared Ogai's literary taste for elegant language, an attachment to the classics, and a conception of literature that emphasized poetic qualities and philosophical implications.[15] The writers associated with *Mitabungaku* opposed the predominant literary stream of "naturalist" novelists, who were partially inspired by such late nineteenth-century European naturalists as Zola and Maupassant.[16] Japan's "naturalists" advocated a plain style of prose close to spoken language, an abandonment of literary traditions, and a concept of literature as a vehicle for describing objectively and without idealization the "truth" of human life. They tended to interpret truth, first, as the overwhelming importance of sexual motivation in human behavior, more or less like their French counterparts, and second, as the exclusion of fictive elements in their stories, which of course had little to do with the European naturalism of Zola, Maupassant or any other Western writer. This philosophy produced the Japanese literary phenomenon of the "I novel" *(watakushi shōsetsu)*, in which the author relates his own experiences in daily life, tells of troubles with women in and out of his family, and avoids all intellectual interpretations and philosophical generalizations.

Ogai vigorously opposed the Japanese "naturalists." Culturally, he deplored their disregard of Japanese tradition. He also rejected their narrow interpretation of French naturalism, an interpretation he knew to be distorted. Among the critics of "naturalism," Ogai especially insisted on a more refined style, greater breadth and depth in subject

15. They were supported by a group of poets including Yosana Akiko in short poems, Ueda Bin in the translation of Western poetry, and Kinoshita Mokutarō in poetry and essays.

16. Although both Japanese and European schools are called "naturalists," they actually differ in several fundamental ways, as explained here and in chapter 6. To distinguish between them, we have placed the word referring to the Japanese school in quotation marks.

matter, and a literature of intellectual sophistication and abstraction. In 1907, he wrote "Half a Day" ("Hannichi"), in half a day, describing the struggles between his wife and his mother and the ethical dilemmas of being caught between the two. This blatant criticism of the two women closest to him imitated the style of the I novel, but differed in an important way from the typical "naturalist" presentations: Ogai did not merely record minute details of daily existence but sought to express his personal philosophy of life.

Another of Ogai's works, his well-known *Vita Sexualis* (1919), parodied the "naturalists" and their novels of sexual desire. In this book, Ogai used stark clinical language to describe his sexual experiences of adolescence, hoping to demystify the "naturalist" writings about sex. Contemporary Japanese society, however, misinterpreted Ogai's intended satire and initially regarded *Vita Sexualis* as part of the highly popular "naturalist" school. The government even banned its sale. Ogai's superior, the vice-minister of war, publicly criticized the work, apparently not comprehending its more philosophical questions about the role of sexual desire in human life. Actually, Ogai's mocking of the popular sexual novels and his general disdain for the "naturalists" reflected his more conservative side. Ogai implied that sex, like other matters, should be expressed within a framework of coherent cultural forms.

In May 1910, the police discovered an alleged conspiracy to assassinate the emperor and the next month arrested several hundred socialists. The police accused twenty-six of plotting the assassination, including Kōtoku Shūsui, an early socialist and anarchist leader active in journalism and politics and the most talented disciple of Nakae Chōmin. Despite government censorship of the press, news of Kōtoku's arrest leaked to the public. Although Mori was head of the Army Medical Corps, he in November 1910 published "Tower of Silence" ("Chinmoku no tō"), an allegorical short story that condemned the government's blatant abuse of power. He sharply criticized the suppression of new social and political ideas, contending that literature as well as science would die if new ideas opposed to the temporary mainstream in a given society could not be openly expressed.

Never had a high bureaucrat of the government so explicitly attacked the official policy line of the Meiji oligarchy—and remained in office. Ogai's opposition to the government's political arrest of Kōtoku required great courage. But his protest had little impact. All twenty-six were convicted of high treason in a hasty trial held in secrecy. Evidence suggests that only four people were involved in the plot, and Kōtoku was not one of them. Yet, in January 1911, the government sentenced twenty-four of the convicted to death. Twelve death sentences were commuted to life imprisonment, and in February, twelve of the accused, including Kōtoku, were executed.

A further explanation of Ogai's personal philosophy of life occurs in "As If" ("Kano yō ni"), published at the beginning of 1912. Its young aristocrat hero at first argues for the relativity of moral and political values, but then states that because no values are absolute and because society requires some system of values, one can only behave as if the traditional values were absolutely true. The hero uses this theory to justify his compromises in life and his difficulty in taking a stand vis-à-vis history. At the end of the essay, however, the hero's "as if" philosophy is harshly criticized by his artist friend: "If your philosophy leads to a dead end, why don't you break it by throwing yourself into something?"

Ogai loosely borrowed the "as if" philosophy from Hans Vaihinger, who was influential in Germany in the early twentieth century, and applied it to come to terms with his own moral and political conflicts, to smooth over some disturbing inner questions, and to purchase a kind of serenity.[17]

But the final remarks by the artist in the story show Ogai's acute awareness of the philosophy's limitations and suggest his admiration of those who "break it" and choose alternatives—the artist in the story, Kōtoku Shūsui, and perhaps the German woman in Ogai's life. Although Ogai's real life proceeded on the pragmatic basis of "as if," the scope of his thought extended beyond. His sensitivity to the tensions inherent in consciously acting "as if" traditional values were absolute may, indeed, have been a source and a motivation for his literary works.

General Nogi's junshi in September 1912 marked another turning point in Ogai's literary activities. One month later, Ogai published "The Testament of Okitsu Yagoemon," the first of his historical short stories. One indication of the warm feelings between the two military

17. Vaihinger, on the other hand, in his *Philosophy of As If* strongly emphasized distinctions between truth and falsehood, stressing that fictions contradict observed reality and falsify experience even when they function "as if" true (Handy, pp. 221–22).

men is that when Ogai was demoted to the position in Kokura, and was departing from Tokyo, Nogi came to see him off. Nogi's presence was an expression of personal kindness but also of sympathy, and indeed empathy, for the younger friend's public humiliation. These personal bonds undoubtedly contributed to the impact Nogi's seppuku had on Ogai. It moved him deeply and reactivated his connections with traditional forms.

Many of the historical stories that Ogai wrote after Nogi's death dealt with questions of self-control and death, suggesting an attempt to justify Nogi's act, or at least to point out its more significant aspects. "The Sakai Incident" ("Sakai jiken"), written in 1914, for example, described the seppuku in the late Tokugawa period of Tosa soldiers who had killed eleven French sailors landing at the port city of Sakai. Twenty soldiers, promoted to the rank of samurai at their own request, had been ordered to commit the bloody suicide before the French officers. The Westerners endured watching eleven suicides before asking that the spectacle be halted. In this story Ogai underlined the disciplined self-control of the samurai traditions in contrast to the highly emotional reactions of the French. His other historical stories gradually expand beyond the Tokugawa period and the samurai world, but always evoke the quality of traditional life and the vigor of the personalities it nurtured. Ogai's literary goal was not simply to justify General Nogi's anachronistic suicide or to defend values generated by Japanese culture that differed from those in the West. His stories were part of his own personal struggle to discover creative power and vitality in traditional values for himself and for Japan. They were his real answer to Dr. Naumann, the answer he was unable to provide at the time of the debate in Munich thirty years earlier.

In 1916, Mori entered the final period of his life. In March his mother Mineko died at the age of seventy. In April, the fifty-four year-old Mori retired as chief of the Medical Affairs Bureau, an office he had held for ten years. Two other deaths that year, of Meiji authors Natsume Sōseki and Ueda Bin, must have emphasized to Mori his own aging. But he remained outside the bureaucracy only slightly more than a year. In late 1917 he was appointed general director of the Imperial Museum and Archives, and in 1919 he became director of the Imperial Art Academy.

During this period, Ogai concentrated his literary efforts on studies of Tokugawa scholars, particularly doctors and Confucianists, writing his best-known historical biographies, of Shibue Chūsai, Izawa Ranken, and Hōjō Katei. Many view this trilogy as Ogai's most accomplished writing. He perfected his prose to attain, according to such writers as Nagai Kafū and Ishikawa Jun, the highest expression of modern Japanese style. He created a new literary form, a biography interwoven with the author's description of the act of writing the book. And Ogai strongly identified with his heroes, invigorating his descriptions and bringing alive persons from the distant past.

Although Ogai dreamed of retreating to the mountains and living in total seclusion, he fulfilled it only vicariously through his writing. In his biography of Hōjō Katei, he commented that the Tokugawa Confucianist's ability to live for a time as a secluded scholar, to accomplish what he, Ogai, could not, was one reason for choosing him as a subject. Ogai envied the ability of all three scholars—Chūsai, Ranken, and Katei—to devote themselves totally to classics and history. The major figures of these powerful literary works resonate with feeling, perhaps because the author so desperately wanted to live their lives. Through these three volumes more than any other, Ogai symbolically transcended his own life.

The author Akutagawa Ryūnosuke met Ogai while the older man was researching the biography of Hōjō Katei. Their encounter is recorded by one of Ogai's literary disciples, Kojima Masajirō. Akutagawa described Mori as "an awkward person to deal with." Ogai was constantly puffing on a cigar, but each time he finished one and took another he quickly closed the box. Akutagawa, who longed for a cigar, was never offered one and could never ask for one. Several days later Akutagawa visited Ogai at his home, finding the author with about twenty old letters spread on the tatami mats of his study. Ogai explained that they were undated letters of Hōjō Katei. Since they were the best primary sources available about Katei's life, Ogai was arranging them chronologically by their contents. When Akutagawa wondered out loud whether such a task was possible, Ogai is reported to have replied, "At least not impossible. I employed the same method with Chūsai and Ranken and succeeded then." Self-confident and well in control of the situation, Ogai expressed more than a little condescension toward Akutagawa.

Early in 1922, Ogai's health began to deteriorate. In June he stopped his official work, and in early July he dictated his last will and testament to Kako. Dictation was not unfamiliar to Ogai. He had translated many books by dictation, producing works of such high literary quality that they hardly seem translations. By rejecting in his testament "all formalities" at burial and insisting that he "die simply as Mori Rintarō of the province of Iwami," he was renouncing more than his official, military-bureaucratic achievements. He also in effect denied the meaning of his literary fame, and perhaps his creative opus, under the name of Mori Ogai. In any case, the official powers denied his request and buried him with the ceremonies appropriate to his rank and achievements.

The testament raises questions about the identity he ultimately sought for himself. Did Iwami, his birthplace, symbolize for the dying man something far more important than all his accomplishments as a great leader of the Meiji intellectual enlightenment? Perhaps. At one point in "Reveries," Mori describes sleepless nights in Berlin when "I felt I was nothing more than an actor performing on stage," and he seems always to have retained those feelings of playacting. After leaving Iwami, Mori burst forth on the great stage of Meiji Japan. As a gifted actor, he brilliantly played different roles assigned to him by groups to which he belonged and by himself. When his theater came to its end, Mori left the stage to become a simple man again as he faced his death, a man without roles, as at the beginning of his life.

Only through documents released thirty years after his death when his copyrights expired, did it become known that he had suffered from tuberculosis. Thus, even at the end of his life, Mori strikingly combined a defiance of authority, in insisting that he be buried as an ordinary man from Iwami, with a submission to cultural prejudice, in hiding the fact of his tuberculosis to protect the family name. This stance was somehow typical of Mori Ogai—never simply one position or its opposite, but always a combination of positions at a high level of accommodation and integration. The reasons for Mori's accommodationism might be found in his high integration into given groups, such as his family and the army, and his lack of commitment to an absolute value that went beyond the day-to-day world. He justified these accommodations, as we have seen, through his philosophy of "as if."

Mori thus personified Meiji society. He and Meiji Japan compromised and balanced between two cultures; both felt tensions and stress resulting from their accommodations. We should be careful, however, not to underestimate the subtle complexities with which Western and Japanese traditions were intertwined. Although their elements can be isolated, it is not unlike separating the precipitate from the distillate of a single equilibrium. Both cultures were mixed in the Meiji state. Extracting their disparate components may help our analysis, but it also detracts from understanding the subject of study as a whole. Mori's personal blending of Japanese and Western cultures was among the most sophisticated of his time.

His attachment to medicine was probably the closest he came to a "pure" Western ideology and was most pronounced just after his return from Germany. But Mori also conceived of literature in Western terms, as a cognitive means of interpreting human existence, which differed greatly from the traditional Japanese idea of literature as entertainment. He was in fact largely responsible for introducing this concept into Meiji society. On the other hand, his writings, as we know, drew heavily on traditional Japanese themes and images. In family relations, Mori was strongly immersed in traditional forms, particularly in his relationship with his mother and in his role as the eldest son and family head. But even these personal relations expressed an intermingling of cultures.

Mori's integration of two disparate cultures, however, contained an inherent instability. The process of balancing is not static but constantly changing, and the coherence of the moment can break down and lead to the individual experience of despair. This is the vulnerable point, the Achilles' heel, of accommodationism. Mori experienced such despair on at least two occasions, during the conflict over his affair with the German woman and during his mid-career demotion and exile to Kokura. These two conflicts, however, were not simply between modern and traditional elements or between Japanese and Western cultures. His family relied on traditional ties to terminate his affair with "Ellis," but its goal was to ensure his success as a "modern man" in the new Meiji state bureaucracy. Similarly, his demotion to Kokura occurred in a bureaucracy that fused modern and traditional elements and resulted in part from his being too modern in his earlier absolute advocacy of Western medicine and his continuing literary activities. On both occasions Mori dealt with his despair by writing about the experience (in "Ballerina" and in "Who is Ogai Gyoshi?"). Great writer that he was, he could transmute depression and despair into creative forms.

In describing his approach to death as one of neither fear nor desire, Mori went on to explain: "In my youth I felt keenly that I wanted to solve the puzzles confronting me before reaching the final destination of death. But that desire has gradually dimmed. I still see the unsolved puzzles, and I still believe they must be solved. But I am no longer in such a hurry to solve them" ("Reveries"). Mori was aware that he had accomplished much, but in old age he also must have recognized the extent of his actual achievement. Perhaps this recognition allowed him in this testament to strip away everything, to refuse categorically all identification with high-ranking bureaucrats, even to cast off his literary name of Ogai. "Death is a very serious matter which ends all. However powerful the state may be, I believe that it cannot act against my will." And then: "I would like to die simply as Mori Rintarō of the province of Iwami." He repeated the phrase not merely as a desire but as a command, and instructed that his tombstone be inscribed only "GRAVE OF MORI RINTARŌ." And finally: "These are the words that I leave with my one and only friend, and no one shall interfere with them."

COMMENTARY / S. Katō

Ogai's relationship to political power through Yamagata Aritomo represents a general pattern of a relatively liberal intellectual seeking to change government policies through his tie to a major powerholder. Such personal advisers are often prominent men of culture who approach the center of political decisions over the head of the bureaucracy. They commonly exert for a limited time considerable influence on political and administrative matters and remain conservative in the sense that they never attempt to radically change the system itself. The fulfillment of their reformist intentions, and sometimes their very lives, depends on the often unpredictable will of the ruler. An ancient example of this relationship is Seneca's association with Nero. More recent examples include Michel de Montaigne's association with King Henry IV in sixteenth-century France, and Arai Hakuseki's relationship with the sixth shogun and his powerful adviser Manabe Akifusa, in early seventeenth-century Japan.

Working within the power structure holds the possibility of achieving some liberalization of government policies. But on the other hand such efforts are under constant pressure from conservative elements both within the bureaucracy and outside the government. The liberal within a conservative power structure is in an extremely vulnerable position that requires compromises which may undermine his own objectives. In critical situations, such as wartime, the apparent collaboration of eminent liberals with the government can be used as a symbol to weaken liberal protests against conservative and rightist policies. Although this was not a major issue with Ogai, it did occur with liberals in Japan's Shōwa Research Group during the 1930s and with liberals in the United States government during the 1960s.[18]

On a more personal level, Ogai and Montaigne resemble each other not only in their relationship to political power but also in certain philosophical attitudes toward life and death that are often considered to be typically Japanese. For example, they shared a skepticism toward doctrines. Montaigne commented on men of knowledge: "Moy, je les ayme bien, mais je ne les adore pas" (p. 415). Ogai wrote in a similar way about his search for an ideology: "Standing at a crossroad, I met many teachers, but no master whom I could follow" ("Reveries"). This feeling was the basis of this theory of "as if," which is very reminiscent of Montaigne.

Montaigne and Ogai also expressed similar attitudes toward certain human values. Both stressed the virtues of self-control, courage, upright conduct, rationality, and an austere life-style. They also subscribed to a kind of elitism with a strong sense of noblesse oblige, in which self-control in an extreme situation might become a total numbing of all feeling, and suicide might be considered the most dignified act for a man. They wrote about their attitudes toward death in similar words. Montaigne noted that "Nature's hand" prepares us for death: "conduicts par sa main, d'une douce pente et comme insensible, peu à peu, de degré en degré, elle nous roule dans ce misérable estat et nous y apprivoise" (p. 89). The wise man, according to Montaigne, avoids neither life nor death: "ny de fuir la vie, ny de refuir à la mort" (p. 94). Ogai also neither aspired for nor feared his own death: "Thus, neither fearing nor yearning for death, the old man dreamed unrealized dreams and lived out his last days" ("Reveries").

Montaigne and Ogai both agreed with Horatius: "Mors ultima linea rerum est." What these men shared was a belief that the "end of

18. Konoe Fumimaro, prime minister from 1937 to 1939 and 1940 to October 1941, formed the Shōwa Research Group in 1936 to provide progressive advice on policy. The group not only was unable to prevent the growth of militarism but helped legitimate it.

things" does not necessarily imply for everyone fear, or a desperate attempt to extend life. In the West, and for Montaigne, the culture that nurtured this view was roman or stoic; in Japan, and for Ogai, it was the samurai culture.

COMMENTARY / R. J. Lifton

Ogai, to the end, lived out his particular version of the mode of accomodation, with its central principle of continuity. The accommodationist fundamentally does not seek either a return to an imagined past (as does the restorationist) or a radical plunge into an imagined future (like the transformationist). Rather he seeks an inner modus vivendi for blending imagery of past, present, and future, and calls forth a psychological spirit of compromise.

But during a time of historical transition, such as the Meiji or post–Second World War eras, the mode of accommodation can become extremely demanding in its psychological choices, the unclarity of relationships between self and society, and the fragility of emerging psychic combinations. That is why we can speak of accommodation's occupational hazard as despair. The despair has to do with uncertainty about ultimate attachments of the self—about forms of symbolic immortality being so painfully crafted, explored, and modified. The hazard is all the greater for the gifted accommodationist like Ogai who requires of himself that he remain open to the full complexity of personal and historical imagery.

Although accommodation sounds much more muted, less exciting, than either restoration or transformation, Ogai demonstrates to us how intense—and creatively productive—it can be. For the talented accommodationist is temporally and culturally "all over the place." He can do special things, and he pays the price.

Thus, Ogai could seem to enter the mode of restoration in his sympathetic identification with Nogi's suicide, but then creatively incorporate its very pastness into a larger principle of cultural continuity. On the other hand, his scientific medicine was uncompromisingly iconoclastic and, in effect, transformationist. But science, too, as his primary Western identification, became part of a larger continuity— one associated with necessary change and evolving personal and cultural forms. And throughout, his ultimate and inclusive allegience was to the collectivity of Japaneseness, to what I have elsewhere called the immortal racial and cultural substance that forms the psychological basis of nationalism. This mode of (biosocial immortality) had long been central to the Japanese and was uniquely energizing as an organizing principle for the Meiji Restoration.

It is interesting to compare Ogai's accommodationism to the very different approach of Albert Camus, who had a similar range of historical, ethical, and creative interests. Camus, after complex experiences with a number of the main political and intellectual currents of his generation—notably Marxism and existentialism—also came to express himself strongly for continuity and for "limits" and against the kind of revolutionary transformationism that inevitably resulted in violence and killing in the name of ideology, or in what Camus called "crimes of logic." But in contrast to Ogai's "as if" philosophy, which essentially required that one deal with uncertainty by going along with prevailing philosophical assumptions, by behaving as if they were true, Camus (1954) preaches exactly the opposite. He stands for the rebel: "A man who says no: but whose refusal does not imply a renunciation" since "He is also a man who says yes as soon as he begins to think for himself."

Camus's model of autonomy—based on a continuous stance of potential rejection of existing arrangements, including and especially those of one's immediate group—is directly antithetical to the longstanding Japanese sense of mutuality and even merger between individual and immediate group. There is still a quest for biosocial immortality in Camus's stance, but one's "group" becomes humankind—an ideal collectivity of men and women united by their critical stance toward the status quo. That kind of universalism via resistance to the immediate has been an extremely difficult stance for Japanese to assume.

Only in his deathbed instructions could Ogai, finally and belatedly, say "no" to the stringent, often suffocating and hypocritical, rules and ritual of Japanese officialdom to which he had always subsumed himself during life. In asking to be buried simply as Mori Rintarō he was laying claim to his own death—in this case not so much to the moment of dying as to the person who had "just died." It must have meant much to him to do at least that.

Could he have been reacting to a deep sense of personal unease, a feeling bordering on guilt and shame, having to do with his having succumbed so much to his military-national "group" at the expense of more individual realization? That kind of "existential guilt"—or animating relationship to guilt—reflects the inner sense of gap between the man one is and the man one could be, and is at the heart of the human capacity for spiritual growth. (The principle is obscured rather than illuminated by sharp distinctions between "guilt cultures" and "shame cultures.") There is surely pathos in Ogai's capacity to gain access to his dimension of self only in dying—all the more so since Japanese society eventually made its own claim, or rather continued that claim on Ogai, and buried him with all the ritual he rejected. Yet his final assertion by negation is part of his legacy, reflecting the pain of a hidden vision beneath his achievement.

4 / NAKAE CHŌMIN (1847–1901)

"One Year and a Half"

Nakae Chōmin

FROM THE WRITINGS OF NAKAE CHŌMIN

One day I visited Dr. Horiuchi and inquired how many days and months before my death. I asked him to speak truthfully and hide nothing. With much to do and enjoy, I wanted to use completely every last day. To make plans for my remaining days I asked how long I had to live. The rather innocent Dr. Horiuchi thought for a few minutes and then replied quite uncomfortably, "One year and a half; perhaps two years if you take good care of yourself." I told Horiuchi that I had expected to live only five or six months and that in one year I could certainly reap a rich harvest from life. This is why I chose the title One Year and a Half.

Some of you may say that one year and a half is very short; I say it is an eternity. But if you wish to say it is short, then ten years is also short, and fifty years is short, and so, too, is one hundred years. If this life is limited in time and that after death is unlimited, then the limited compared to the unlimited period is not even short: it's nothing. If you have things to do and enjoy, then isn't it possible to use quite well one year and a half? As fifty and one hundred years disappear, so, too, does the so-called one year and a half. Our life is nothing but a single empty boat on a nonexistent sea.

Thus, I received a death sentence of one year and a half. Since then, what are the pleasures of my daily life? For the present, because I am a traveler and have no books, I amuse myself by reading the local Osaka press (the Asahi *and* Mainichi *newspapers) as well as the more familiar* Yorozu Chōhō *newspaper from Tokyo. Through these three papers I maintain contact with the outside world.*

Recalling the excellent entertainment provided by vocal parts of the puppet performance, I decided soon after my arrival in Osaka to attend the bunraku, *the puppet theater, and convinced the manager of my hotel to join me. . . . My wife had heard* Chūshingura *performed twice before, and I three times. Nonetheless that evening I never tired of the show, and, indeed, the more I listened, the more amused I became, proving how truly superb the performance was. Tsu-dayu's countenance and deep voice, reflecting his dignity and elegance, created with astounding precision the character of Oishi Kuranosuke, deputy lord of the Akō Castle. He was joined by Ro-dayu, speaking the Kantō dialect exactly like a native, who played the straight-forward and courageous character of Heiuemon. And who could have surpassed the graceful voice and coquettish singing of Koshiji-dayu in imitating the female character of Okaru? It was the most magnificent theater imaginable, and I have already viewed it three times. One year and a half is decidedly not so short. Did not Confucius himself say that if one learns the way in the morning, then one can die in the evening without regret?*

If time had stood still, I would have had before me an eternal life, with neither death nor sickness. But this was not so, and gradually my last year and a half passed away. A swelling in my throat which had been slowly expanding began to constrict my breathing and disturb my sleep. My wife and friends recommended that I return to Tokyo for medical care and then come back to Osaka. But after examining me, Dr. Horiuchi forbade such a trip, saying that it would be extremely dangerous in my condition and that I would surely suffocate during the train ride. According to the doctor, the only possible treatment was a tracheotomy, a relatively simple operation in which a hole is cut in the windpipe and a metal pipe is inserted to permit respiration. But my wife, being fearful and undecided about the operation, sent a telegram to my cousin, Asakawa Norihiko, a medical doctor, asking him to come. After considering my case, Norihiko agreed with Dr. Horiuchi's conclusions, and on May 26, in the presence of Norihiko and one Dr. Ishigami, director of the Osaka Institute of Contagious Diseases, Dr. Horiuchi performed my tracheotomy.

After the operation I rented a room in a house directly in front of the hospital so I could continue receiving treatment from Dr. Horiuchi. This house belonged to the Asao family and was located in 1-chome Imabashi, facing a canal. To its right was the Kōrai Bridge, and to its left, the Takaiji Bridge. From its front gate, which looked to the east, I could see the Tenjin Bridge rising from the water. In the evening, lights from both banks reflected brightly on the canal, and it seemed as though I were living in a house built on water. Dr. Horiuchi visited me daily to dress my wound, and I faithfully obeyed his instructions to rest. Although the tracheotomy incision was small, it was nonetheless an operation. At first I felt considerable pain, and whenever I coughed, phlegm, instead of coming from my mouth, flowed directly from my breast. My voice was completely dry and no longer resonated. I could speak to people only by approaching them very closely. I had obviously become a disabled person. Moreover, this surgical operation was far from a fundamental cure; it would only prevent my suffocating to death while I lived my remaining one year and a half.

After news of my tracheotomy became known in Osaka and Tokyo, I received a daily stream of letters asking about my recovery. I had my wife reply that my progress was excellent. Many people, unaware of the meaning of a tracheotomy in cases of cancer, automatically assumed that the operation had successfully cured my disease and sent letters of congratulations. The "year and a half" was known only to my wife and myself. Even my two children sent postcards and letters from Tokyo saying, "dearest Father, in due course you will recover." As a father I adopted a stoic philosophy; I had to protect my secrecy. Ah, but human beings are such fools.

My wife, who never once complained about my one year and a half, demonstrated a deeper understanding of human beings than I had expected. She listened to me faithfully and tried to enjoy the present. In that way, she seemed to console herself. Even while we were at the hospital, she somehow appeared cheerful, as if she were relaxing at a hot springs. I passed the days leisurely and eventually my wound healed completely, leaving me with only a cough. On June 18, I left the hospital to return to Kozuba Inn in Nakanoshima.

(One Year and a Half [Ichinen yūhan], pp. 166, 167)

Although the spirit is not indestructible, the body, which provides the foundation for the spirit, is composed of many elements that are indestructible.

When Napoleon and Toyotomi Hideyoshi died, the gaseous elements which composed their bodies perhaps were absorbed by birds in the sky. And maybe the solid elements dissolved in ground water, soaked into the roots of a radish and finally appeared in some person's stomach. Although elements continuously change their locus of existence, they never cease to exist. Thus when a person dies, his previously alive and moving body begins to decompose and its elements begin to disperse, but none of the individual elements are ever destroyed.

According to this logic, there should be no hope of reaching heaven and no fear of condemnation to hell. It is impossible to receive another body and be reborn. The only second generation for oneself in this world is one's children.

Whether you say there are many gods or only one, no god existed before the beginning. Although we do not know what existed before the present world, there is no doubt that the elements which formed the previous condition evolved into the present one. Even without the intervention of such a dubious thing as God, these elements which exist without beginning or end change incessantly from state to state through the process of combination and recombination and thus create the history of the world.

(Sequel to One Year and a Half [Zoku ichinen yūhan], p. 220)

In April 1901, one of Japan's foremost progressive political theorists and newspaper commentators, Nakae Chōmin, began to experience severe throat pain and difficulty in breathing. Suspecting cancer, he consulted a doctor, who confirmed his fears. The diagnosis was cancer of the larynx. The doctor estimated that the fifty-four-year-old man had at most eighteen months to live. Chōmin must have expected that his last months would not be pleasant.

Throat cancer is a particularly debilitating disease. It imposes on its victims unrelenting stresses, both physical and psychological, as the body gradually deteriorates. One of the first functions lost is verbal communication: doctors often perform a tracheotomy to alleviate breathing difficulties and inserted a tube into the windpipe, thereby depriving the patient of the ability to speak. This condition of blocked communication but sustained consciousness commonly lasts for months as the person's health gradually decays.

Chōmin's tracheotomy was performed in May, a month after he received the diagnosis—his "death sentence," as he called it. For the last seven months of his life, Chōmin was confined to bed and communicated with visitors by writing with chalk on a piece of slate. The breathing tube sticking out of his throat made his life awkward and uncomfortable. He could eat no solid food and survived only on tofu, soft bean curd. And because of swelling in the area around his larnyx, Chōmin was unable to sleep on his side or his back. He had to lie on his stomach and support his forehead by folding both arms on the pillow, while painfully raising his neck. Only in this torturous position could Chōmin rest.

Despite his suffering during this period of enforced convalescence and physical deterioration, Chōmin wrote two remarkable books, *One Year and a Half (Ichinen yūhan)* and *Sequel to One Year and a Half (Zoku ichinen yūhan)*, in which he recorded his last words on politics, politicians, and philosophy. Neither physical pain nor the knowledge of imminent death prevented him from completing the work—a work that Chōmin called the expression of his "true self." Indeed, the realization that his life would soon be over drove him to finish his writing. He was concerned totally with this world—with how to live and how to die—and not with the world beyond. Chōmin reasoned that if one year and a half is short, then ten years also is short, and ultimately any limited time of life, compared to death, must be considered either as nothing or as eternity. His focus on the relativity of time is one frequently expressed by dying people in many cultures.

In convalescing after the tracheotomy, he sought to use well the limited time left him. He viewed the famous play of the forty-seven masterless samurai, *Chūshingura*, in his beloved puppet theater, the bunraku. His comment that "It was the most magnificent theater imaginable"—followed by the Confucian maxim, "If one learns the way in the morning, then one can die in the evening without regret"—suggested that puppet theater was more than mere pleasure for Chōmin. It was an experience of transcendence.

Chōmin derived great satisfaction from reading the daily newspapers. They allowed him to continue to feel connected with the particular world of the living that had engaged him for many years in his own activist journalism and general commitment to libertarian causes.

Chōmin's frantic writing also symbolized his connection to living. His first volume, *One Year and a Half*, presented in a diary style his life and thoughts beginning with the discovery of his disease in April and ending in August. Chōmin wove progress reports of his illness with a running commentary on current events, and he mixed biting criticisms of Meiji politicians and society with subtle discussions of shamisen music and philosophical remarks on life and death. The second volume, *Sequel to One Year and a Half*, was written in late September in Tokyo, while Chōmin was struggling with constant pain, coughing fits, and failing eyesight. The book, subtitled "Without God, Without Soul" (*Mushin mureikon*), explored problems of atheism and materialism, and partially fulfilled Chōmin's longstanding aspiration to develop and record systematically his personal philosophy. In a final, almost superhuman burst of energy and determination, Chōmin completed the treatise, without referring to other books, in approximately ten days. Thus, he was able to see the publication of his last two works before his death in December 1901—ten months short of his promised one year and a half. Reading and writing on his deathbed, Nakae Chōmin was determined that his last offering to the world would have a certain quality of completion.

Unlike many dying people who withdraw into resentful self-absorption, Chōmin retained his wit, humor, and warmth. After his surgical operation for cancer, one of his disciples visited Chōmin and tried to encourage him by saying that another famous columnist, Fukuchi Ochi, who had been hospitalized with a similar disease, was said to have lived for six years. Chōmin responded immediately, "Well, then, his life is four times longer than mine." And he laughed. The visitor, who was just leaving, said, "Please take care of yourself."

"No, I won't take care of myself," replied Chōmin, "because it is impossible to be cured anyway. As long as I am alive, I will eat tasty food, hear good shamisen music, and write whatever I think" (Ishikawa, p. 411).

Chōmin's two last books demonstrate his remarkable ability to maintain his quality of mind. Even in his last moments, when he was unable to speak and could hardly move, he held firmly to his convictions. When his relatives had called in an old priest to offer Buddhist prayers and last rites, Chōmin refused to cooperate. He was determined to die as a materialist.

In the political realm as well, Chōmin defied a power almost as absolute as death, the Meiji state. He devoted most of his time, passion, and ingenuity to the defense of freedom and people's rights (jiyū minken) against the extension of state power over individuals. Chōmin and his fellow activists promoted the Western idea of "the state serving the people"; the government emphasized the more traditional concept of "the people serving the state." The Meiji oligarchs, who had once fought against the feudal hierarchy of Tokugawa society, did not simply perpetuate the Tokugawa system. They instituted a form of paternalism in which all subjects were in principle equal before the emperor, a dramatic shift from the previous system. Circumscribed pockets of egalitarianism, such as the military and the educational systems, were established as a means to recruit elites and strengthen the state. But they did not hesitate to restrict individual rights when they considered it necessary. For Chōmin, however, full equality and freedom were the goals. He never wavered in his view of the individual as the ultimate value. He not only argued for universal suffrage but fervently attacked the general discrimination against the Japanese outcast (burakumin).[1] "Enthusiastic about egalitarian ideas, you do not accept the aristocrats above you. But if you do not respect the outcasts below you, where are we to find real egalitarianism?" ("Shinmin sekai" ["The World of Outcasts"], in Shinonome shinbun, February 14 and 25, 1888). And he was consistent. He insisted that the maid in his home eat at the same table as the family, a practice almost unheard of at the turn of the century in Japan. His absolute egalitarianism was exceptional anywhere and extraordinary in Meiji society.

---

1. The Japanese outcast refers to a group that during the Tokugawa period was an officially recognized class at the bottom of the social structure. Discrimination against this group continues in various forms today (see De Vos and Wagatsuma.)

But Chōmin's egalitarianism also reflected his marginality in that society. When Japan embarked on industrialization using Western models, two main types of leaders—both nationalistic in spirit—predominated: the promoters of westernization, who wanted the nation to learn from the West to join the club of colonizing powers, and the upholders of a kind of Japanocentrism, who emphasized the virtues of past traditions and remained hostile to Western influences.

Chōmin represents the small minority of individuals who criticized the West on the basis of Western ideals. He could fully subscribe to progressive Western ideas because he felt relatively free from rigid samurai values; he could uphold his principles throughout his life because he did not seek to remain a member of the ruling clans and factions and therefore was not obliged to compromise with them. Chōmin recognized and perhaps even cultivated his marginality to guarantee his individual freedom. His contribution to Meiji Japan and to history was founded on his commitment to egalitarian individualism in principle and in action.

In the fall of 1847, a son was born to the Nakae family, a samurai family of the lowest rank in the domain of Tosa. He was named Tokusuke at birth, was called Takema for most of his childhood, but after 1887 referred to himself almost exclusively as Chōmin, the name we use here.[2] His birthplace was the castle town of Kōchi in Tosa on the island of Shikoku, the smallest of the four main Japanese islands, nestled between Honshū and Kyūshū. Tosa was one of the outer and more autonomous feudal domains that played a key role in the politics of transition from Tokugawa to Meiji government. Tosa thus completes the list of major groups involved in Japan's emergence into the modern world in the late nineteenth century: the Tokugawa shogunate, the imperial court, and the three domains of Satsuma, Chōshū, and Tosa.

Although it became the home base for a faction of fanatic restorationists, Tosa differed in two major respects from Satsuma and Chōshū, its traditional rivals on the islands of Kyūshū and Honshū. First, Tosa was less powerful economically than either Satsuma or Chōshū, although it certainly figured among the more wealthy do-

2. Nakae adopted the name Chōmin to express a particular sense of self, as Mori was able to do with his use of Ogai. Its meaning is explained later in the text.

mains at the close of the Tokugawa period. Second, it was ruled by a feudal family that felt bound by obligation to the Tokugawa in return for having received control over the Tosa territory after the battle of Sekigahara in 1600.[3] Both factors contributed to Tosa's official emphasis on compromises and mediation between the protagonists in the pre-Restoration period. Tosa leaders realized they had little chance of gaining national rule from the Tokugawa through military means but hoped they could enhance the domain's influence through negotiations.

In the 1850s and 1860s, the years of Nakae's childhood and adolescence, Tosa, like many areas of Japan, was embroiled in political conflict. The intrusion of the West confronted nearly every level of Japanese society with what was often perceived as a threat of extinction. In Tosa, young samurai in particular were swept up in frenzied calls to expel the foreigners. The domain's official reaction, however, differed significantly from those of other domains. Soon after Commodore Perry's arrival in 1853, Yoshida Tōyō, Tosa's chief minister, instituted administrative reforms in the domain's economic, educational, and defense programs. Yoshida even organized a mixed military force of 10,000 samurai and commoners, known as the People's Corps (*minpeitai*), before Takasugi Shinsaku formed his combined army, the *kiheitai*, in Chōshū in 1863 (see chapter 2). The Tosa militia never battled against the West—its original purpose—but instead fought against the shogunate a decade later. Yoshida's policies made him the target of both ends of the political spectrum in Tosa.

Our knowledge of Chōmin's childhood, and of many periods of his life, is seriously limited by a lack of information. Chōmin kept no diary and wrote no autobiography. The only contemporary biographical work and the primary source on Chōmin's early life is *Chō-min sensei*, compiled by his disciple Kōtoku Shūsui.[4] But Kōtoku was a poor Boswell. He did not systematically collect the writings or investigate the life of his teacher. The small book he wrote was based on what he learned from living and working with Chōmin. Moreover,

3. The battle of Sekigahara marked the military unification of Japan under the army of Tokugawa Ieyasu, the final in a series of victories over antagonistic domains from western Japan.

4. "*Sensei*" is a term of respect for teachers, often translated as master, but used also to refer to doctors, politicans, lawyers, and others of high social status.

Kōtoku was much concerned with tracing his own anarchist-socialist beliefs back to Chōmin, whom he wanted to consider a revolutionary. The disciple thus framed the problem of interpreting the historical role of his teacher. Kōtoku's political actions after his teacher's death furthered both these perceptions of Chōmin and the dissemination of *Chōmin sensei*.

The rise of antiliberalism and militarism in the 1930s halted all academic research on Chōmin, whom the government considered a dangerous character even after his death. Research in the postwar period, however, has helped fill some of the gaps in knowledge about him. He has been studied by liberal thinkers who identify with many of his ideals, and by some Marxists who interpret him as a bourgeois democrat fighting against autocracy. But many questions about his life remain unanswered and perhaps unanswerable.

Some information about Chōmin's childhood is available. Kōtoku cites his mother's description of him as a quiet, gentle, studious young boy who especially loved reading. Another account, probably somewhat exaggerated but still indicative of Chōmin's character, states that on hot summer days the young boy, as an antidote to drowsiness, would lower himself in a bucket into a well so that he could continue his reading in a cool, pleasurable environment. The story, which may or may not be true, suggests both his free, eccentric spirit and his love of reading. He is said to have had another strange habit of throwing his rice bowl or tea cup to destroy it after every meal. His mother, who was unable to stop him, was forced to use lacquer utensils for meals. Guests who knew his habit used to bring porcelain dishes, instead of the usual toys, to satisfy his destructive pleasures. This was not simply impulsive violence on Nakae's part, but suggests a pattern of subverting proper behavior, one that was sanctioned and rewarded by his family and close society, and was directed against specific social norms. Although he was otherwise a child of mild temperament, he was known to react violently to children who mistreated his younger brother. Some authors contend that Chōmin's later conviction to defend the weak in society began with the defense of his brother.

During the political turmoil at the end of the Tokugawa period, violent struggles often erupted between the two dominant factions in Tosa—one supporting the Edo shogunate and the policy of opening the country (*sabaku-kaikoku*), and the other, the "loyalists," supporting the policy of expelling the aliens in the name of the emperor (*sonnō-jōi*).

Nakae was then a student in his early teens. Although the record is sparse, he seems to have concentrated more on his studies than on the political fighting around him. Yet he could not have been ignorant of the conflicts, especially since the jailyard in which many radical loyalists were punished was close to his home. He is said to have witnessed one particular incident in which three loyalist samurai were ordered to commit seppuku. We cannot be certain just how Nakae reacted to this event. One scholar suggest that it contributed greatly to Chōmin's aversion to the samurai ethos and symbols. In any case, by the time he was fifteen, in 1862, when Tosa chief minister Yoshida was assassinated by loyalists, Chōmin was undoubtedly aware of Japan's internal chaos and external threats.

In the complex bureaucratic hierarchy of Tosa samurai during the Tokugawa period, the Nakae family was not only in the lowest ranked group, the so-called footsoldiers (*ashigaru*), but the lowest subdivision of that group, the class generally assigned to manual labor. Just barely included in the elite samurai class, the footsoldiers received low stipends of three to seven koku, which sustained a meager existence, particularly in the inflation of the mid-nineteenth century. In the Nakae family, the normal hardships were exacerbated by the assignment of the father, Motosuke, to the Edo office of the Tosa lord. Not only was Motosuke rarely at home during the childhood of his eldest son, but as punishment for what were described as "indiscretions" he committed in the capital city, the family's already low stipened was further decreased. Consequently, Chōmin and his mother bore most of the responsibility for the family's welfare.

In 1861, when Chōmin was fourteen years old, his father died. As the eldest son, Chōmin became legal head of the household and his mother assumed full responsibility for his upbringing and education. We have no record of how Chōmin reacted to his father's death, but it brought about an early combination of freedom and responsibility along with a close, collaborative relationship with his mother. In contrast to Nogi, Nakae did not have a strong father who had to be opposed. He could pursue his literary interests with few obstacles and little guilt. In early adolescence, he decided his goals and set out to fulfill them.

Education was a central concern throughout Nakae's life. In 1862, the year after his father's death, Chōmin entered the domain school for samurai, Bunbukan or "Literary and Military Arts," which had opened that year to replace the old domain school. This school was part of the reformist plans of Yoshida Tōyō to strengthen the domain's defenses against the West by learning Western methods. It was the first domain school to teach the English and Dutch languages. Nakae took advantage of these offerings and gradually shifted his focus away from the traditional Chinese classics. In 1861, Tosa authorities chose Nakae, then eighteen, and other advanced students to go to a progressive school in Nagasaki to learn the ways—particularly the military ways—of the West. Tosa radicals, who several years earlier had opposed the reformist plans of Yoshida as contaminating Japanese purity, had assumed power and were implementing a program nearly identical to Yoshida's.

In the mid-1860s, the city of Nagasaki, Japan's connection to the West for more than two centuries, gained new meanings and functions. Most of Japan's politically active elite gradually realized that the West was not a force that could be repelled with samurai techniques or endured like a passing typhoon. It had become commonplace to believe in the necessity of adopting Western techniques to ensure Japan's defense against the West. Western military methods were widely perceived as critical factors in the shifting international and domestic power relationships. For this reason, Nagasaki, with its well-established training centers in various forms of knowledge, soared in importance in the eyes of the rival domains as well as the Tokugawa shogunate.

At the same time, new sources of information about the West were breaking Nagasaki's monopoly on Western teaching. It was no longer necessary to travel to the far city on the western coast of Kyūshū to obtain "Dutch knowledge," since French, British, and American knowledge were becoming more available through various other channels. Students of the West began to concentrate in Edo following the establishment in 1857 of the Institute for Investigation of Alien Books (Bansho shirabesho). Still, Nagasaki continued to serve its crucial function as a center of foreign learning that attracted students from all over Japan. Nagasaki held out the distinct advantage of being much less controlled by the shogunate than Edo. Indeed, during the 1860s, Nagasaki's cosmopolitan environment provided a training ground for antishogunate loyalists, who were also increasingly independent from their own domains.

Western knowledge had long been understood to be a source of power that could be used against not only foreigners but also against the establishment order in Japan—the reason that the Tokugawa government, from the beginning of the seventeenth century, imposed strict controls on Dutch learning. A number of Japanese students of the West, viewed with suspicion as potential subversives, were assassinated by fanatical superpatriots as well as by domain and Tokugawa governments. The attitude that anything foreign is dangerous became institutionalized in Tokugawa Japan and found anxious and sometimes violent expression in reaction to individual Westerners in Japan during the last years of the regime. Japanese ambivalence to the introduction of new ideas and techniques was not unique but perhaps unusually intense. The political expression of that ambivalence could be found in the simultaneous use of those new ideas to strengthen the existing order and to destroy it.

Nakae's decision to study a foreign language was made in the midst of that general psychological and political ambivalence and was influenced by several factors. It was one of the new paths of advancement open to a lower samurai, since late Tokugawa Japan did not consider such practical learning appropriate for the truly elite samurai. It also connected the young man with the most exciting issues of the day, and with a new kind of access to knowledge and to a sense of personal power. In addition, Chōmin had a talent for languages and must have derived considerable satisfaction from his rapid progress.

When he arrived in Nagasaki in 1865, Chōmin was supposed to continue his studies of English, but for unknown reasons switched to French. This decision affected the entire character of his life as he integrated the French language and thought into the core of his identity. In Nagasaki, Chōmin befriended several important political activists from Tosa: Gotō Shōjirō, a protagonist of the future freedom and popular rights movement; Iwasaki Yatarō, the supervisor of Tosa students in Nagasaki and future founder of the Mitsubishi *zaibatsu* or big financial combine in Meiji Japan; and Sakamoto Ryōma, who shortly after played a critical role in uniting the Chōshū and Satsuma domains against the Edo shogunate. Chōmin was particularly impressed with Sakamoto, in whom he recognized potential greatness. But once again, despite ample opportunities, Nakae did not become active in the political organizing then underway in Nagasaki.

After two years in Nagasaki, Chōmin borrowed money from Gotō—Iwasaki had refused his request for a loan—and took a foreign boat to Edo. It was 1867, the eve of the Meiji Restoration. In the capital city, Chōmin enrolled as a student in Japan's most advanced private school for training in French language, but after several months was dismissed for "bad conduct," apparently his habit of frequenting the neighborhood brothels. Chōmin then went to Yokohama to continue his language lessons under the tutelage of a French priest. Although living with the priest did not seem to diminish his interest in brothels, it did seem to improve his French. When the ports of Hyōgo and Osaka were opened in December of that year, the French government selected Chōmin as interpreter for its special representative in Japan, Léon Roches.

From our present perspective, Chōmin at the age of twenty seems rather young to be serving as the interpreter to France's ranking diplomat in Japan. But in the pre-Meiji samurai world, once a male passed his initiation rite of *genpuku* in his early teens, he was an adult and no further restrictions were made solely on the basis of age. More important, Chōmin possessed a rare skill in Japan of the 1860s, the ability to speak French. He was also in the right place at the right time. Dramatic opportunities were opening up for many young samurai with particular talents.

Léon Roches at the peak of his diplomatic career was an impressive man. Historian Meron Medzini described him as a "proud man, fiercely patriotic, shrewd and artful, and an individualist who kept his own counsel and tended to spurn advice from others" (p. 74). Roches had risen from the lowly rank of military interpreter to achieve an impressive diplomatic career, serving as consul general at Trieste, Tripoli, and Tunis. In October 1863 he arrived in Tokyo as France's foremost diplomat in Japan.

The policies that Roches adopted are characterized as *politique personnelle* because of his overwhelming personal role in their formulation and enactment. To expand French trade interests, which he considered his main goal, he emphasized French cooperation with other foreign powers and French moderation toward the Japanese government. His primary policy innovation was to affiliate himself and his government with the Tokugawa shogunate as the only legitimate ruler of Japan.

The Western powers "opened" Japan during the last half of the nineteenth century primarily for concessions on trade. And when the

British, French, Dutch, and Americans saw the antagonism between the Satsuma and Chōshū domains and Edo developing into a civil war, they agreed on a policy of military nonintervention. This strategy fit their common interest of minimizing the extent of Japanese internal conflicts so that trade would not be jeopardized. The nonintervention agreement, however, did not stop foreign manipulations motivated by national interests. France, under Roches's leadership, aggressively advised the shogunate on how to reorganize its administration and modernize its military techniques, hoping to reinforce the tottering Tokugawa power structure. And the British encouraged Satsuma and Chōshū to unite the country by doing away with the shogunate.

In the last months of 1867, political events rapidly evolved into a national transformation. In November, the shogun relinquished his powers to the emperor in a compromise proposed by the Tosa domain lord, and to a certain degree arranged by Tosa political activists such as Gotō and Sakamoto. The leaders of Satsuma and Chōshū, however, persisted in advocating the use of force to overthrow the shogunate. Although some Tosa activists (including Itagaki Taisuke, who later became an opposition leader against the Meiji oligarchy) shared the belligerent Satsuma-Chōshū pre-Restoration policy, many Tosa leaders sought to avoid a large-scale civil war through some compromise solution. The latter group feared that outright warfare would weaken Japan's position vis-à-vis the foreign powers and would mean simply replacing Tokugawa authority with the equally monopolistic power of Satsuma-Chōshū.

The compromise agreement, however, did not satisfy the more radical loyalists in various domains. In January, they engineered a small coup d'etat, gaining control of the imperial palace in Kyoto. The young emperor then proclaimed an edict of imperial restoration. Later that month, at the battles of Toba and Fushimi, the imperial loyalists defeated the Tokugawa forces and soon afterwards seized the Tokugawa palace in Edo. In April the new government issued the "Charter Oath" through the imperial court. This short document, based on the ideas of Sakamoto and Gotō, powerfully combined the new with the old. Henceforth, Japan would abandon "absurd customs of olden times" and adopt international standards of behavior. The oath's fifth and final point stated that knowledge would be sought throughout the world in order to strengthen the foundations of imperial rule.

Chōmin, as interpreter to Roches, accompanied the French envoy first to ceremonies opening the port of Hyōgo to foreign trade, and then to Osaka and Kyoto, where they remained until March or April. Neither Roches nor Chōmin kept a personal record of his experiences. Diplomatic correspondence, however, shows that Roches participated in one particularly important incident. In mid-February, Tosa soldiers, in an outburst of antiforeign agitation, murdered eleven members of the crew of a French gunboat in the port city of Sakai, near Osaka. Roches transformed this incident into a foreign crisis for the new government by demanding the execution of those responsible as well as monetary compensation. His demands arose out of a desire not only to obtain justice and maintain French prestige but also to soothe his wounded sense of self-esteem over the total failure of his policy of supporting the shogunate. As we mentioned in chapter 3, twenty soldiers were ordered to commit seppuku in front of the French officers and Roches, and eleven completed the gruesome ritual before the proceedings were halted at the command of the captain of the French ship. We are not certain that Chōmin was present at the Sakai incident but he was surely involved in it. The mass seppuku, orchestrated for Westerners, must have made a profound impression on him.[5] Chōmin continued to serve Roches until the latter was recalled by his government in April 1868.

As Roche's interpreter, Chōmin experienced the Meiji Restoration mostly as a spectator, though from a front-row seat. He witnessed the demise of the Tokugawa regime not from the standpoint of his radical or moderate Tosa compatriots, but through the eyes (and voice) of the French envoy, who quite explicitly sympathized with the shogunate. Roches dealt with the political situation primarily in terms of French trade interests. Chōmin overtly supported no one—neither the Satsuma-Chōshū forces, the shogunate, nor the emperor. He undoubtedly had sympathies, but he probably learned a great deal about transcending immediate ideological conflicts that he later put to good use in dealing with the antagonisms of Japanese political parties. More directly, Chōmin probably learned much through conversations with Roches about French political ideals of liberty, freedom, and equality—and through his own observations about hypocritical

5. Because the soldiers involved were from his own domain of Tosa, Chōmin probably experienced considerable conflict between his identities as Tosa samurai and interpreter to the French diplomat—and may well have been left with considerable death guilt.

French violations of those same ideas. Yet through it all, as one of Japan's leading scholars of French language and culture and still just twenty years old, he probably came to identify strongly with French political and cultural tradition.

Chōmin's life in the first years of the Meiji period had two strong involvements which became the reference points for his later life: French intellectual culture and Japanese popular culture. His continuing stipend as a Tosa samurai allowed him to pursue his studies of French law, including the problems of translating French philosophical and legal concepts into Japanese. In 1869, he became director and French instructor of a small private school (juku), and the following year he began to teach French at the college that later became Tokyo Imperial University.

At the same time, Chōmin immersed himself in the art forms of Japanese chōnin culture.[6] He frequently attended the puppet theater and faithfully studied the shamisen, becoming quite skillful at playing the four-stringed musical instrument and singing the accompanying long epic songs known as nagauta. These interests provided an earthy, indigenous counterpoint to his specialized and even esoteric studies in French lexicography. Chōmin the westernizer was thus solidly grounded in the two streams of Japanese traditional culture—the literature of the Chinese classics and the entertainment of the common people. His active involvement in chōnin culture fit his background and upbringing as a low-ranking samurai, in an environment in which the two subcultures were fused. Many expressions of chōnin culture, in fact, strongly criticized the samurai order and probably contributed to Chōmin's tendency to challenge the establishment system and to identify with the common people. This antielitism of chōnin culture shared some elements with French ideological egalitarianism, so that Chōmin's two very separate cultural interests had at least a point of spiritual connection.

In 1871, Chōmin decided that he needed to leave Japan to advance

6. During the Tokugawa period, a mass-participant, urban culture emerged and flourished in major cities. Known as chōnin bunka ("the culture of townspeople"), it was closely associated with the rise of Japan's bourgeoisie, especially the Tokugawa merchant and artisan classes who were increasingly oriented toward the pursuit of pleasure in the world of entertainment (the "floating world" or ukiyo). The art forms of chōnin culture included puppet theater and new popular dramas of kabuki, the music of the shamisen, the woodblock prints known as ukiyo-e, and a thriving popular literature.

in his studies of the French language. His conclusion reflected an important trend in the first years of Meiji. Leaders and prospective leaders were sent abroad to absorb Western skills and technologies in all fields—politics, science, culture, and the military. In 1869 and 1870 alone, 116 students were dispatched abroad from the various domains and 58 from the central government, the imperial court, and private concerns. By 1873, nearly 400 students were studying abroad. The most famous expedition was the Iwakura Mission of 1871, led by Iwakura Kengai, a Kyoto noble who sided with the antishogunate forces and emerged as a leading figure of the Meiji government. Half the Japanese cabinet left the country with him for eighteen months. Its primary goal was to hold primary negotiations on revising the trade treaties. In particular, the Japanese government wanted to restore its right to tax foreigners and abolish foreigner's special rights to use foreign judges and to land troops in Japan. But the mission's most important goal was to search for modernizing models that Japan could follow.

Chōmin's application to the mission was characteristic of him. Rather than following the customary channels of speaking first with Tosa officials in the government, he appealed directly to Okubo Toshimichi, a high-ranking official originally from Satsuma responsible for the overseas tour. To obtain an audience with Okubo, who was not easily accessible to a young teacher-student, Chōmin first befriended a driver of Okubo's cart. With the driver's aid he is said to have jumped before Okubo's carriage one day, declaring that he had learned all the French that was possible to learn in Tokyo, and that he had the need and the right to go to France. Okubo reportedly demanded to know why Chōmin had not appealed to the influential government officials from Tosa. Chōmin replied that he had no intention of serving the Tosa clan, that he would only serve Japan. Okubo apparently liked that answer and arranged to include Chōmin among the stipend students accompanying the Iwakura mission—though only after consulting with Itagaki Taisuke and Gotō Shōjirō, the two most powerful Tosa samurai in the Meiji government. The incident illustrates not only Chōmin's boldness and autonomy and the force of his ambition, but also his nascent nationalism and his sense of commitment beyond his domain. One biographer, Kuwabara Takeo (p. 31), notes in reference to this episode that "one can almost say that he [Chōmin] was oblivious to the authority derived from high social rank." But it might be more accurate to say that he consistently subsumed considerations of hierarchy to other goals, which was truly remarkable in early Meiji Japan.

Chōmin was assigned to the Justice Ministry to study the French legal system and in November 1871 left Yokohama for America and France. The following October he arrived in Lyons, and six months later he was in Paris. Chōmin had arrived in France at a time of political transition. The Paris Commune had fallen in the spring of 1871 and France was still establishing the Third Republic. Although France under Napoleon III had recently lost a war with Germany, Hegel and Marx had not yet crossed the Rhine. Auguste Comte still dominated the Parisian intellectual world, which remained optimistic about the future of scientific progress and confident of the basic visions of the century that produced such thinkers as Rousseau, Newton, and Kant.

Chōmin's first objective in Lyons was to master the French language. Despite his advanced ability, he decided to relearn the fundamentals of the language by attending a primary school. Later in Paris, he followed his own course of study. Instead of investigating the technicalities of French law as instructed by the Justice Ministry, he spent most of his time reading philosophy, history, and literature. This rejection of official authority was facilitated by the distance between France and the Japanese bureaucracy. It also reflected Chōmin's strong commitment to his own inner voice over the call of either samurai values or obligation to the Ministry.

Chōmin thus used government sponsorship for his personal goals. In his free moments, he visited other Japanese scholarship students, particularly Saionji Kinmochi, a young samurai studying at the Sorbonne. Saionji, whose family is famous in Japanese history, became one of Japan's leading political figures until his death in 1950. In Paris, however, Chōmin's language ability gave him a decided advantage over many other students; it allowed him to communicate relatively easily with all classes in French society. Chōmin especially enjoyed drinking cheap wine at lower class bars, which gave him insights into Parisian life, while perhaps reminding him of his own connections with Japan's chōnin culture.

Chōmin gained much of his French political education from a political philosopher and activist, Emile Acollas (1826–91), who had become Saionji's teacher. Acollas, an ideological follower of Rousseau, became dean of the faculty of law at the University of Paris under the Paris Commune and was an uncompromising defender of human freedom. The French philosopher not only inspired Chōmin intellectually, sparking in him a lifelong dedication to the principles of eighteenth-century French liberalism, but impressed on him the importance of the popular press. Acollas's impact is revealed in Chōmin's citation of him in a later political essay alongside Mill, Montesquieu, and Kant—entirely out of proportion to his position in French intellectual history. Chōmin even seriously considered abandoning his career as a teacher to remain in France as a journalist. But his government recalled him because of economic problems in Japan; also, his mother was ill. Chōmin, however, had learned the crucial social role of press. He not only became one of Meiji Japan's most prominent editorial writers but founded numerous publications dedicated to defending principles of popular rights and criticizing the government in power.

Chōmin differed from most of the elite government students sent to Europe in two fundamental ways. First, very few students became wholesale believers in a system of Western values; Chōmin's espousal of nineteenth-century materialism and his commitment to the political radicalism of Rousseau were exceptional. The typical government student, like Inoue Kowashi, obediently followed the instructions of his home ministry and remained loyal to the ideology of the Meiji government.[7] Inoue exemplified the model intellectual in the pattern of Japanese spirit and Western technology. Chōmin, who was convinced of democratic ideals, waged his personal wars against that Japanese spirit, which often proved to be reactionary, authoritarian, and hypocritical. We might say that the glory of the Meiji state and the misery of the people were largely caused by the many Inoues and very few Chōmins.

In addition to his egalitarian beliefs, Chōmin consistently applied that principle to the actions of all men in all societies. Tani Kanjō, a leader in the Meiji government, once deplored that those who learned the English language tended to idealize England, those who learned French admired France, and those who learned German identified

7. Inoue, of the same generation as Chōmin and in France at about the same time, actually studied Western legal systems in detail. He returned to Japan to become an able and shrewd bureaucrat of the Meiji government and helped draft the constitution.

with Germany. But Chōmin was different. He distinguished between behavior and values. He harshly criticized Western actions that contradicted Western principles. For example, in an 1882 *Jiyū shinbun* article, he outspokenly condemned the Anglo-French imperialism he observed in southern Asia when returning to Japan. "The British in Port Said and the French in Saigon are extremely arrogant, treating the Turks and Indians almost as dogs and pigs. . . . The Europeans, who call themselves civilized people, consistently behave like that. . . . They don't know that the Turks and Indians also are human beings" (Nakae, 1974, p. 239). This unflinching attack on the West expressed what became a fundamental belief. Twenty years later, on his deathbed, he wrote in *One Year and a Half*, "The people's rights are the highest principle, and freedom and equality are the ultimate justice. They cannot be monopolized by the West" (pp. 175–76). Chōmin criticized the Western powers not from the particularity of Japan's national interests competing with the West, but from the universality of Western values transcending the geographic West. Chōmin spanned Japanese and French cultures without being politically or morally restricted by either. He persistently pursued his individual ideals.

After returning to Japan, Chōmin concentrated on education for several years. After a short visit with his mother in Kōchi, he arrived in Tokyo and established a private French language school in his home. He soon expanded its curriculum to include politics, law, history, and philosophy. Chōmin's school was an independent personal base. He scorned the government schools, branding the scholars they graduated as "useless" for the progress and improvement of society. Nevertheless, in early 1875, Chōmin accepted the directorship of one such government institution, the Tokyo Foreign Language School. He served there for three months until a dispute with the Ministry of Education on educational reforms prompted his resignation.

Chōmin's policies as director of the Tokyo Foreign Language School provide some insights into his conception of Japanese culture. He insisted that classical Chinese be included in the curriculum of all students, arguing that since the Chinese classics were an integral part of Japan's cultural heritage, all educated Japanese should have a good command of them, as educated Europeans knew Latin and Greek classics. Bureaucrats in the Ministry of Education, however, refused Chōmin's proposal and he resigned in protest. The conservative government opposed Chōmin, the radical reformer, because he insisted that students have a grounding in classical Chinese culture.

This episode suggests that Chōmin was a traditionalist not only in his attraction to chōnin culture, but also in his conscious attitudes toward the cultural legacy of Japan. But the question of his traditionalism is more complex. We might say that a training in Chinese classics developed not only language skills but also talents and habits for digesting foreign ideas. The more deeply involved in this tradition, the more likely that a Meiji westernizer could fully grasp Western ideas. We see this in the case of Chōmin as well as in gifted novelists like Mori Ogai and Natsume Sōseki. The Meiji writers who were least nurtured by the Chinese classics, such as the "naturalists," tended to be superficial in their contacts with European culture (see note 16, chapter 3). It is therefore a mistake to regard the Tokugawa traditional legacy as incompatible with a westernizing cultural process. The former often helped the latter.

Chōmin also followed his own educational precepts. Soon after returning from France, he began an intensive program of improving his already superb classical Chinese. In part, his educational policies might have been based on a French model that emphasized the classics along with eighteenth-century liberalism. But although Chōmin drew on cultural roots to energize his progressive appeals, his use of classical Chinese also restricted his audience largely to the elite. For example, two of Chōmin's most important works, including his translation of Rousseau's *Social Contract*, were written in such a highly sophisticated style that they were virtually inaccessible to readers who lacked a classical education. The strict traditional style of Chōmin's writing thus belied its fervently progressive contents.

Yet, Chōmin's combination of Western philosophy with Japanese literature, of Western political ideas with a Japanese style of life, did not create overwhelming psychological conflicts. A usual explanation would be that he successfully "compartmentalized" the different elements of his sense of self. This capacity for compartmentalization—for segmenting off seemingly unrelated or even antagonistic psychic forms so that each functions more or less independently—has been noted to be particularly strong in Japanese. But our observations on Chōmin suggest a second possibility: these elements can be brought together by the symbolizing process and inwardly recreated in ways that blend whatever can be blended and mute or disregard what cannot. Such blending tends to be neither rational nor irrational but holistic, occurs mostly outside of awareness, and is probably responsible for a good deal of impressive, if imperfect, cultural assimilation—not only by Japanese but by many in relation to the West.

After leaving the Tokyo Foreign Language School, Chōmin became a translator in the experimental Japanese senate, the *Genrōin*, for eighteen months. He was discharged in 1877, also because of a difference of opinion with his superior, and he never worked for the government again. Chōmin then concentrated on teaching and managing his private school. The school was important in Meiji Japan not only because of the large number of students it trained—nearly two thousand in twelve years—but also because of the attitudes it fostered. Chōmin did not simply teach a series of disconnected courses; he taught the world view he had learned in France. Many of his students became frontline critics of the government, including several of Japan's early socialists. Chōmin's school, however, never developed into a major university as did those of Okuma Shigenobu (Waseda University) and Fukuzawa Yukichi (Keiō University). Perhaps Chōmin never aspired for it to become a major university. In fact he closed the school in 1886 for several probable reasons—his basic antipathy toward established institutions (even his own), his relative lack of business acumen, and his impulse toward change. It is difficult to imagine the restless Chōmin as the staid president of a stable university in good standing with the government.

In early 1881, Chōmin took his first steps into the world of Japanese politics, joining the movement for freedom and popular rights at its peak. Organized primarily by Itagaki and Gotō, who had left the Meiji government in 1873 in a dispute over whether to dispatch a military force to Korea, this movement provided the major opposition to the regime during the 1870s and 1880s. By 1881 the freedom and popular rights movement reached national proportions by drawing on, first, the support of disenfranchised samurai and, then, of farmers and merchants. This opposition group demanded two changes in political structure: elected assemblies on both local and national levels, and a national constitution.

Chōmin and Saionji joined the political battle by establishing a daily newspaper, the *Free Orient* (*Tōyō jiyū shinbun*), and becoming its respective editor and president. With his new public platform, Chōmin rapidly became known as a radical libertarian. Within one month of the paper's first issue, however, the government intervened, forcing Saionji to resign and the paper to fold. This effectively, if only temporarily, halted Chōmin's verbal attacks on the Meiji oligarchy. Earlier, in 1875, the government's fear of newspapers led it to enact strict censorship laws and controls on the press. When two reporters of the *Free Orient*, for example, claimed in a front-page article that Saionji had been ordered to resign by imperial decree, they were simply imprisoned—one reporter later died in jail. Chōmin reacted more prudently to the Saionji incident, criticizing the government in his highly complex and intellectual style of Chinese prose. His article did not precipitate his arrest but neither did it have a popular impact.

Government pressure, however, did not discourage him. In February 1882 he began to publish a bimonthly political journal from his school. Titled *Discussions on Western Political Principles*, it aimed at introducing Western political and social thought into Japan. In it Chōmin published his serialized translation of Rousseau's *Social Contract*, which for the first time provided many government critics with a solid ideological basis. During this same period, Nakae became more closely aligned with the Freedom party, which had formed at the end of the previous year as the key political organ of the freedom and popular rights movement. In mid-1882, he joined the board of editors of the party's newspaper. But when party leaders Itagaki and Gōtō visited Europe at government expense, Chōmin rebelled. He attacked their complicity with the designs of the Meiji oligarchs, and in October 1882 resigned from the paper and the party. In October 1884 the Freedom party disbanded because of scandals among the leadership and riots associated with party members in the provinces. When Chōmin reentered the political arena two years later he was only tenuously connected with the former party leaders from Tosa.

His second period of political activism began in 1886 when he promoted a national meeting of freedom and popular rights supporters. A major factor in his return to politics was the government's promise in 1881 to convene a national assembly by 1890. On the issues of the assembly and the constitution, Chōmin and the Meiji government stood at opposite poles. Chōmin demanded that an election be held for a national assembly so that elected representatives could draft the constitution. But the government intended first to draft the constitution and proclaim it as a gift of the emperor and only then allow the election of a parliament to ratify the imperial document. Chōmin demanded that local government leaders be chosen by popular election; the central government intended to appoint prefectural governors.

In short, Chōmin championed a decentralization and popularization of power, as opposed to the clans of Chōshū and Satsuma, which sought to maintain their monopoly of the political system. At stake was the political structure of Meiji Japan and the country's future course. In the end, the Japanese state emerged as a constitutional monarchy, but its constitution severely restricted the functions of the elected parliament. Symbolically presented by the emperor to the people, the Meiji constitution placed greater limits on the exercise of rights by the ruled than on the use of power by the rulers. Given Japan's internal and external circumstances in the late nineteenth century, Chōmin's alien ideas might not have been acceptable to either rulers or ruled. But through his efforts, libertarian principles became more familiar to a large segment of the Japanese people as at least a vision of possibility.

By the late 1880s, Chomin was writing mainly political essays and short stories. His most famous short book was *Political Discussions of Three Inebriates* (*San suijin keirin mondō*, 1887). It portrayed three drunks arguing the politics of the times. One was a right-wing militarist an arrogant and somewhat crude ultranationalist, whose name—Gōketsu—has been translated by Dardess as "Swashbuckler." Another was a radical pacifist and libertarian, somewhat pedantic Western-oriented scholar, whose name—Shinshi—has been translated as "Highbrow." The third character was Nankai Sensei— literally "Mr. South Seas"—which vaguely suggests Chōmin's native country, Tosa, as well as his own name. He was the realist moderator of the all-night discussion of Japan's domestic and foreign politics, a tippler who was always willing to ponder and pontificate on government when lubricated by brandy.

Through his three drunks, Chōmin brilliantly analyzed Japan's political dilemmas and accurately anticipated future scenarios. Nankai promised to "write down the important points [of the discussion] one by one before I get too drunk in the hope that someday I can put together a little book for my own pleasure and for the delight of others" (Dardess, p. 213). Chōmin's relationship to these character was complicated. He certainly had elements of the brandy-loving, superrational Nankai Sensei, but he also displayed tendencies toward nationalism and radical libertarianism. Indeed, it was his personal experience with these ideologies that gave vitality to the three characters.

In *The Three Inebriates*, Chōmin evoked different aspects of his own self. Perhaps least central to him though not without importance, was his parodied conservative side, represented by Swashbuckler, who wanted to use military power to solve all of Japan's problems. Swashbuckler favored sending an army of conservatives to conquer a foreign country. If the army won, argued Swashbuckler, it would set up a separate conservative state, and if it lost, they would all die. In either case, he noted, Japan would be rid of its conservatives and could institute true reforms. There is more than a suggestion here of what happened in the Second World War. Chōmin used Swashbuckler to criticize ex-samurai progressives who wept bitter tears when forced to relinquish their swords. Highbrow was a more direct self-parody, involving longwinded speeches and labyrinthine confusion in applying Western ideas to Japan. Highbrow's idealism, like Swashbuckler's militarism, was literally suicidal. Highbrow advocated an absolute pacifism with no defense against enemy attack other than dying from foreigner's bullets.

Nankai, as the man in the middle, opposed both aggressive militarization and idealistic pacifism. He responded to the inevitable question of how a weakly armed Japan would handle an attack by a strong country with his "theory of a small country" (*shōkokushugi*): if Japan did not seek to expand, but instead followed practices that did not provoke outsiders and always took the side of international justice, then even without being heavily armed the likelihood of an attack by another country would be very small. If the unlikely ever happened, according to this theory, then the only choice would be to fight to the last of the Japanese people. Nankai's small country theory, whatever its limitations, would have at least avoided the carnage of the Second World War.[8]

But the words of Cassandra were not heeded. Imperial Japan, aspiring to become a big country, followed the pattern of Western colonialist powers and embarked on a course of military adventures that terminated in the collapse of 1945. Chōmin was seeking a path by

8. Nakae's small country theory resembles at least the military aspects of policies initially imposed on Japan by the occupation after the defeat in the Second World War—and supported by much Japanese antiwar sentiment.

which Japan could avoid being either colonized or colonizer—either (in Camus's terms) victim or executioner.

In one paragraph of the essay, Nankai encouraged Highbrow to continue his advocacy of democracy:

At the present time the idea of an emperor and a nobility is deeply rooted in the minds of men, and only in your mind, Highbrow, do the seeds of democracy grow. If you are truly devoted to democratic thought, speak out, write books, and sow the seeds of democracy in the minds of the people. After a hundred years or so they will probably germinate throughout the land. Be sure to do this right away if you hope to reap the rich harvest of democracy.

(Dardess, p. 284)

Here we feel ourselves close to Chōmin's own motivations. He sensed the unlikelihood of realizing his egalitarian goals in his lifetime, but related his efforts to a suprapersonal future.

The year 1887 marked a turning point in Chōmin's life. In addition to producing his three brilliantly illuminating drunks, he also began to refer to himself regularly as Chōmin. *Chō* means "a great number" and *min*, "people," so that his name signified his determined identification with the common people. He also tried to live that identification in concrete ways. In one recorded incident, he paid a group of ten rickshaw workers their daily wage to go drinking with him for the rest of the day. In such actions Chōmin might have been expressing his sense of absurdity about the world and a certain amount of self-mockery and frustration concerning his own relatively elite status and the futility of his efforts to help the really poor. He gained the reputation of an eccentric.[9] But Chōmin did care about demonstrating in practice the ties to common people he preached.

In December 1887, the government's recently passed Peace Preservation Act interrupted Chōmin's efforts to raise popular consciousness. It forbade assemblies deemed dangerous by the police and gave the police the right to evict dangerous individuals from within about eight miles of the imperial palace in Tokyo. Under this law nearly 500 people who criticized the government, including Chōmin, were removed from Tokyo. Many members of the opposition regrouped in

9. In the prewar period especially, this characterization interfered with his standing as an independent creative thinker, as did official suppression of his work. Only recently has the extent of his intellectual achievement become widely recognized.

Osaka. Chōmin, as editor-in-chief of a new opposition newspaper, continued to attack the government for not adopting democratic reforms. During this period he wrote a famous editoral calling for the total liberation of outcasts as well as many columns on egalitarian liberalism.

In 1889, with the promulgation of the Meiji constitution, the government lifted restrictions on mobility and Chōmin began to commute between Osaka and Tokyo.[10] Many Japanese welcomed the new constitution, but Nakae persisted in denouncing the document and demanding that it be totally revised by the yet-to-be-elected parliament. In particular he criticized the constitution's ambiguities about the rights of parliament, the cabinet's obligations to parliament, and procedures for treaty ratification and budget approval. To clarify these issues through constitutional reform, Nakae decided to run for election to the first Diet as a candidate from Osaka. His fame as a public speaker and newspaper commentator ensured his election.

In November 1890, the first session of Japan's bicameral Diet convened. Chōmin once again participated in the opposition's top level political manueverings, while attempting to revive the old Liberal party. He helped establish the Constitutional Freedom party (*Rikken jiyūtō*) and unsuccessfully sought to unify it with the other opposition group, the Progressive party (*Kaishintō*). From the beginning, he assailed the poor quality of parliamentary debate and was totally frustrated in his goal to revise the constitution. In February 1891, when the Tosa faction of the Liberal party compromised with the government to allow approval of the budget, thereby averting a dissolution of the Diet, Chōmin resigned in protest.

Quitting the Diet meant leaving politics. Without official party support, Chōmin was unable to raise sufficient funds for his political work. Increasingly strict government surveillance of opposition members also hindered his activities. Then, in late 1891, his mother became ill again, putting an additional strain on his limited finances. To resolve these monetary difficulties and simultaneously build a foundation of freethinking entrepreneurs, Chōmin decided to go into business. He vowed that until he achieved his fund-raising goal and could return to politics, he would "not speak one word of politics and not

10. Travel between the two cities was greatly facilitated by the recently completed Tokaido railway.

cross the gateway of a politician" (Kuwabara, p. 30). At the same time, at the age of forty-four, he gave up his established pattern of drinking.

His willed transformation was both internal and external. His disciple, Kōtoku Shūshi, and Chōmin's eldest daughter described his home life in these years as a model existence: he read, sported with carp, climbed Japanese plum trees, and played with his children and taught them strict manners. But one suspects he experienced more conflict than he showed, and that he might also have been bored.

Chōmin first ventured into the business world by founding lumber and paper enterprises while managing a newspaper in Hokkaido. In 1893, after returning to Tokyo, he invested in various private concerns, including railroads and brothels. As a free-enterprise capitalist Chōmin exemplified the entrepreneur in shrewdness, trustworthiness, and perseverence. But although the Sino-Japanese War generally stimulated Japanese business, few of Chōmin's ventures succeeded. Moreover, some of his investments contradicted his principles. His most controversial investment was his stubborn bid in 1898 to establish a brothel in Gunma prefecture, whose strong Christian movement had succeeded after seventeen years of lobbying to persuade the local government in 1893 to become the first prefecture to outlaw prostitution. Chōmin directly challenged the prefecture's policy and its Christian basis. He defended his investment in the brothel as the entrepreneur's right to provide needed service and decried government attempts to regulate his business activities. Kōtoku cites a letter from Chōmin in which he speaks of the ideals not only in his foreign and economic policies but in his prostitution policies as well: "Licensed prostitution is a real need, and its management causes no wrong. All jobs are equal" (p. 26).

Chōmin was again "breaking tea cups," but in a way that was socially and politically reckless. Instead of investing in a brothel in one of the more permissive prefectures where it would have caused little notice, he chose a prefecture in which a public uproar was inevitable. Kuwabara, in his discussion of the brothel affair, points out that while Chōmin followed Rousseau in political philosophy, he resembled Diderot in personality. (In eighteenth-century France, when Rousseau proposed abolishing prostitution, Diderot and Voltaire opposed the idea as unrealistic.) Chōmin's attitude toward brothels was also rooted in their important role in Tokugawa popular culture and art. But he seemed to have little sensitivity to the exploitation of women, economic and sexual, throughout most of chōnin culture.

His investment failures only dragged him into deeper poverty. Yet he would not accept money from others, especially not from Iwasaki Kyūya, head of Mitsubishi, who was willing to provide Chōmin with funds, but whose father had refused to lend him money thirty years earlier in Nagasaki. Despite his personal difficulties, Chōmin continued to express his belief in the growth of small- and middle-sized industries as contributing to greater individual freedom and as opposing the alliance between government and big business.

In 1897, at fifty-one, he staged his last political comeback, almost single-handedly establishing of the People's party (*Kokumintō*). Japan's victory two years earlier in the war against China had fueled nationalistic sentiments, and the Freedom party was cooperating completely with the government. Chōmin hoped to create a popular political party that could challenge the rule of the Meiji oligarchs, particularly Itō Hirobumi, who was leading his third cabinet. But partly because of financial shortages, the People's party failed, disappearing with hardly a ripple. Two years later, Chōmin joined a second attempt to counter Itō's political organization (the *Rikken seiyū kai*). The opposition group, called the People's League (*Kokumin dōmei kai*), also advocated expansion in Manchuria and Korea. Whether Chōmin actually supported this policy is still being debated by scholars. At this time, Chōmin assumed editorial activities for another newspaper, the *Daily Evening Newspaper* (*Maiyū shinbun*), but he was forced to curtail his work at the end of 1900—because of severe throat pain.

In March 1901, Chōmin resigned from his newspaper duties while continuing his entrepreneurial ventures. On the train from Tokyo to Osaka, where he was to investigate an investment possibility, his throat pain suddenly intensified. He visited an Osaka doctor who diagnosed his illness as cancer of the larnyx. Two months later, still in Osaka, he underwent a tracheotomy. He died in Tokyo in December. His body, in accordance with his will, was donated to medical research, a relatively rare practice at the turn of the century. And as he requested, the funeral ceremony was performed in Aoyama cemetery in Tokyo with no religious rituals and the grave left unmarked.

Although Chōmin completed two books in his last months, his early and abrupt death clearly cut short his attempt to develop and articulate his political philosophy. In 1886, Chōmin had published *Treatise on Philosophy* (*Rigaku kōgen*), a general survey of Western philosophy.

Believing that "there has been no philosophy in Japanese history," he gradually detached himself from Rousseau and in *Sequel to One Year and a Half* began to summarize his own metaphysical views of the world. The result combined eighteenth-century philosophies of materialism (from the encyclopedists) and atheism (from Voltaire) with nineteenth-century scientism. But he did not live long enough to elaborate the philosophical foundation he sought for his basic political principles. Chōmin might well have felt that his life was short of complete.

Although Meiji society in many respects recognized the preeminent talents of Nakae Chōmin, it also judged him a failure. His private school did not become one of the elite universities of modern Japan; his political campaigns did not produce any major social transformations; his publications were almost all shortlived; his business ventures were dismal flops. His only success was the influence he exerted on society through translations, newspaper editorals, essays, and books.

Forever dissatisfied with Meiji society, and restless in his own political and social arrangements, he was steadily nurtured by loving relationships with his wife and children. This was extremely important for him, as he had the protean man's need for areas of stability. He also had the innovator's nostalgia for the old and the timeless. When he felt pain he tended not to withdraw but to act. And though he did so at times impulsively or in ways that were self-defeating, his life and literary legacy suggest a notable lack of despair. In all, he was a remarkable example of Meiji-style integration—a blending—of the most diverse and different kinds of external and psychic forms, in the service not only of the existing Japanese collectivity but of a Japanese and broadly human collectivity that did not yet exist.

COMMENTARY / R. J. Lifton

Chōmin, like Ogai, sought to keep his death his own—to preserve a private area of experience from the omnivorous claims of his society. But unlike Ogai, Chōmin asserted that principle not only when dying but in his living acts, especially in his consistent pattern of oppositional behavior. Chōmin was the rare Japanese of the Meiji era who died and lived saying no. I think Camus realized how hard that was to do in any society.

A completely private death probably does not exist anywhere. In legislating religious and other practices around dying and postdeath ritual, societies reflect widespread psychological needs for placing death in a larger context of collective human continuity. Where individual psyche and collective symbolizations are more or less in harmony, as in much of the premodern world, both the dying person and the survivor could probably blend with prescribed practices without too great a sense that they violated authentic individual experience. But with the modern-historical emergence of the individual—less at home in his symbols, more uncertain and probing in his beliefs, confused by the more varied images available to him—that blending is no longer possible. Some of the most painful experiences of dislocation occur in the process of dying. Consider the situation in Japan and America.

As early versions of modern individuals, Ogai and Chōmin, in dying, struggled against being consumed by prevailing social and religious practices. Their society kept individuals tightly within its formations and closed ranks further with its orchestration of dying and funeral practices. One can still see related patterns in contemporary Japan. Now it is not so much the power of the state and its social order that closes in on the individual but rather that of the immediate institution, especially in the case of the all-enveloping commercial companies, some of whom even employ full-time funeral directors to take care of all the details when company employees die. But providing this pragmatic function can hardly guarantee authentic individual experience, nor prevent a painful sense of being swallowed up by the hypocrisies of institutional practice. (That kind of experience was brilliantly portrayed by Kurosawa Akira in his film, *Ikiru*, though the institution perpetrating the death-linked insults was a small government office rather than a large business firm.)

In America, institutions can do something of the same, but the more striking intruder on death is medical technology. Ivan Illich (1976) captures something of the ultimate quality of that process when he says that

Therapy reaches its apogee in the death-dance around the terminal patient. At a cost of between $500 and $2,000 per day, celebrants in white and blue envelop what remains of the patient in antiseptic smells. . . . the religious use of medical technique has come to prevail over its technical purpose. . . . . the conjuring doctor perceives himself as a manager of crisis. In an insidious way he provides each citizen at the last hour with an encounter with society's deadening dream of infinite power.

(Pp. 97–98)

I believe that Illich underestimates the profound anxieties of doctors themselves in the face of death. It would seem that healers, dying patients, and prospective survivors are caught up in a pattern of technicism that outwardly replaces ritual and leaves just about everybody empty, guilty, and angry. But Illich is surely right when he says that "Western man has lost the right to preside at his act of dying" and "mechanical death has conquered and destroyed all other deaths."

The two situations may be more similar than they appear at first glance. The Japanese institution in question draw on prevailing technology; and American technicism operates through social institutions. To avoid being devoured in death, I believe that an individual must, like Chōmin, feel himself related to a larger principle that transcends impinging groups and their practices. For Chōmin that principle, of course, had to do with ideals of individual rights. And his capacity in turn to hold onto those ideals seems to depend on the depth of his relationship to more traditional Japanese artistic and educational principles.

Real innovation depends on powerful grounding, and Chōmin seems to have been grounded in Japanese cultural tradition to a degree that could not be true of later westernizers. His powerful burst of creativity just before death, insistence on authenticity in dying, and his eclectic, highly idiosyncratic testament (with its impressive admixture of tones of Buddhism, Confucianism, Japanese this-worldliness, and general humanism) all suggest the extent to which he could integrate disparate historical forces in laying claim to his own life no less than his death.

COMMENTARY / S. Katō

Chōmin was a marginal man in Japanese society who became an individual with principle. As a marginal man he was outside the center of power yet within Meiji political movements. As an individualist, he became familiar with French ideas and language and was deeply convinced of the rationalism of the Enlightenment. These conditions enabled him to become an irreplaceable observer of modern Japanese politics.

A marginal man is neither an outsider nor an insider. In contrast to outsiders, he has firsthand knowledge about his own society; in contrast to insiders, he can maintain an intellectual distance from that society. The combination of knowledge and detachment, which provides the basis for a relativization of the prevailing value system, can make the marginal man an excellent objective analyst-observer of society. This is the case of many creative poets, artists, writers, and social scientists, both in the past and the present.

But because the marginal man is not entirely integrated into society and is not a core member of any organization, his direct influence on society is limited. He sometimes must confront the full force of social pressure, which requires a strong conviction in personal principles. Marginality is thus closely related to individuality—and is often associated with strength as an observer but weakness as a man of action. Chōmin, for example, was brilliant in his farsighted analysis of Japanese political reality, but he always failed in his actions in parliament and in business.

The plight of the marginal man is especially acute in a society which is group-oriented, traditionally homogeneous, highly organized and controlled, or ideologically monolithic. Chōmin's Japanese society was, and has remained, group-oriented and homogeneous. Contemporary Soviet society is highly controlled and ideologically monolithic, while North American society is highly organized and controlled. In the Soviet Union, creative writers are often alienated marginal men. And Jewish intellectuals, who view themselves as removed from the center of the American power structure, have made a major impact on American arts and letters. In premodern Japanese Heian court society (especially from the tenth to the twelfth centuries), which was tightly organized and completely closed to the outside, a great many creative writers of court literature were women who knew everything in their small society (and nothing of the outside world) but had no access to power.

The marginal man does not identify with his own society but tends to associate himself with another culture—either another country or the past or the future. Meiji intellectual leaders, such as Chōmin, Ogai, Natsume Sōseki, and Uchimura Kanzō, were associated with foreign cultures: French, German, English, and American, respectively. German and French romantic poets, mostly marginal in early nineteenth-century bourgeois society, identified with the cultural values of the aristocratic society of the past. Revolutionary poets in Russia and China, such as Vladimir Mayakovsky and Lu Hsün, on the other hand were marginal men who associated with a future society.

Associating oneself with another society, however, does not always result in creativity. Drieu La Rochelle, for example, with his strong sympathy for fascism, was clearly a marginal man in the French intellectual world before the Second World War. He collaborated with the German Occupation and then killed himself when France was liberated. His writings are certainly not remembered as particularly insightful or outstanding.

For a marginal man in a group-oriented society, personal integrity assumes immense importance, especially at death. Chōmin's uncompromising attitude toward his own death may be considered representative. He did not submit to pressure from outside groups, did not become a showman for the mass media, and did not dramatize his death. Chōmin's death was a simple but powerful testimony of his integrity as an independent individual.

5 / KAWAKAMI HAJIME (1879–1946)

"The Great Death"

Kawakami Hajime

FROM THE WRITINGS OF KAWAKAMI HAJIME

From a letter to Comrade Suzuki

Physically I am quite a coward. I can remember as a child walking with my grandmother and moving off the road to wait for rickshaws to pass, even when they were far away. Because of this careful attitude, I was never injured, except once when I cut my finger peeling a persimmon. And then I apparently cried violently. Its scar remains even today. I have not cut myself since—and I hate to see blood or to feel pain. For such a coward it is almost impossible to take part in what Marx calls the "clash of human bodies." In today's situation I might be better off simply withdrawing from it all and hiding in the forest. But I have no such intention. I will remain until the end in the ranks of the courageous youth. Even if I stand at the very rear I will continue to support my side and will never betray the X X X X X. . . . [1] Although it may be rather difficult for me to achieve, I want to complete my life actively expressing the energy and spirit that remain in this old body. . . .

In my childhood, I was told that I would not live to be an adult; and at the age of twenty-six I once risked death. Unexpectedly, I have now lived for more than fifty years. It has been a gift of chance. I will do my best to spend whatever additional days I am granted working for the ultimate cause. The night of the anniversary of Karl and Rosa.[2]

(Autobiography [Jijoden], vol. 1, pp. 260–61, 262)

"On the assassination of comrade Yamamoto Senji" ("Dōshi Yamamoto Senji kyojin ni taoru")

Eulogy: "Standing before the body of comrade Yamamoto, I would like to express with deepest respect my farewell.

"The precious blood which you shed calls forth from our comrades throughout the nation a more profound dedication and a hundred times, even a thousand times, more perseverance in our struggle. We, the comrades you left behind, must be keenly aware of why, how, and by which class you were murdered. We

1. Kawakami explains in a footnote: "When this letter was published, these six characters were deleted to meet censorship requirements. But I have long since forgotten the original text and what these six X's represented."

2. Karl Liebknecht and Rosa Luxemburg were leading Marxist activists and theoreticians who helped found the German Communist party. After attempting a revolution by force in January 1919, they were arrested and killed by government soldiers.

may grieve deeply over our separation from you, but your death is definitely not in vain. The countless comrades who follow you will never allow it to be so. As one of them, I express my heartfelt respect for you and my infinite gratitude for your invaluable and selfless sacrifice for the sake of the entire movement."

Today, that distant past seems almost like a dream. But as I copy anew the sentences of my eulogy, the events gradually become clear. I remember that just before the funeral ceremony was to begin I stopped for a moment in the room where Yamamoto's body lay. Mr. Hososeko, who used to be called Secretary General, handed me brush, ink, and paper, and requested that I prepare the eulogy. I had just viewed Yamamoto lying in his coffin. The expression on his face was almost as always. He died without disease, and the only visible mark was a trace of coagulated blood on his forehead, the wound he received when he fell to the entranceway floor while struggling with his assassin and being stabbed in the heart. It was just after paying my last respects to your body that I wrote the eulogy. My words—"The precious blood which you shed calls forth from our comrades throughout the nation a more profound dedication"—must have been a direct expression of my own personal reactions at that moment. —One can write many eloquent words. But if, after a period of time, they are not reenforced by deeds, they will never be written on a scroll and hung on wall for posterity. Fortunately, I can look back on what I have written and feel no such shame. It is something for which I am thankful.

Because of Yamamoto's position as a lecturer at Kyoto Imperial University, some people considered him a disciple of mine. But he was in fact never directly influenced by my thinking or by me. . . . From his family background and academic speciality, Yamamoto had no obligation to die in the forefront of the proletarian class struggle at the hands of an assassin. It was not an inevitable fate—yet he nonetheless died a tragic death. I have never been able to overlook this. His death was probably the most powerful stimulus that inspired my active participation in the proletarian movement.

(*Autobiography*, vol. 1, pp. 267–69)

"Feelings at beginning to write my autobiography"
("Jijoden o kakihajimeta koro no shinkyō")

I am now sixty-six years old. Even though I was allegedly born with three diseases, always came out poorly in my high school medical examinations, was warned by the doctor after each checkup in college to take better care of my health, and was refused insurance after graduation and marriage because of my deteriorated condition, I am now, despite this persistently weak disposition, approaching the age of seventy. Each time I learn of the death of my younger and healthier friends, I feel it very strange that I am still alive. My weak self has nearly accomplished the life assigned it by heaven. Now, I can die at any moment. In fact—and I have felt this way since my youth, and even more so now—I may die any time. But thinking this, I feel that there are other things to write and other books to read and that I would like to leave behind more of my own writings.

I have already finished recording my life from the time of the Unselfish Love Movement until the New Workers-Farmers party (Shinrōnōtō). This gives me some satisfaction, but I have not written a word about the period from the dissolution of the New Workers-Farmers party to my entrance into the Japanese Communist party. I would like to write that now. . . .

Today is May 27, 1944. The day is quiet and so is my spirit. At the side of my small desk are some full-blooming, slightly drooping red and white peonies that Mr. Sakamoto brought yesterday.

With many red and white peonies arranged in a vase
The old man of the hut is writing.

Hardly thinking at all I composed this poem. Somehow I find things to eat and time to write quietly. And with flowers arranged about me I feel as if I am living in a paradise more luxurious than that shown in the Amida Sutras. Feeling this supreme bliss, I continue my writing.

(*Autobiography*, vol. 2, pp. 85–87)

ew Japanese opposed the Pacific War. One who did was Kawakami Hajime, the most popular and perhaps the most controversial Marxist theoretician in prewar Japan. In 1933, at fifty-three, Kawakami was arrested and jailed for illegal membership and activities in the Japanese Communist party. He was released in late 1937 in a much weakened physical state and thereafter abstained from political activism. On August 15, 1945, news of an important radio broadcast revitalized the sixty-five-year-old man. He reacted sharply to his wife's remark that the broadcast would probably call for them "to fight to the last Japanese," telling her, "Don't talk nonsense. It's surrender." Kawakami had long awaited that conclusion. At noon came Emperor Hirohito's unprecedented announcement: Japan indeed surrendered and accepted the conditions of the Potsdam Declaration.

The imperial proclamation of defeat elicited a variety of reactions. While a few extreme militarists solemnly committed seppuku, many officers were stealing goods from the disintegrating army's storehouses. Writers and intellectuals who had collaborated with the government in war propaganda were shocked almost to the point of collapse by the sudden turnabout. Most people, however, accepted defeat with a mixture of resignation, relief, sadness, and anxiety about their future under the occupation. Kawakami, by contrast, rejoiced when he heard of the surrender, for it meant the defeat of Japanese militarism and the end of its expansion abroad and oppression at home.

On the day of surrender, Kawakami composed two poems:

> Ah, such happiness,
> At somehow living long enough
> To see this rare day
> When the fighting has ceased.

> Now I, too,
> Will crawl out of my sickbed
> To see the light
> In the sky that is clearing.

(Suekawa, p. 264)

Kawakami had achieved one of his major personal goals, to live to the end of the war. The poems express his sense of being a survivor who had been reborn. He looked hopefully toward a new era.

The occupation forces immediately set in motion a wide-ranging reconstruction of Japanese institutions aimed at preventing a resurgence of militarism and implanting a tradition of democracy. For Kawakami the most important consequences of the new political liberalism were the legalization of the Japanese Communist party (JCP) and the release of political prisoners. For the first time in Japanese history, the JCP, the only political party that had consistently opposed Japanese imperialism, emerged from underground. Three men assumed party leadership: Nosaka Sanzō, who returned from exile in Yenan, and Tokuta Kyūichi and Shiga Yoshio, who were released from Japanese prisons.

Kawakami wrote two poems, one as homage to Tokuta and Shiga and another to Nosaka, which were published in the party newspaper *Red Flag* (*Akahata*) on December 19, 1945, and January 17, 1946, respectively. The poems contrast the personal triumphs of individual party heroes with Kawakami's sad resignation to his own impending death—all in a highly lyrical, romantic style:

> Through eighteen years in prison,
> Six thousand days in isolated cells,
> Lived these fighters.
> Never curbing their will
> Until they saw again the sun.
> Comrade Tokuta,
> Comrade Shiga,
> How vigorous they are:
> Great men in Japanese history.
> I envy them.
> I trust them.
> I respect them.
> These jewels of mankind.
>
> An ailing old man of seventy
> In a lonely, humble hut,
> Lying on his deathbed,
> Sends them from afar, his heart.
> (Sumiya, 1962, pp. 307–09)

Tokuta would soon become ill and die and Shiga would later leave the JCP to found a new communist organization, the Voice of Japan

(Nihon no koe). But the war's end brought at least a moment of euphoria, to Kawakami and others of the left.

In the autumn of 1945, after eight years of forced seclusion and total abstention from political activities, Kawakami found himself a focus of public attention. He received visits from scores of newly freed prisoners, including many he had never met, for whom Kawakami was an almost sacred symbol of continuity. His translations of basic Marxist texts, including *Das Kapital*, as well as his own voluminous writings on Marxist theory, formed an important core of intellectual leftist thought in Japan. And Kawakami's resistance to ideological backsliding had made him an inspirational model for others imprisoned by the government during the war.

As the JCP reentered the political arena, Kawakami felt a powerful urge to join its activities—to emerge from isolation, appear in public, express himself freely without censorship, and help mold Japan's postwar transformation. Physically, however, that was impossible. He was extremely weak and confined to bed. Food was still scarce in the fall of 1945, and medical care, when available, was inadequate.

Kawakami, in fact, felt near death, as he made clear in poems he sent, together with pictures of himself, to a few close friends:

> Now with no hope of standing again,
> I wish only to accept death calmly.
>> (Suekawa, p. 266)

And,

> Day and night confined to bed
> To survive would be useless.
>> (P. 267)

Kawakami's resignation was not without despair. He thought constantly of death, but he persevered. One of Kawakami's last students at Kyoto University, Nawa Tōichi, after his release from prison in October 1945, met his former professor several times. They discussed the coming transformation of Japan, the political problems likely to occur, and the future of the emperor system. Kawakami had to carefully avoid exertion or excitement. According to Nawa, the elderly man spoke in a firm but quiet voice, stressing that intellectuals must participate actively in Japan's imminent "bourgeois democratic revolution" and in formulating its values and policies. In December, with every movement now painful, Kawakami asked his younger friend his advice whether to try to become politically active. Nawa replied that he wanted his teacher to live as long as possible and therefore it was best to minimize all strains. He suggested that it would be sufficient for Kawakami to allow his name to be used.

But another former student, Horie Muraichi, when asked the same question, urged Kawakami to write something for the party. Kawakami then agreed, but the efforts he made, while helpful to the party, might have hastened his death. Nawa, who later realized this, felt a kind of death guilt.

Even today I wonder whether my answer was correct. Every time I think about it I become very sad. But I felt then that *sensei* himself was waiting for the answer. I now recall that in order to lighten the heavy burden on my heart.

(Nawa, p. 250)

Kawakami's last writings provide important insights into his thoughts and feelings at the end of his life. In addition to the poems dedicated to party leaders, he prepared a memorial message for a meeting on December 20, 1945, to commemorate the death of Yamamoto Senji, the Diet member from Kyoto who was assassinated in 1929 after openly opposing the government's repressive Maintenance of Public Order Act *(Chian iji bō)*. Yamamoto's death had a powerful impact on Kawakami. In his postwar memorial "Speaking Before the Grave of My Deceased Friend Yamamoto Senji" ("Bōyū Yamamoto Senji kun no bozen ni kataru"), Kawakami again expressed both hope and sorrow. Noting that the occupation forces had repealed the repressive law opposed by Yamamoto, Kawakami continued, "Now, perhaps, the common people comprehend the full meaning of the fight for which you gave your life." Kawakami concluded the passage, which was read for him in his absence, with his own statement of farewell: "I am almost at the end of my life. Even writing this short passage is extremely painful physically. I must apologize that I can say no more" (Sumiya, 1968, pp. 259–60). Kawakami's commemorative statement for Yamamoto was of course political, but also personal and moral, reasserting his own commitment to that same struggle.

Finally the acute food shortage, the bitter cold of the Kyoto winter, and old age itself were too much for him. On January 30, 1946, at the age of sixty-six in his small Kyoto house, Kawakami Hajime died of pneumonia, "calmly as if asleep," as one observer reported. Not far from his home, on the slope of East Hill (Higashiyama) was Hōnen-in, a temple of the Pure Land Buddhist sect, where he often used to stroll and where he told his disciples he wished to be buried. The wish was not then carried out because of the high price of a burial plot within the temple grounds. Years later his disciples, relatives, and friends collected enough money to erect a memorial stone to Kawakami and his wife Hide in the Hōnen-in Temple. They inscribed on the stone a short poem by Kawakami written in 1932 when he joined the JCP:

> Looking back along the path
> That I have struggled to follow,
> I see so many mountains climbed,
> So many rivers crossed.
>
> (Sumiya, 1962, frontispiece)

Kawakami Hajime is remembered as one of the most vocal and influential intellectuals of the left in Japan from the time of the First World War to the early 1930s. Although he was neither the first socialist nor the first Marxist theoretician, he was the first professor of an imperial university to express publicly his sympathy for socialism, then lecture on Marxist theory in the classroom, and finally commit himself to the JCP's underground political activities.

Kawakami was also widely recognized as a prolific author and newspaper columnist, dedicated teacher, competent scholar, political symbol, and sensitive poet. As a newspaper columnist, Kawakami wrote eloquently and persuasively about social problems, such as the gap between the luxury of the nouveaux riches and the poverty of the working people. During the 1920s, Kawakami's lectures at Kyoto Imperial University attracted throngs of leftist students from all over the country. He transformed Kyoto into a mecca for that generation of the Japanese left. In this way, his prestige as a professor at an imperial university helped legitimize and publicize socialist and Marxist causes which had previously been ignored by Japan's intellectual establishment.

Kawakami was also one of Japan's first economic theoreticians. He analyzed, commented on, paraphrased, and translated numerous economic works. His studies provided a solid foundation for subsequent Marxist scholarship. Indeed, we may consider him the founder in Japan of the academic study of Marxism, which dominated the social sciences in the prewar period until suppressed, and which reemerged prominently after the war.

Kawakami's transition from scholar to political activist, widely reported in the press during the late 1920s, made him an important political symbol as well. But by the time he officially joined the Communist party in 1932, government suppression and police infiltration had reduced the party to shambles. As an underground group the JCP created a mysterious halo around itself, stressing its role as the moral symbol of the militant left more than its role as a political organization. In a similar way, Kawakami's action, though politically ineffective, was seen as personally heroic—all the more so because he held to his beliefs through imprisonment. Unlike many other leftists and liberals, Kawakami successfully resisted police pressure toward *tenkō* (literally "changing direction"), which from the late 1920s until the end of the war referred to a formal renunciation of socialism, communism, or liberalism, and a "patriotic" endorsement of militarism and the government. Kawakami became a personal model of ethical behavior for the left in general and for the Communists in particular.

Finally, Kawakami was a prolific and accomplished writer of both poetry and prose. During the thirty years before his arrest, he published at least one article a month and an average of two books a year. After his release from prison in 1937, while in forced seclusion in Kyoto, he composed poems of circumstance and compiled a five-volume autobiography recounting the events of his dramatic life. Kawakami's autobiography is without doubt one of the best of its genre in modern Japanese literature. He lyrically integrates the story of his personal life with that of Marxist politics and vividly evokes the experiences and emotional conflicts of a man who lived by principles. As a writer, which he was more consistently than anything else, Kawakami sensed that his personal struggles had historical meaning. His autobiography expressed his conception of his role in history.

Kawakami Hajime was born on October 20, 1879, into the new Japan of the Meiji period, a member of the first post-Restoration generation.[3] Unlike Nogi, Ogai, and Chōmin, who directly experienced the

3. We refer to Kawakami Hajime in his youth as Hajime and in adulthood as Kawakami. He never adopted an alternative name.

conflicts surrounding Japan's transition, Kawakami knew the To-kugawa period only as history. Five years before his birth, his family had received compensation in exchange for relinquishing its samurai status. In 1877, two years before his birth, the new national army crushed the Satsuma Rebellion, the last vestige of violent samurai op-position to the Tokyo government. His childhood coincided with the early period of the "cultural enlightenment," when Japan sought to eliminate the remnants of Tokugawa society and aggressively im-ported Western styles in all aspects of life—military, political, economic, communications, even fashion. Japan was an imperial na-tion intensely seeking recognition as part of the international commun-ity.

Hajime's father, Sunao, was a lower retainer for the Mōri clan of Chōshū who fought in the Chōshū militia during the Restoration. Under the Meiji regime, he became head of a small village in Yamaguchi prefecture at the western tip of Honshū, and principal of the local primary school. Sunao's character is reputed to have fit the literal meaning of his name—simple, sincere, and honest. He was so sincere, it is said, that he never once throughout his entire life opposed the will of his mother. Hajime felt very close to his father. He recalled in his autobiography, "I am truly happy that I have not a single bad memory about my father." He wrote that he did not envy those who received large estates from their fathers, that although his family was relatively poor in the early years of Meiji, his father had left him good memories. Hajime's image of his father was of a faultless man who fulfilled his filial piety and obeyed his Buddhist prescripts. This ex-tremely idealized image was not only a psychological burden in Kawakami's lifelong search for spiritual truth, but also a stimulus to that search.

Although Kawakami described his childhood as a period of dream-like, fairy-tale bliss, he was in fact surrounded by conflict from birth. Indeed the confusion in family relationships suggests something close to an early Meiji version of a Gilbert and Sullivan operetta. Nine months after marriage, Sunao separated from his wife and sent her home, when she was already several months pregnant. In the fall of 1879, when a young boy was born, Sunao, as permitted by Tokugawa custom, retrieved his heir. Hajime was then raised in his father's house by his grandmother. In his autobiography, Hajime wonders whether being denied his mother's milk and fed thin rice gruel instead was the original cause of his lifelong physical weakness. Certainly the thought itself symbolizes the deprivation he experienced in early childhood at being separated from his mother. This sense of deprivation, in a culture virtually constructed around maternal nurturing, was to become another lifelong image, and here too Kawakami managed to convert his pain into a source of energy.

Sunao remarried soon after separating from his first wife, but the new wife was said to have rejected her baby stepson and perhaps partly as a consequence, her relationship with her mother-in-law rapidly deteriorated.[4] After she gave birth to Sunao's second son, he dismissed her and brought back his first wife. But Hajime, now three years old, remained grandmother's baby. He continued to sleep with his grandmother in her separate cottage near the main house, while his stepbrother slept with Hajime's real mother.

His grandmother spoiled him greatly, never scolding him for spilling things on the tatami mats or for breaking dishes; his demand for her was such that she found it difficult to get away from him even long enough to enter the bath. This exaggerated attachment probably resulted from Hajime's original maternal deprivation. But in her mid-fifties, his grandmother had frequent epileptic fits during which she would lose consciousness, froth at the mouth, and her arms and legs would go into violent contortions. Hajime's early imagery must have combined absolute need with old age, bizarre illness, and death. It is the kind of early experience that can impart lifelong sensitivity to death and suffering and special mixtures of vulnerability and potential achievement.

Hajime entered elementary school at an early age, where he performed well and won several prizes. He later wrote that his abilities were no better than the average village boy and that the prizes were due to his father's influence in the school and the village—although

4. It is quite possible that there was a power struggle between the two women around the little boy. The stepmother's apparent hostility toward the child might have resulted not only from the fact that he was not hers (and held a position in the family superior to that of any child she could produce) but also from her inevitable defeat by the grandmother in the contest for substitute mother, and perhaps for her husband's affection as well. In those days, and even now, the position of the younger woman in such struggles was extremely difficult, all the more so because a second wife and stepmother could probably expect even less support from her husband in such a contest (especially a husband noted for his filial piety) than under ordinary circumstances.

Hajime's accomplishments in life suggest otherwise. In that comment we can infer a combination of public humility, genuine self-doubt, and ambivalent feelings toward his father and the latter's relationship to the village politics of the time.

Hajime's maternal grandfather, whom he often visited and was very fond of, also influenced the young boy. The grandfather was a prominent scholar, author of Japanese and Chinese poetry, painter, and secretary for the feudal lord's family during the Tokugawa period. His love of poetry was such that as a young man, although his family was poor, he traveled the long distance to Edo to meet the famous Confucianist Satō Issai, receiving from him a handwritten poem. The grandfather's scholarly and artistic talents tended to reinforce and shape the traditional cultural patterns instilled earlier in Hajime. The grandfather surely influenced the career choices of Hajime's younger brother and a cousin, both of whom became painters, and Hajime's own later integration of scholarly, aesthetic, and traditional patterns with radical politics.

In 1888, Hajime graduated from elementary school and proceeded to the Iwakuni School, one of five schools financed by a prefectural education society to prepare students for middle school. This institution provided a way for sons of low-ranking former samurai without adequate financial support to get ahead in early Meiji society. Yamaguchi prefecture, which included the old Chōshū clan, had close connections with the new national government and therefore was among the first to establish a local educational society. The local group served the government's policy of using the educational system to produce and recruit talented young men who could then become bureaucrats and scholars working for the national goal of a "rich country and a strong army." This association exemplifies the Meiji programs which decentralized many functions in order to centralize more power in the hands of the Tokyo government.

As a young boy, Hajime accepted the ideals of the education system. His boyhood hero was Yoshida Shōin, the celebrated leader of the samurai-scholar activists without office (shishi) who were devoted to the Restoration cause. The Meiji government idealized the shishi image as a symbolic model for the new elite, stressing two characteristics: selfless devotion to the emperor, and a strong sense of duty in state affairs. The shishi ideal was particularly deep-rooted in Yamaguchi prefecture, the home of Yoshida Shōin and his disciples.

From an early age, Kawakami incorporated into his basic identity an ideal of selfless nationalism that persisted throughout his life. As a young economist, for example, he supported a theory of state-controlled mercantilism rather than economic liberalism. And in his thirties, when he was sent by his university to study economics in Europe, he wrote a thoroughly nationalistic series of articles on Europe and Japan. Even when he later adopted Marxism and rejected the concrete shishi ideal of devotion to the emperor, its spirit of dedication remained strong within him, as did his sense of duty to the Japanese state.

In 1893, at fourteen, Kawakami left home for the first time to attend middle school in the prefectural capital of Yamaguchi. The separation seems to have been most difficult for his grandmother, who was then sixty-six and expecting to die soon. At his departure, she told him through tears, "This is farewell" (Kore ga oitomagoi da). Thereafter, when he returned home for vacations, every time he stood up to leave the room, his grandmother repeated the same phrase. She in fact did so for another thirty years, and lived long enough to see her grandson rise to become a famous professor at Kyoto Imperial University. But the story suggests how much Kawakami was immersed in emotions around partings and transitions.

While attending the middle and upper schools in Yamaguchi, Kawakami devoted himself to literature and politics. Initially he wanted to become a major literary figure. He read widely and particularly liked the long emotional poems of Shimazaki Tōson, which reflected the influence of Western romantic poetry in the expression of lyrical sentiment. These poems represented a break from previous Japanese literary forms and became very popular among Meiji youth.

Kawakami never lost his love for Tōson's poetry, but as he approached graduation from upper school he shifted his focus to the more "practical" subjects of law and politics. His choice reflected Meiji society's conception of a "successful" student as one who joined the central government and became a statesman serving the nation. He was deeply impressed by the nation's first party cabinet and the elegant appearance of politicians in high silk hats. His mother's brother in Tokyo, one of Japan's first lawyers, provided a model of conventional success. Thus, just before entrance examinations, Kawakami decided to apply to the law department of Tokyo Imperial University.

He wanted to become a statesman. Such last-moment switches were rare, but he could not be dissuaded, not even by his German instructor who warned that he had the nature of a poet and not a legalist. Kawakami was finally allowed to apply to the law department and after cramming with one of the best students in his class, he passed the exam and was admitted.

Kawakami arrived in Tokyo in 1898, three years after Japan's defeat of China. Two intellectual currents then predominated in the capital city: national chauvinism and social criticism. Military victory over China had precipitated Japan's emergence onto the world scene and vastly enhanced feelings of nationalism. At the same time, Japan became more open to social trends in other countries, including ideas critical of capitalist development. In 1897, for example, the first groups organized in Japan to study, publicize, and implement the new concepts of labor unions and socialism. The nineteen-year-old Kawakami was deeply responsive to these currents.

In his first step toward independent thought and action, he moved from the home of his successful uncle, where he initially lived, to his own small room of three tatami mats, an area about six by nine feet, in a student boardinghouse.[5] He attended few classes, preferring to spend his time reading literature, as he had at school in Yamaguchi. He also started two activities that altered his life directly and indelibly: attending the many free lectures on social and political issues held in Tokyo, and studying the Bible. He checked the newspapers daily, planning his schedule according to that day's lectures. In this way, he learned about social problems from leading intellectuals critical of the government—Kinoshita Naoe, Uchimura Kanzō, Kōtoku Shūsui, Tanaka Shōzō, and others. Kawakami considered these men his real teachers more than the professors inside the walls of the university. From them he first learned about democracy, socialism, and Christianity. He became aware of social problems and began to question society's goals as well as his own. This reflective, self-critical aspiration toward moral improvement that emerged during his university days became an enduring theme of his life.

At the age of twenty, that theme became organized around the Bi-

5. Despite this move he continued, according to custom, to be supported by his uncle throughout his student days. Such aid, of course, was not without reciprocal obligations. When Kawakami later graduated and began working, he provided his cousins with room and board for a period of time.

ble. In his autobiography Kawakami stated that the Bible had a greater influence on him than the Analects of Confucius, greater than any
book he had ever read. He had little previous connection with religion
and approached Christianity with naive directness. He did not simply
read the New Testament; he believed in it. He sought to follow the
literal meaning of Christ's teachings in the Sermon on the Mount and
interpreted the following verse (Matthew 5:39–42) as the "command
of absolute unselfishness":

> But I say unto you, That ye resist no evil: but
>> whosoever shall smite thee on the right cheek, turn to
>> him the other also.
> And if any man will sue thee at the law, and take away thy
>> coat, let him have thy cloak also.
> And whosoever shall compel thee to go a mile, go
>> with him twain.
> Give to him that asketh thee, and from him that would
>> borrow of thee turn not thou away.

In "The History of My Spirit" ("Watakushi no kokoro no rekishi"), an
essay written in prison, Kawakami recalled his initial reactions to
those verses:[6]

To this absolute unselfishness, I unconditionally bowed my head. I hardly
reflected on reasons why but simply felt in my heart, "That's it! That's it!" I
believed that this attitude of absolute unselfishness truly had to be man's ideal
behavior. And I felt from the bottom of my heart the overpowering demand
that my own behavior literally had to follow this ideal. But at the same time,
I felt fear, "With that attitude, it's impossible for you to live in this world.
You would soon give up your life."

(Kawakami, *Gokuchū nikki*, vol. 1, pp. 255–56)

Kawakami records that reading the Bible made him aware of death
and caused him to question how he should live: "This was the beginning of my spirit (kokoro)."

6. *Kokoro* refers to one's deepest emotions; it is also translated as "heart" or "true
mind" and associated with sincerity or "wholeheartedness."

Kawakami's sense of "That's it!" suggests what is sometimes called a eureka experience: a sudden personal breakthrough in which one discovers, through a new influence, a way of articulating what one has strongly but inchoately sensed. These experiences always involve an important ultimate component, a sense of connecting—or reconnecting—the self to an immortalizing principle. Thus Kawakami related the Bible's "turn the other cheek" attitude of gentle acceptance to a longstanding Japanese principle of selflessness. His personal experience was part of a more general process of reactivating old Japanese feelings by means of vitalizing images from the West. This has been a key psychological process during the hundred years of Japan's overall modernization.

Kawakami never officially joined the church. But during his last year at Tokyo University he confronted a social problem that provided him with an opportunity to act on his new religious ideals. Since the late 1880s, wastes from the Ashio copper mine, located to the northwest of Tokyo in Gunma prefecture, had contaminated the Watarase River and polluted irrigation water and fish, destroying the livelihood of thousands of peasants. In November 1901, Kawakami attended a speech delivered by a fiery politican named Tanaka Shōzō on behalf of the victimized farmers. To Kawakami, Tanaka seemed to personify the absolutely unselfish man. The presentation so stirred the student that he impulsively donated his coat and muffler to the society aiding the Ashio victims. The next morning he hired a rickshaw and delivered all his belongings to the farmers suffering from the cold winter. He thus united his thought, feeling, and action, and realized his idealistic goal of selfless giving. His parents, however, were less than overjoyed. His mother pointed out to him that the clothing he had given away was the result of her labors and not his. But Kawakami believed that obeying spiritual commands, as Christ said, had to supersede obligations to parents.

Although he entered Tokyo University with the aim of becoming a government official, Kawakami graduated in July 1902 with the goal of becoming a journalistic critic of the government. The next November he married a woman from his home prefecture of Yamaguchi. But he was unable to find employment at a newspaper, and his uncle resolutely disapproved of a journalistic career. Two months later, in January 1903, a professor at the Tokyo Imperial School of Agriculture hired him as a lecturer in economics. Characteristically, Kawakami entered academic life with great ambitions. From the start he aimed at becoming an overseas student for the Ministry of Education, a doctor of economics, and ultimately a university professor. He began his career lecturing on basic economic theory, industrial economics, and transportation theory at various schools scattered around Tokyo—the Agriculture School, the Tokyo Special School (later Waseda University), the Taiwan Society School, the Peers School—all positions arranged for him by his professor. Just to keep up with the different classes he was teaching required disciplined preparation nearly every day of the year. He also served as editor for the *National Academic Society Journal (Kokka gakkai zasshi)*, published by members of the law faculty of Tokyo Imperial University. He worked prodigiously, earned a good income, and carried out a younger man's traditional obligations to a sponsor by helping to arrange his professor's personal library, performing some secretarial work, and ghostwriting several articles.

In October 1905, Kawakami began writing his first major newspaper articles. The series, entitled "Discourses on Socialism" ("Shakaishugi hyōron"), was published under a pseudonym in the *Yomiuri shinbun*. Because of its provocative content and the mystery of the author's identity, the series attracted widespread attention and contributed to a significant increase in *Yomiuri* readership and sales. The first few articles introduced basic concepts of socialism, followed by several others that systematically criticized existing socialist movements in Japan.

These articles had considerable importance for the still young socialist movement in Japan. The first socialist party (Social Democratic party) was founded in 1901 by Christian socialist leaders Abe Iso'o (1865–1949), Kinoshita Naoe (1869–1937), and Katayama Sen (1859–1933), and was promptly banned by the government. Then around the time of the Russo-Japanese War, a socialist, antiwar journal, the *Commoner's Newspaper (Heimin shinbun)*, was founded and published by Sakai Toshihiko (1870–1933), a Marxist, and Kōtoku Shūsui, Nakae Chōmin's disciple who later became an anarchist. Kawakami in his "Discourses" in the *Yomiuri*, distinguished three main factions—none of them satisfactory to him—the Christian socialists, the Heiminsha socialists, and the "state socialists." The third group is more accurately termed the social policy school, derived from German political economists and based in the law faculty of Tokyo Imperial University, where Kawakami was trained. It supported a system of private enterprise with active government regulation to reduce social conflict, which Kawakami equated with a form of socialism (see Bernstein, 1977, pp. 52–55).

Before the First World War Japan's socialists were mostly Christians or ex-Christians (with only a few exceptions, notably Sakai and Kōtoku), who tended to be motivated largely by spiritual and humanitarian concern for the underprivileged. They embraced various ideological currents, including syndicalism, social democracy, anarchism, and Marxism, and were loosely linked around common opposition to militarism, war, and the centralized oligarchy. But they were nonetheless isolated in the Meiji imperial state with no effective ties to the workers, farmer, or farm tenants. And their activities were severly restricted by official censorship and police harassment. At this time Kawakami was not a socialist. But his *Yomiuri* series demonstrated strong sympathy for some aspects of the socialist cause, particularly its humanitarian elements.

Just before beginning the *Yomiuri* series, Kawakami was living in a row-house apartment with his wife and baby son and his uncle's son and daughter as boarders. Because studying during the daytime was impossible due to constant commotion, he usually worked through the night, until his neighbors rose just before daybreak and disturbed his concentration. Kawakami found this situation increasingly intolerable, and in October, when he started writing the *Yomiuri* articles, he sent his wife and son to his parents' home in the country to reduce distractions. He felt driven by his studies and wanted to devote himself totally to reading, thinking, and writing. Soon after his family left, however, his interest and motivation in his work waned somewhat and he began reading religious books. His doubts about life and self once again emerged strongly and he questioned whether his economic research was not just another form of self-glorification, the very opposite of absolute unselfishness.

It was then that he picked up Tolstoy's *My Religion* at a secondhand book store, and was profoundly affected by Tolstoy's attempt to live the words of the Bible. *My Religon* spoke to Kawakami's unease, his sense that something was wrong in his life and had to be changed. The separation from his wife, on whom he depended for psychological bal-

ance, left him vulnerable to his own inner turbulence.[7] Reading
Tolstoy provided a way for him to articulate and order his personal
conflicts. It also helped him solve the dilemma of where to take his
readers—and himself—after his comprehensive critique of socialist
movements in Japan.

At the beginning of December 1905, in the last four articles of his
series, Kawakami introduced his conception of ideal socialism, which,
he proclaimed, could be achieved only through widespread spiritual
change leading to a belief in "the totally unselfish pure love of others"
(*jun muga jun taai*). The conception was of course biblical and
Tolstoyan. But it arose even more directly from his encounter with a
small splinter sect of Pure Land Buddhism known as the Movement
for Unselfish Love (Mugaai undō). He first communicated with the
sect's leader, a young priest only three years older than Kawakami, in
late November when struggling over the conclusions of his critique of
socialism in the *Yomiuri*. On December 4, he met the priest and decided to join the group. The following day, according to the leader's
instructions, he resigned his various teaching jobs around Tokyo and
sold all his belongings except for his Bible and a volume of Shimazaki
Tōson's poetry. He then wrote his thirty-sixth article for the *Yomiuri*,
confessing his own identity to the public and declaring his determination to abandon all economic pursuits so he could follow the truth of
selfless love and seek ideal socialism. (The disclosure that the author of
the series was an unknown twenty-six-year-old lecturer in economics
shocked *Yomiuri* readers as much as Kawakami's ideal socialism baffled
them. But the series helped establish his reputation as a brilliant
economic journalist.)

On December 8, Kawakami entered the "Garden of Selflessness"
("Muga en"). He understood the group's theories in terms of his own
ideas about total unselfishness based on the Bible. To love others was
for him an absolute command—and he demanded that other members
of the group obey that command. He criticized them for various
reasons, including their tendency to sleep during the day instead of
devoting all their powers to the spiritual cause. Kawakami soon separated in disgust from the group to carry out his own missionary work.

7. Kawakami's wife later claimed that had she remained she might have helped
him control his inner conflicts and avoid the subsequent experience that took place.
But one reason for sending her away might have been his unconscious desire for the
freedom to plunge into some form of religious experience.

That night, determined to exist "without sleep and without rest," he had an intense mystical experience. He later described it as "the great death" (*taishi ichiban*), a Zen term meaning the death of the private self or ego. For several days, he lost all sense of feeling in his skin, hands, and legs. In his autobiography, Kawakami wrote "This [experience] solved my doubts that had lasted many years and allowed me to live the forty years from then until today in happiness." This moment of religious transcendence for Kawakami became a point of reference and a source of energy for his basic humanism and moralism. It left him with a permanent image of truth, of absolute blending of immediate and ultimate experience—that is, of perfect centering. In surviving his direct confrontation with nothingness, disintegration, and death, he felt revitalized and almost invulnerable. His religious experience thus enabled him to feel part of a transcendental source of power and confirmed his belief in the truth of absolute unselfishness. He referred to his body thereafter as a "public instrument of society" (*tenka no kōki*). He then returned to the Movement for Unselfish Love and remained for about two months, until February 1906, when the discrepancies he felt between his personal ideals and the bizarre reality of the organization caused his final separation from the group.

The *Yomiuri* immediately hired Kawakami to report on economic affairs. A year later, he resigned to found an economics journal that opposed advocates of a free economy and free trade. In accordance with his moral notions of serving the state rather than than the self, he called for protectionist policies and a state-centered economy. He went through a period of intense nationalism as he groped for a way to make sense out of his commitment to unselfishness in terms of economics. A contemporary socialist, Sakai Toshihiko, assailed Kawakami's eclecticism as "an incomplete mixture of Neo-Confucianist humanism, Buddhist spiritualism, socialist economics, and status quo compromising" (Sumiya, 1962, p. 114). But Kawakami was searching for his own voice, seeking his own idiosyncratic path to selflessness. He was looking for a framework in which his spiritual and scholarly ideas would blend.

In 1908, Kawakami was appointed lecturer in economics at Kyoto Imperial University and entered his first stable working environment at the age of twenty-nine. There, for the next twenty years, his scholarly pursuits and spiritual goals led him first to academic Marxism and then to political activism. During the first five years of his university career, before leaving Japan for two years' study in Europe, Kawakami studied classical nonsocialist economics, and his ideas were still deeply rooted in the intellectual milieu of the late Meiji period when nationalism swept Japan following the war with Russia. Kawakami's nationalism was constructed around a principle of total personal service for the general good, "for the sake of the state." He wrote two economics textbooks, translated several technical economic works by Western scholars, and explored general problems of integrating Western knowledge into Japanese culture. He favorably compared the ethics of Japanese nationalism to those of Western individualism, as summarized by biographer Sumiya Etsuji (1962):

In Japanese patriotic morals and nationalistic ethics, the state is the *goal* and the individual is the *means*, giving rise to a selfless patriotic altruism, while in Western individualist ethics and commercial morals, the state is the *means* and the individual is the *goal*, giving rise to the Western ethical perspective.

(Pp. 133–34)

He did call for a combination of the two traditions, but fundamentally he considered the Japanese way to be more compatible with his principle of selflessness.

Kawakami's ardent nationalism was reinforced by his stay in Europe, from 1913 to 1915. He pursued his research on economic history and theory in Germany, France, and England. Critical of much that he encountered, Kawakami fully embraced what he called Japan's "special" nationalism. That theme is expressed in his impressions of Europe published as a series of articles in an Osaka newspaper, and later collected in a book, *Looking Back on the Homeland (Sokoku o kaerimite)*. And he was remembered by Shimazaki, his boyhood idol, whom he met in Paris, as a student who emphasized "the great and able nation of Japan."

After returning to Japan, Kawakami wrote another series of articles in the Osaka *Asahi shinbun*, from September to December in 1916, which described and analyzed conditions of poverty he had observed in Europe. He then compiled and published the articles as a short book entitled *Tales of Poverty (Bimbō monogatari)*, which was an immediate bestseller in Japan. The work occupied a pivotal position in

Kawakami's intellectual development and became a classic treatise in the history of economics in Japan.

Tales of Poverty was divided into three sections: "What are the living conditions of poor people?", "Why are there so many poor people?", and "How can poverty be permanently cured?" His description of the malady was more convincing than his suggested cure. In the last section he proposed three possible solutions to poverty: first, reform public morals—that is, have the rich voluntarily abandon their luxurious ways; second, implement a social policy that would eliminate the gulf between rich and poor; and third, establish national ownership of all industry, as Japan had done in education and in the military. Kawakami supported the first solution. Overcoming poverty became a matter of individual ethical decision. Problems of distribution would be resolved, he believed, only if people shifted from egoism to altruism.[8]

Tales of Poverty was epoch-making in establishing poverty as an accepted topic of public debate. Until then, those Japanese who discussed social problems and socialism were mostly Christians and ex-Christians, a small minority of ideological dissidents in the homogeneous nationalistic society created by the Meiji regime. In this sense, Christians resembled socialists in their isolation from the masses and their exclusion from the establishment.[9] Kawakami, who had received his doctorate in economics and been appointed a professor at Kyoto Imperial University while in Europe, was an authentic member of the intellectual establishment. *Tales of Poverty* did much to legitimate social protest against poverty and social criticism in general.

Tales of Poverty was also the first economic analysis of poverty published in Japan. Earlier socialists had discussed poverty mostly in political and journalistic terms or in the abstract language of political philosophy. But only rarely had they used concrete data and social scientific analysis. Academic economists, while introducing and commenting on Western economic theories, almost totally ignored

8. In this sense, Kawakami's moral concern transcended his nationalism. But genuine selflessness and dedication can also be associated with nationalism, even when the latter takes aggressive and jingoistic directions, as it did in Japan in the 1930's. Selflessness thus can be associated with both the traditional, more or less rightist and restorationist world view and the Marxist, leftist, and transformationist world view.

9. The predominance of Christians in early socialist movements in Japan resulted not only from Christian humanitarianism, but also from the almost inevitable alliance between two dissident groups subjected to heavy ideological and political pressure.

poverty as a subject of study. Kawakami was the first to provide the Japanese reading public with both data and analysis on the special phenomenon of poverty in the midst of abundance in industrialized nations. Despite the weakness of its conclusions, *Tales of Poverty* opened Japanese eyes to the universal problem as no work had previously done.[10]

Kawakami's concern with poverty anticipated later social trends in Japan. Unlike Europe, Japan (and United States) had profited from the First World World War. Industries expanded, population concentrated in urban areas, and agriculture became increasingly commercialized. Yet, despite doubling its industrial output, Japan at the end of the war was still a half-industrialized country. Quantitative changes in the economy did not produce immediate structural changes in society. And when the booming international trade ceased at the end of the war, depression set in, following a pattern similar to that in Europe. The depression affected farmers and tenants in the countryside, especially in silk-producing areas.[11]

It was then that Japan's trade union movement began to develop. But radicalization of the Japanese working class did not occur on the scale of the West, and trade unions were not a base for radical politics. Unlike their more numerous Western counterparts, factory workers in Japan were much less organized and could return to their families in farming villages if they lost their jobs in the cities.

Conditions after the First World War contributed to a radicalization of Japanese intellectuals. College graduates for the first time encountered difficulties in finding jobs in industry and government. A growing number of unemployed but highly educated urban youth condemned the gap between the rich and the workers and tenants. They responded sympathetically to various new cultural trends, including the rise of socialist movements in Western Europe and the Communist Revolution in Russia. The liberal ideas propounded by Yoshino Sakuzō found more followers. The various Marxist movements cen-

10. In that sense, *Tales of Poverty* resembled the 1891 "Rerum Novarum" of Pope Leo XIII which warned society of social injustice and proposed moralistic solutions. In Japan, however, Kawakami's treatise coincided with the decline of Christian socialism. At the same time, the book initiated his own search for a more effective way to change society.

11. Silk was the largest single export commodity in Japan during the early twentieth century; the sharp drop in demand for silk abroad caused severe suffering in Japan's rural areas.

tered on the underground Communist party founded in 1922 increased in numbers. Students became increasingly conscious of their political rights and of the authoritarianism of the government.

There was also experimentation in literature and the arts. In the 1920s, the New Sensibility School (*Shinkankaku ha*), including writers Kawabata Yasunari and Yokomitsu Riichi, opposed the style of proletarian literature and used Dadaist elements to reconstruct a reality based on personal perceptions.

Kawakami both contributed to and was influenced by the leftward shift of intellectuals during the interwar years, a time characterized as the period of Taishō democracy. His first phase of academic research focused on capitalist economies and lasted until 1919. In that year, he terminated publication of the original version of *Tales of Poverty*, then in its thirtieth edition, and prepared a new edition in which the last section was significantly revised. Retaining his original discussions of conditions and causes, he eliminated the plea for moral reform and replaced it with a more radical statement, including "one doctor's monologue" on the necessity for operating on sick societies. Kawakami now advocated fundamental changes in social structure, an important turning point on his path to Marxist doctrine.

The Japanese government has never more clearly shown its Januslike qualities than during these Taishō years. In foreign affairs, Japan cooperated with Western powers, sending the liberal Nitobe Inazō to the secretariat of the League of Nations in Geneva, and signing naval disarmament treaties first in Washington (1922) and then in London (1930). Toward the Asian continent, however, Japan continued to pursue an expansionist policy, annexing Korea in 1910 and making its twenty-one demands on China in 1915. Japan retained its extraterritorial rights in China and from 1918 to 1922 intervened militarily in Siberia, but failed to establish a stronghold.

Domestically Japan made some democratic advances, installing the first cabinet headed by a majority party leader in 1918 and passing a law for universal male suffrage in 1925.[12] The government allowed some degree of freedom of expression by liberalizing censorship policies, and decreased the number of army divisions in 1925 because

12. Before 1925 voting rights were awarded to those persons whose tax payments exceeded a certain level. The 1925 law removed these tax requirements for male Japanese, but continued to deny voting rights to women and Koreans and Taiwanese living in Japan.

of financial pressures. But the regime also intensified nationalistic in-doctrination by increasing its control over primary and middle schools in 1919. It also bestowed on the police a formidable tool for oppression by passing the Maintenance of Public Order Act in 1925 (meant to avoid changes that might result from universal suffrage) and by ex-panding the Special High Police Force established in 1911.

A comparison with the Weimar Republic is instructive. In Japan, the oligarchical powers were forced to adopt liberal policies internally and externally during the 1920s because of the postwar international situation and mounting opposition from the urban middle class. But the basic legal structure of political institutions, their inherent au-thoritarian and antidemocratic qualities, remained intact. In contrast, Germany's political institutions in the 1920s were democratic, though the political traditions inherited from the prewar empire were not. Hence the differences of the 1930s: Taishō democracy gradually shifted to supernationalistic militarism without revising the Japanese Constitution or altering the establishment, while the Weimar Republic was abruptly replaced by the Nazi regime whose leader came from outside the old power structure. Although there was continuity in the Nazi case as well, especially in a formidable political-intellectual tradi-tion of anti-Semitism, it required a radical political upheaval to im-plement the new program with diabolical thoroughness and pseudoleg-ality. This points to another difference between fascism in Japan and Germany. Although both were highly romantic, the Japanese version was considerably less systematic and much less a comprehensive ideology.

Kawakami's revision of his solution to poverty marked the begin-ning of his second phase of academic research, his critique of capitalism and his evolving Marxism. Between 1919 and 1928, the year he resigned from his professorship, he progressed from Marxist economic theory to Marxist historical and philosophical ideas to Marx-ist political action. His transition in the early 1920s occurred in an at-mosphere of vigorous intellectual debate over socialism, democracy, methods of historical research, and Marxism and communism.

After the October Revolution in Russia in 1917, the ideological background of socialist movements in Japan became increasingly Marx-ist. Earlier Christian overtones diminished, as did anarchist trends represented by Kōtoku Shūsui who was executed by the government in 1911, and by Osugi Sakae who was murdered by an army officer in

1923. Now the Christian minority was more or less accepted by the interwar urban society, which was more oriented toward the West. Christians no longer needed political radicalism and militant radicals no longer needed Christian inspiration. Marxism supplied Japanese intellectuals not only with a political ideology to combat social injustice but also with an intellectual tool for systematic analysis of their contemporary situation against a broad historical background. They experienced Marxism both as political idealism and social science—and in many cases as a form of religious dogma.

The Japanese Communist party was formed one year after the Chinese party, in the framework of the Communist International (Comintern). The party's goal was defined as "bourgeois revolution," oriented toward the democratization and demilitarization of imperial Japan. The JCP's program—at least provisionally—resembled in many ways the reforms imposed by the occupation after the Pacific War, including land reform, dismantling of the zaibatsu, demilitarization, abolition of censorship—except on one point: abolition of the emperor system.

As an illegal underground organization, the JCP was subject to constant oppression by the special police, which in the first half of the 1930s succeeded in almost totally destroying its organization. From the beginning, the JCP had two important characteristics: its link with and control by the Moscow-centered Comintern, and its invisibility to the Japanese public. The Comintern was far removed from the Japanese scene, and its political directives to the JCP were often unrealistic. Nevertheless, many prominent JCP members, including Kawakami, adhered to Comintern directives with unquestioning obedience. But these manipulations damaged the organization and inflicted enormous sacrifices on its members. The party's invisibility, on the other hand, gave the JCP the special charisma we have mentioned. More and more publications and organizations secretly affiliated with the JCP, and its influence increased in socialist movements and among leftist intellectuals in general. The invisible party thus created a visible world—or, in Buddhist terminology, behind the appearance of conventional (hōben) Marxism expressed in institutions and public actions ruled a hidden, esoteric communism.

Psychologically, the Communist party connected with deep-seated doubts concerning militarism, ultranationalism, and social oppression. At the same time the party provided vivid and compelling im-

agery of rebirth and revitalization through revolution. Like many leftist intellectuals in Japan and elsewhere, Kawakami experienced both
kinds of imagery with great force.

In 1923, Kawakami published *The Historical Development of Capitalist
Economic Theories*, which greatly elaborated on ideas expressed in *Tales
of Poverty*. The book followed the progression of his own studies of
capitalism, first reviewing British economic theories, then critically
describing their historical development, and finally arriving at John
Ruskin's altruistic economic philosophy. Leftists did not receive the
work hospitably. Two young second-generation Marxist theoreticians, who had recently returned from Germany with dogmatic
ideological weapons, attacked Kawakami for not fully comprehending
dialectical materialism and for emphasizing historical ethics more than
materialism—in short, for not understanding Marxism. In fact,
Kawakami did not understand Marxism and admitted it. One critic,
Kushida Tamizō, pointed to deficiencies in the professor's theory of
value, his failure to distinguish between price and value, and his
evaluating all labor according to human sacrifice. Kushida argued that
Kawakami's theory ignored the concept of surplus value, which became the capitalist's profits, and was more appropriately called a value
theory of human sacrifice. Kawakami's emphasis on sacrifice, of
course, derived from his belief in absolute unselfishness and his ideal
conception of the individual's serving the state as an instrument of the
public interest.

The other critic was Fukumoto Kazuo, who returned from Germany in 1923 with a rigorously orthodox Marxist theory. He wrote
widely in leftist publications, attacking "unorthodox" interpretations
of Japanese intellectual leaders, and one of his first targets was
Kawakami. It was indeed symptomatic of Japanese intellectuals, ever
sensitive to new currents abroad, that a theoretician of revolution with
no practical experience could quickly gain hegemony in Marxist
ranks. Fukumoto became the dominant ideologue of the JCP, as his
radical communist elitism replaced the policy of a broad popular front
advocated by its former leading theorist, Yamakawa Hitoshi. This
period in the history of the JCP became known as "Fukumotoism" and
ended abruptly in 1927 when Comintern denounced both Fukumoto's
and Yamakawa's interpretations.

Kawakami reacted to his younger critics by submitting to their attacks and internalizing their criticisms. His impulse to capitulate was

probably related to his highly self-critical search for truth and virture as well as to a certain form of dependency that required him to find authorities to follow in that search. As he recalls in his autobiography, instead of defending his non-Marxist ideas, he devoted himself totally to studying Marx and Engels, particularly the text of *Das Kapital*. The results of that Marxist immersion were formidable: *Fundamentals of Economics (Keizaigaku taikō)* in 1928, *Introduction to Capital (Shihonron nyūmon)* in 1932, and a translation of *Das Kapital* (with Miyakawa Minoru) in 1931. These volumes were ground-breaking contributions to economic and Marxist thought in Japan.

During the 1920s, Japanese minorities and dissidents were subjected to a series of repressive measures. In 1923, following the great Kantō earthquake around the Tokyo area, which killed 132,000 people and destroyed large areas of the city, rumors spread about ostensible violence by Koreans, socialists, and members of labor unions. Many Koreans in Tokyo were murdered in the mob violence that broke out, and some socialists and labor union activists who had been imprisoned were killed by soldiers. The government, interpreting the earthquake and its aftermath as a warning about the possibility of a large-scale social disaster, stepped up its pressure on all forms of opposition. The Maintenance of Public Order Act of 1925 prohibited all organizations and activities that aimed at changing the *kokutai* ("national polity") or tampering with the private property system. The government first used the act in January 1926 when police arrested thirty-eight students from all over Japan, including members of the Student Social Science Study Club, a Marxist group to which a number of Kawakami's students belonged. Eighteen were convicted and sentenced to jail; another seventeen were rearrested in the next government roundup and also convicted.

In February 1928 Japan held its first election with universal male suffrage, and Kawakami joined the campaign of Oyama Ikuo, a member of the Workers-Farmers party *(Rōnōtō)*. Kawakami disliked the travel, the speeches, and the incessant police harassment, but he felt an obligation to continue electioneering. Despite the expanded electorate, however, only one JCP-related candidate running on the Workers-Farmers ticket was elected, Yamamoto Senji, a zoology professor from Kyoto Imperial University.

Kawakami's campaign effort for Oyama was not only unsuccesful, but contributed to his departure from the university. After the elections, the government arrested about 1,600 "undesirables" accused of violating the Maintenance of Public Order Act, including members of three JCP-related groups: the Workers-Farmers party, the Labor Union Council, and the Youth Proletarian Federation. In April these three organizations were banned, and the Ministry of Education increased its efforts to root out leftist university professors. Kawakami was among those forced to resign.

The first event in his conversion to activism was his arrest at a meeting held in Tokyo in December 1928 to establish the New Workers-Farmers party, a replacement for the party banned in April by the government. Kawakami wrote that this was the last open meeting held in support of the JCP until after the war. The police arrested many participants, but Kawakami's detention in particular attracted widespread domestic and foreign attention because of his imperial professional status. Kawakami described the arrest as a "milestone in my life."

In March 1929 came the second event, the assassination of the leftist politician Yamamoto Senji by a right-wing fanatic. Yamamoto was stabbed to death on the very day the Diet passed a series of repressive amendments to the law (Maintenance of Public Order Act) against which he had spoken out. Less than one month before his assassination, Yamamoto had intervened with the police to have Kawakami released after his second arrest, which occurred in Kyoto. Then, at Yamamoto's funeral ceremony in Tokyo, the police once again prevented Kawakami from speaking just as he began the eulogy for his close friend.

Yamamoto's death left Kawakami with a survivor's indelible image. One of Kawakami's students recalled, "Whenever I saw *sensei*, he always used to say that Yamamoto Senji was a truly great man. I never met anyone who praised Yamamoto the way *sensei* did." Kawakami gave special meaning to Yamamoto's death in terms of expressing one's convictions whatever the personal consequences:

I think that someone who publicly states what he believes, although he recognizes that he may be murdered, is the greatest of men *(ichiban erai)*. Yamamoto was someone who could do that and he was truly great. He must have known that opposing the repressive revision of the Maintenance of Public Order Act meant death. Nonetheless, Yamamoto valiantly opposed the bill—a great, great man. When I was a young student in Germany, the First

World War began. The first day of the war, I was drinking tea in Berlin's *Unter den Linden*. Tens of thousands of people were demonstrating about the declaration of the war. All Berlin was in a furor of war fever. In those circumstances, one doesn't even think about things like pacifism. But Liebknecht made a speech in parliament opposing the war. Not everyone could do this; only the great man can unwaveringly persist in his own beliefs.

(Yasuda, pp. 220–21).

Throughout his writings, Kawakami used Yamamoto's death as a call to arms. We recall the survivor motif in his eulogy to Yamamoto—his insistence that "We, the comrades left behind, must be keenly aware of why, how, and by which class you [Yamamoto] were murdered," and his expression of "infinite gratitude for your invaluable and selfless sacrifice" (*Jijoden*, vol. 1, pp. 267–68). Not only did he point to Yamamoto's death as "probably the most powerful stimulus which inspired my active participation in the proletarian movement," but also explained, "I reached the stage where I could finally and completely understand the words of Lenin that 'rather than writing about the experiences of the revolution, one should participate in it'" (pp. 277–78). Kawakami identified with Yamamoto as a friend and fellow professor-activist. He felt he should have been equally active; very likely, he also felt that he and not Yamamoto should have been the one killed. The rest of Kawakami's life had elements of a survivor mission. His way of animating his relationship to guilt—of converting guilt into the anxiety of responsibility—was to transform his theory into practice.

From 1929 on, Kawakami became increasingly involved in the political maneuvering of the left. In the second national wave of arrests, in April 1929, the government imprisoned nearly three hundred leftists, bringing those jailed to seven hundred and fifty. That fall, Kawakami joined Oyama of the New Workers-Farmers party in a tour around Kyūshū lecturing on Marxism. In January he moved to Tokyo to edit the party newspaper. The next month he ran for election to the Diet from Kyoto on an antimilitarist platform but was defeated. Gradually, Kawakami became convinced that the New Workers-Farmers party was the wrong strategy and in October 1930 he split with Oyama. Kawakami held to a doctrinaire line that only one Communist party could exist in Japan and that it was necessary to rebuild the organization totally decimated by arrests.

In the summer of 1931 a member of the underground JCP approached Kawakami. After displaying a proper introduction to prove that he was not a police spy, his visitor, a professor in civil law, asked Kawakami for financial contributions to help fund the party's activities. He could not have asked a better person. Sumiya (1962) writes:

The Communist party and its members were thoroughly idealized by Kawakami and he promptly consented [to the request for money]. In the case of the Garden of Selflessness, Kawakami, immersed in selfless love, entered the Garden believing ideally in the movement and its members. In the case of the Communist party, he regarded the party with a respect that verged on worship.

(P. 225)

In Kawakami's determination to contribute to the reconstruction of the party, his Marxist beliefs blended with his personal doctrine of self-sacrifice. Honored that the party had approached him to help, he pressured his publishers to increase his royalties and committed himself to do anything within his power for the sake of the movement.

In the early 1930s, fascism was on the rise at home and abroad. Government oppression pushed the JCP close to extinction. As the party extended its network in search of funds, the police arrested marginal activists and sympathizers, including many academics. At the same time, the Japanese military was extending its power overseas. In September 1931, the imperial army in Manchuria initiated aggression against China, and in January 1932, attacked Shanghai. The war with China was on, and there was upheaval at home. On May 15, an ultranationalist group, mainly young naval officers and army cadets, attempted a coup d'etat. Although they murdered Prime Minister Inukai Tsuyoshi, their other assassination plots failed. The main organizers of the rebellion were apprehended by the Ministry of War, but they received only light sentences as the military manipulated the incident for its own political ends. Indeed, the Inukai cabinet was replaced by a military cabinet led by Admiral Saitō Makoto, marking the end of party rule in imperial Japan. Under the Saitō cabinet, Japan withdrew from the League of Nations in March 1933 to protest the adoption of a critical report on the Manchurian affair.

While rightists rioted in Tokyo in May 1932, the Comintern convened in Moscow. The executive committee of world Communists produced a document known as the 1932 Theses that analyzed the

Japanese situation and redefined the mission of the JCP as that of taking the lead in the bourgeois democratic revolution, which had to precede the socialist revolution. In July, the full text of this manifesto appeared in the illegal *Red Flag*, translated by "Honda Kōzo," Kawakami's underground party name. His decision to translate the 1932 Theses reflected his belief in the document's literal message. He accepted it as a declaration of faith, devoting himself to it as he once had to the Sermon on the Mount. Only absolute plunges of this kind met his extreme demands on himself. This commitment was another step toward resolving conflicts between his roles as scholar and activist, between egoism and altruism, and between what he called "religious" and"scientific" truth.

In August, Kawakami joined the party and went underground. His primary responsibilities were editing the party newspaper and composing new propaganda pamphlets. The fifty-four-year-old professor felt a transcending sense of satisfaction from working with total self-sacrifice for what he believed to be the highest cause. Party membership also gave him complete freedom to write whatever he thought, because illegal propaganda was not subject to the scrutiny of the censor. Yet one senses the futility in Kawakami's jump into the small, fragmented group of JCP members. At the end of October, over two thousand JCP members had been arrested, leaving only a skeleton of a party heavily infiltrated by government spies. Kawakami, because of the extreme difficulties in communicating with others, could not be fully aware of how few party members and leaders had not been arrested. While he secretly composed propaganda about nationalism, the emperor, and Marx, his party completely disintegrated. And as an underground activist, Kawakami was outside his métier, a scholar no longer writing books, a showpiece who could not be shown. On January 12, 1933, the special police caught up with him in the small second floor room in the home of a Japanese-style painter. After only 140 days in the underground, Kawakami was arrested and his writings burned.

That same year, Sakai Toshihiko, one of the founders of the JCP, died in Tokyo; Katayama Sen, a member of the Comintern, died in Moscow; Kobayashi Takiji, a Communist writer, was killed by the police; Noro Eitarō, one of the brightest Marxist historians, was arrested and died in prison. As the Japanese left all but disappeared, the nation's militarists gained total power. Outside Japan, of course, it was the year Adolf Hitler became chancellor and Franklin D. Roosevelt was inaugurated as president.

Kawakami converted his prison experience into a form of witness to his convictions; a struggle around what Erikson called "the meaning of meaning it." We have mentioned his refusal to renounce his political beliefs, unlike many other Marxists and Communists who underwent tenkō, or ideological about-face. We should note that with enough time and systematic technique anyone can be broken down. In terms of police pressure, Kawakami's case was special. He was not only a public figure but an imperial university professor, a member of the elite bureaucracy appointed directly by the emperor (*chokuminkan*), so that cabinet approval had been required for his arrest. He was not threatened or abused to the same degree as other leftists.

Although the authorities constantly badgered him about recanting his beliefs, they did not use physical torture. They pressured him more with the enticement of an early release, the opportunity to rejoin his family, and the demand that he serve Japan. His strength to resist ideological backsliding, however, came not only from his status but also from the religious intensity of his commitment to Marxism and his wife's support. The last was crucial. According to his autobiography, Kawakami asked his wife whether she thought he ought to endure his sentence or submit to the demands of the police to win leniency. She recommended that he remain in jail to keep his self-respect. Kawakami did exactly that and eventually emerged from prison with a sense of having lived up to his own strict internal standards.

The second method Kawakami employed to sustain himself in prison was his work. Prison had certain psychological advantages. He could devote himself totally to scholarly contemplation, knowing that he had no choice. Kawakami was allowed to keep a diary and chose to write about the relationship between science and religion, in particular Marxism and Buddhism. His choice of Buddhism was pragmatic—it was impossible to gain access to books on Christianity, although his elite status allowed him to use the prison library with its ample Buddhist texts. Kawakami was less interested in Buddhism as such than in the general relationship between religious and scientific truth, which he believed was dialectical.

He wrote later that jail was an appropriate place to study religion because of its similarity to a monastery. He was also aware of his uniqueness, especially in Japan, as a Marxist sensitive to religious questions. He believed that his religious experience as a youth had provided him with a strong motivation for becoming a Marxist. Scientific and religious truths were not mutually exclusive for him. Rather than rejecting his mystical experience at the Garden of Selflessness, he integrated it into his sense of self. And this core of religious experience helped sustain Kawakami through his four and a half years of incarceration without renouncing his beliefs.

In June 1937, Kawakami was released from prison. Malnutrition and illness had taken their toll, but he described his worst torture in prison to have been a particular reminder of the death of his friend, Yamamoto Senji. Through a bizarre coincidence, Yamamoto's assassin was incarcerated in the same prison. Kawakami recalled his extreme disgust when their eyes would meet as they both entered the prison bath. The psychological pain probably derived in part from a reactivation of his survivor emotions, especially his death guilt. But imprisonment also undoubtedly served as expiation. He had sacrificed a great deal for others, had paid his debt for not preventing poverty, for not being more effective in the party, for not saving Yamamoto. He could feel that in the realm of action he had done what he could.

As a condition of his release, Kawakami accepted the authorities' requirement that he not break the law again and in fact retire from political activities. At fifty-eight he was thin and weak from the long stay in jail under poor health conditions. He was convinced that if he were arrested again he would not survive. Kawakami made clear that he abandoned political activism not because he no longer believed in Marxism or thought that the Communist party was mistaken, but because he did not want to be confronted with the choice of either renouncing his beliefs and denouncing others or dying as a martyr in jail. He published his statement of political retirement on his release from prison, in which he said that he had attempted everything possible within his physical and spiritual limitations, had fulfilled his obligations, and had at last earned the right to lead a simple private life. Kawakami declared he was going to become "a hermitlike man of leisure," a mode of withdrawal which earlier we noted to be highly respected in Sino-Japanese tradition.

Becoming a wartime recluse had elements of comfortable resignation and even pleasure. The resignation came from a recognition of his personal and his party's limitations, which psychologically eased his acceptance of political inactivity. The pleasure derived from his renewed appreciation, after years of conscience-ridden public struggle and then confinement, of the small joys of everyday life, especially in Kyoto, and doing what he wanted to do—working on his autobiography and writing poetry. He could live out his "other side", the side of the poet, while recording his life as a Marxist scholar. His last years could be for himself.

But at the same time he experienced the imposed restriction on leaving jail as "the close of my life as a Marxist scholar. This one sentence is a funeral song and an epitaph" (Sumiya, 1962, p. 293). In part he felt as if he were already dead, that he had lost a vital dimension—his political self. And he must have also felt at least small stirrings of guilt at not making the ultimate sacrifice, as Yamamoto had, to the party. But through conflict and pleasure, he maintained a strong will to survive long enough to witness the defeat of Japan's militarists.

Kawakami began preparing for death many years before 1946. Indeed, we might consider his release from prison in 1937 and political retirement as marking the beginning of that preparation. In 1944, Kawakami wrote that he thought he was on the verge of death, but that he had accomplished "a dialectial unification of religious truth, which is absolute unselfishness, and scientific truth, which is Marxism. This accomplishment during my lifetime allows me to die without a trace of anxiety." While we might question whether he really accomplished that unification or actually died "without a trace of anxiety," what he did achieve undoubtedly contributed to his readiness for death.

Kawakami's five-volume autobiography brought together his poetic and political sensibilities in a warmly written "life review," the reflections of an elderly man on what he had done and what that had meant. It served as an act of self-completion. It permitted him to reassert his identity. as an author, a persistent and powerful identity that subsumed the various dimensions and concerns of his life. And it enabled him to maintain his work habit, a way of structuring everyday existence, regardless of external and internal pressures and shifts. His autobiography stands as an important literary work, a political statement, a personal testament, and a final protest against the wartime militarist government of Japan.

Looking back on Kawakami's life we can see how exceptional he was in Japan. A typical Japanese belongs to the same groups with lifelong commitments, adapting his ideological stands to changing situations. Kawakami's case was reversed: he changed his commitment to groups while his ideological beliefs remained consistent.

Although not always an accurate observer of social reality, Kawakami was a dedicated observer of himself. Stendhal might have called this consciousness of self egotism. But unlike Stendhal, Kawakami grew up in a highly collectivized society, and needed perhaps more than most the feeling of belonging to a group—whether family, religion, political sect, or nation-state. He desperately tried to overcome his self-absorption by subscribing to the altruistic principles first of "selfless love," then of Marxist theory.

When he perceived an inconsistency with his altruistic faith, he felt compelled to move from one group to the next, because no group could satisfy his strict conditions for absolute altruism. He could not identify with any group for very long, and had to base his identity on the consistency of his own ideological faith, which in turn necessitated his inconsistency in group membership. From Kawakami's own point of view, he never allowed an external force to violate his inner ideological core—his religious and Marxists beliefs.

As he approached death, this religious Marxist seeker, self-centered altruist, group-oriented individualist, poet-socialist fighter, and, despite all, man of integrity, seemed if not fully satisfied with himself at least aware of his completion. Hence his calmness, perhaps even inner peace, in dying.

COMMENTARY / R. J. Lifton

Kawakami conveys the sense of "staying the course" as a scholar-activist and Marxist—of living out those ideals right into his death. In that sense his life had an overall unity, despite its formidable upheavals. His life and death could thus be later recast into the mold of the myth of the hero by the left, with considerably less alteration than was required by the right for its parallel attempt at recasting Nogi's life and death.

One American commentator (Bernstein, 1974, 1977) has stressed the irreducible contradictions in these elements, but that judgment may underestimate the psychological synthesis Kawakami actually achieved. How did he do it? I am not quite sure, but I think there are clues in his extraordinarily effective use of three psychological-cultural elements. The first was a cultural grounding that had roots both in his family (his maternal grandfather was probably an important model) and in samurai tradition in general. Some may now ridicule the figure of an "effete" elderly figure in traditional kimono lecturing at Kyoto Imperial University on Marxism, but the cultural currents behind that picture (aesthetic, psychological, historical) undoubtedly lent considerable power to both the Marxism and the moral energy associated with it.

A second element contributing to Kawakami's rather extraordinary synthesis was his use of a kind of Neo-Confucian self-criticism. One senses the importance of the Confucian principle of self-rectification and certainly the theme common to Confucianism no less than to Christianity and Marxism: namely, insistence on combining theory with practice. That insistence, in more or less traditional Japanese meaning, can be viewed as sincerity. Drawing the principle, emphasized in all these traditions, of subsuming the self to the shared moral vision, Kawakami formed his lasting principle of absolute unselfishness.

But the intensity of Kawakami's commitments and the driving force of his synthesis seems to me to reside in his third psychological element, his unusual sensitivity to death and death imagery. His very vulnerabilities to death and death equivalents, surely initiated by the separations and confusions in his early life and his admitted fears of blood and violence, were turned into sources of strength. A clear evidence of this was his productive survivor sensitivity expressed in relationship to the death of his friend and political colleague, Yamamoto Senji. The "survivor mission" of continuing the struggle in which Yamamoto died remained in effect for Kawakami until his own death, and I doubt whether the image of Yamamoto's assassination was ever very far from his mind.

This kind of creative survivor intensity can often be observed in outstanding social and political leaders—I found it to be a central theme in Mao Tse-tung's revolutionary energies, for instance. Kawakami's extreme eurekalike responses to calls to renewal he could perceive in the Bible, Tolstoy's writings, and the Buddhist sect he temporarily joined were also, I believe, related to his great sensitivity to death and disintegration, and to related images of human suffering (for Kawakami poverty was not just an economic category but a compelling image of degraded human beings). One senses that Kawakami almost went down with his vulnerabilities in this area—at moments he was close to psychological breakdown. Very probably the other two elements I have mentioned—his general cultural grounding and the principle of self-rectification—tempered his passionate immersions into situations symbolizing death and renewal to a degree that eventually enabled him to achieve a measure of stability without divesting him of those passions.

If one is to ask what is most Japanese about all this, I think I would say it is the extraordinary range of elements he had to bring into his synthesis. After all, no outstanding Japanese individual since the time of the Meiji Restoration has been able to escape some such synthesis in his living and dying—all the more so if he is a passionate transformationist like Kawakami.

COMMENTARY / S. Katō

While in prison Kawakami read many works by and indeed identified with the famous Chinese poet Lu Yu (1125–1209). Kawakami noted that Lu Yu was not only a poet (*shijin*), but also a nationalist (*shijin*, literally "a man of politics") and a moralist (*dōjin*). These three elements also formed the basis of Kawakami's self.

In Chinese as well as Japanese traditions, the three elements of poetry, nationalism, and moralism were intermingled in Confucian education: poetry was appreciated not only in aesthetic terms, but also considered as an expression of political ideas, which in turn were regarded as inseparable from the moral quality of the man. Kawakami inherited this cultural legacy and kept it alive in himself until his death. Of these three elements, the moral force (the quality of dōjin), enhanced by his survivor's complex, was the most fundamental, constantly working at the core of Kawakami's self-absorbed personality, driving him toward his activities as a poet and man of political ideals. Kawakami's ideals were at first nationalistic, which is typical for a shijin, but later shifted to Marxism stressing social justice rather than national interests and going beyond the range of the shijin tradition. The more deeply he was rooted in traditions, the more difficult it was for him to become committed to a Western ideology. But the greater the difficulties to overcome, the more stable was the conviction to the Western ideology when achieved. Only after a long time and enormous efforts did Kawakami arrive at the "truth" of Marxism.

In this sense, and perhaps in this sense only, the legacy of Confucian education helped Kawakami as an authentic Marxist scholar. The same background, however, proved to be a serious obstacle on his way to Marxism, concerning the relationship between theory and practice. As a scholar, Kawakami regarded Marxist theory as absolute truth; as a moralist, he felt an obligation to put the theory into practice much in the same way as Confucianists or Christians. This, however, is not Marxism.

In Confucianism and Christianity the theory or principles are expounded as the truth, universally valid at all times in all cutures. Practice of the theory, which is morally required, by no means affects the truth itself, which transcends history. On the other hand, Marx's idea, in the context of nineteenth-century historicism, was that such a universally valid truth cannot exist and that the pretended universality of any theory or set of principles serves the interests of a particular social class. For Marxism as an ideology, "practice" means to analyze the historical situation, define the concrete interests of the working class, and take actions for those interests. Practice generates theory, which in turn guides practice. In such dialectical interactions between theory and practice, the moral satisfaction of the individuals involved is secondary, if not irrelevant.

Kawakami, however, took as absolute first the theory, then the JCP and Cominterm. His practice culminated in joining the almost disintegrated underground party. Because it had no influence over the majority of the working people, it left no room for checking the theory against the concrete historical situation, which in turn tended to produce a deification of the theory. Objectively, Kawakami was far from the theory-practice dialectic, although subjectively he felt a moral satisfaction in his practice. Herein lies the most fundamental difference between Kawakami and Mao Tse-tung. For Kawakami, the JCP was the only avant-garde party, as such representing all the interests of the proletariat, and party membership was almost in itself the goal of his practice. For Mao, the Chinese Communist party was only the vehicle by which he could approach the reality of the Chinese working people, for whom he elaborated his theories and strategies of the peasant-based Chinese Revolution with a flexible political realism.

Kawakami certainly was not alone in his doctrinaire approach to

Marxist theory, his deification of the party, and his lack of real contacts with the working masses. In prewar Japan, more than half the working population was engaged in the agricultural sector; less than 10 percent of the industrial workers were organized; only a part of the organized workers was under the communist influence. Marxism between the two wars flourished mainly among the urban intelligentsia. Isolated from the rest of society, those intellectuals tended to be ideological purists, becoming more and more radical, which of course further increased their isolation. In the absence of any other systematic criticism of the regime, and under fierce police oppression, interwar Marxist movements increasingly became a moral issue for the intellectual elite of that time, with an invisible, and therefore absolute, authority at the center: the JCP. Kawakami personified these general trends—in his weaknesses and his strengths.

Kawakami's theories may not have much to teach us today. As a moral force, however, he is still a great teacher of living and dying with integrity, idealism toward others, and internal peace for himself.

6/MASAMUNE HAKUCHŌ (1879–1966)

Either Buddha or Jesus

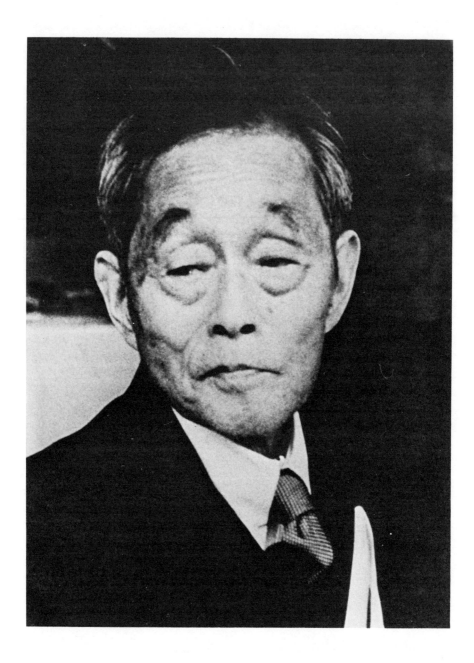

Masamune Hakuchō

FROM THE WRITINGS OF MASAMUNE HAKUCHŌ

"Desires Are Stronger than Death"
("Yokubō wa shi yori tsuyoshi")

Those . . . who can gain eternal peace simply by following the path of a religious life are fortunate. Most people, however, vaguely fear death, and, on occasion, are threatened by death. I, too, from my childhood long ago to my old age today have never been able to escape this fear. Though I have listened ad nauseum to the exhortations of saints, philosophers, sages, and Zen monks of all ages and countries, I still cannot feel that I truly understand their teachings. It is said that the Buddhist priest Hōnen, who founded the Pure Land sect, and Bunyan, who wrote Pilgrim's Progress, *were so obsessed by the fear of death and their relationship to what would come after it that their anxiety nearly drove them insane. The mere sound of church bells was supposed to have made Bunyan shudder in fear. But these two men finally freed themselves from the fear of death, one by aspiring to follow the way of Buddha and one by seeking the salvation of Christ, and they attained a state of eternal peace. I envy them. Because I am either too stupid or too clever, I have never been able to attain that sacred state. Indeed, even at this age, I still fear death. Knowing that I will die sooner or later, I simply live minute by minute, pretending that I have forgotten my inevitable fate.*

(Collected Works of Masamune Hakuchō [Masamune Hakuchō zenshū], vol. 9, p. 470)

"In search of newness, go even to hell"—as a poem, this ardor, this adventurous spirit is interesting. But after all it is only an idle thought of poetry. I imagine that at the hour of my death, I will either chant "Namu amida butsu" ["I sincerely believe in Amitabha"] *or murmur "Jesus Christ." Then it will become apparent which is stronger, the power of Japanese tradition concealed within me or the power of the foreign religion on which I once set my heart.*

(Collected Works, vol. 9, pp. 471–72)

Love and lust are said to be stronger than death. But at times I feel that it is rather the desire for money and possessions that overpowers death. Although the best way to conquer death may be to believe in an afterlife, I sometimes think that another possible method is through our desire to possess. By becoming totally absorbed in an unwavering desire to possess, one may be able to drive away the shadows of death that haunt the spirit.

(Collected Works, vol.9, p.472)

"Gluttony and sexual desire," "wealth and pleasure," "lust for power and lust for conquest": the human heart is like a nest of desires. But we should cherish these desires and strive to use them carefully, for without them, man would become nothing. From ancient times to the present, man as a matter of common sense has respected highly the subjugation of all desires. Yet literature and the arts are like flowers that bloom from the seeds of these human desires

(*Collected Works*, vol.9, p.473)

The discovery of the atomic and hydrogen bombs has produced a fear that their explosion in war will prematurely and suddenly destroy the earth and mankind. Sometime after that destruction, however, a new world and new living things may arise so that life will persist on the earth. If I were the creator, I might regard the making of a world for humans as a mistake and might want to destroy this world and start over again. Imagining such an eternal universe is a gradiose poem in the mind of this miserable man.

(*Collected Works*, vol. 9, pp. 473–74)

In November 1950, Masamune Hakuchō was awarded the prestigious national Cultural Medal for his contributions to Japanese literature extending over nearly half a century. In an essay titled "The Day of Receiving the Award" ("Jushō no hi"), the celebrated author wrote in his typically ironic style, "It was because I lived longer than anyone expected. No other author old enough to be considered for the prize was still alive. I was like something picked up by the side of the road" (Sasaki, p.89). He wondered half-jokingly if he had been awarded the prize as a hint that he had written enough and that it was time for him to lay down his pen. He viewed himself as a historical leftover from prewar Japan, an accidental survivor. Yet he lived another twelve years, always continuing to write.

In mid-June of 1962, at eighty-three, Hakuchō complained of severe weakness throughout his body. Resting in his quiet country home in Karuizawa, a summer resort area some one hundred and twenty kilometers northwest of Tokyo, did not improve his condition. The previous month an extensive medical examination had revealed nothing unusual. By August, however he had lost his appetite and developed a strange feeling in his upper abdomen. That month he was admitted to the Tokyo hospital affiliated with the Japan Medical School, but his condition continued to deteriorate. On October 6, doctors diagnosed his illness as cancer of the intestine. Since about 1957, he had spoken often of his death; now he knew that he was dying.

At that time he told a close friend, "God will certainly embrace me and guide me to heaven." He also asked that his funeral ceremony be held in a church. He specifically requested that the ceremony be performed by Uemura Tamaki, president of Japan's YWCA and the daughter of Uemura Masahisa, one of Japan's early Christians and the man who had baptized Hakuchō more that sixty years earlier. She not only agreed to Hakuchō's request but visited him daily over the remaining two weeks of his life to discuss Christian ideas with him. On October 28, Masamune Hakuchō died. Two days later, Uemura Tamaki performed the funeral rite as Hakuchō had requested in the Japanese Christian Church in Kashiwagi.

Hakuchō's last-moment embrace of Christianity culminated his lifelong struggle with that religion. Many biographers cite his request for a Christian funeral as evidence of his fundamental belief, but Hakuchō's entire relationship with Christianity was actually fraught with ambivalence. His fear of death drew him to the religion, but his skeptical iconoclasm kept it at a distance. Throughout his life and his writings Hakuchō used this iconoclasm as a vehicle for approaching truth. His persistent doubts about Christianity became a source of creative energy, part of a more general cynical stance at the core of his sense of self. Only when near death, as he relinquished his struggle for truth, could Hakuchō accept Christianity as a means of quieting his fear and facilitating his dying.

This is not to deny the importance of Christianity in his life. His early involvement in it left a profound personal imprint and gave him a central point of reference in his efforts to understand and articulate basic human questions. Although he always insisted that the Bible was a "dreamlike fable" that did not portray the truth about human nature, Hakuchō never ceased reading and studying that fable. He felt constantly confronted by the moral questions raised by the Bible, and quoted from it extensively in his essays, perhaps more than any other Japanese novelist.

Hakuchō's preoccupation with death became particularly marked after the Second World War. One early postwar essay was titled "The Agonies of the War Victims" ("Sensaisha no kanashimi"). Others, such as "The Victory of Death ("Shi no shōri") in 1949 and "The Fear-of-Life Map" ("Jinsei kyōfu zu") in 1954, dealt more explicitly with his fear of death. Another short essay published in 1954, titled "Desires Are Stronger than Death" ("Yokubō wa shi yori tsuyoshi"), excerpted at the beginning of this chapter, expressed the conflicting themes that possessed Hakuchō in his last years of life: a profound fear of death; a disdain for believers of all sorts; and a feeling that at the moment of death he would need to believe in something. Hakuchō noted that though most people vaguely fear death and occasionally feel threatened by it, since childhood he had "never been able to escape this fear." He explained that he was raised by his grandmother, who chanted Buddhist sutras each morning with him. Hakuchō claimed that these chants and other stories of the Buddhist afterworld gave rise to his early fear of death and anxiety about an afterlife. He also described his envy for those who by beliving in Buddha or the Christian God can appease their fear of death and attain a state of inner peace.

For many years Hakuchō had maintained an uneasy truce with religion—drawing on it, rejecting its transcendent concepts, "because I am either too stupid or too clever," and mocking believers in Christianity and Buddhism. He lived as much as possible in the present moment ("minute by minute, pretending that I have forgotten my inevitable fate"), but with a premonition that when he finally faced death he would surrender (*Masamune Hakuchō zenshū*, vol. 9, p. 470). His only question was to which spiritual adversary: "I imagine at the hour of my death I will either chant "*Namu amida butsu*" or murmur "Jesus Christ" (pp. 471–72). Hakuchō's choice of the "foreign religion" suggested a central paradox that existed throughout his life.

Masamune Hakuchō established his literary reputation in the prewar period as one of Japan's great "naturalists," writing in a style of concrete, day-to-day realism. Although he virtually stopped writing during the war, he returned to the literary world after Japan's interlude of militarism, producing a huge quantity of work. He continued to write in his dry, iconoclastic style of "naturalistic realism."

But in his sparse, ironic prose, he no longer distinguished the various genres of novel, essay, and criticism from one another. This continuity with his prewar literary identity contrasted sharply with the great majority of writers whose pre- and postwar works differed radically in style and content, reflecting the far-reaching social and ideological transformations. For Hakuchō's basic sense of reality in both life and literature remained rooted in the detail and flow of ordinary existence.

Although Hakuchō was exceptional in his struggles with Christianity, his attitudes were like those of ordinary Japanese people: a highly pragmatic approach to daily life, a deeply rooted skepticism about abstract ideas, and a reluctance to become committed to any absolute value beyond everyday reality. The Japanese as a people were secularized even before industrialization began in the late nineteenth century, a people highly integrated within a community—sometimes encompassing the entire nation—beyond which their vital concerns rarely extended. Like his "naturalist" contemproaries Hakuchō was influenced and perhaps inspired by European naturalists of the late nineteenth century, notably Zola (see chapter 3). But "naturalism" did not produce Hakuchō's down-to-earth realism; rather his realism provided a framework for accepting the concept of "naturalism." Similarly, his pragmatic and cynical view of life were the source of his resistance to the sublime, all-embracing Christian teaching that so attracted him in his youth. His life and writings thus embodied a conflict between what he called his "dream," which was Christianity, and his immediate reality, which was everyday triviality. His life was a battleground between the severe demands of a transcendental religion—which he said, in effect, he could not endure—and direct pessimistic insight into the human condition.

Hakuchō was conscious of his beliefs and their contradictions. His confrontation with Christianity seemed to play a decisive role in his acute sensitivity to the world around him. His dream sharpened his sense of reality. Christianity thus contributed to his becoming one of the most powerful proponents of a this-worldly approach to life that was in essence opposed to Christianity and its emphasis on an after-life. Hakuchō became, we might say, the conscience of the indige-nous, popular world view, not because he was one of the great silent majority of modern Japanese, but because he belonged to a marginal articulate minority of those who lived with the majority without really belonging to it. That relationship was a function of both his literary talent and his encounter with Christianity. Hakuchō's literary ap-proach, which ignored vast social transformations, thus symbolized Japanese continuity.

Masamune Hakuchō was born in 1879, the same year as Kawakami Hajime, in a small farming and fishing village midway between Okayama City and Akō City on the coast of the Inland Sea.[1] His par-ents were well-to-do landholding peasants, part of the local elite of the small village of about three hundred families. The family had lived on the same plot of land for two centuries, something not uncommon in rural Japan even today. In the past, they had produced medicines and shipped pottery made in the region. But the main source of income de-rived from providing local peasants with farm land and such fishing equipment as nets and boats. As rich landowning peasants, the Masamune family embodied some of the contradictions of the To-kugawa class society in the mid-nineteenth century. The family be-longed to the rising entrepreneurial class, and one indication of its in-creasing wealth and status compared with the impoverished samurai class is that for three generations prior to Hakucho's, the head of the Masamune family had married women of the samurai family of Okada from across the Inland Sea.

1. Although he was known as Tadao as a young boy, we commonly refer to Masamune throughout the text by the given name Hakuchō, which he adopted as a young adult.

Hakuchō's nonsamurai, elite rural origins were an important theme throughout his life. The second floor of the Masamune home over-looked the calm waters of the Inland Sea on one side and steep wooded mountains on the other. Hakuchō used the environment of his home and his village as the scene for many short stories, including "Two Families" ("Ni kazoku") and "Near the Cove" ("Irie no hotori"). This heritage contributed to his later critical stance toward Tokugawa cul-ture as well as to his acceptance of the critique mounted by Japanese "naturalists" toward city life and Christianity.

The two previous heads of the Masamune family had been childless and had therefore adopted other family members as heirs. Uraji, Hakuchō's father, and his wife, however, were prolific: Hakuchō was the first of ten children. One child died in infancy; the other six boys and three girls were a talented group. On the male side, the second son became a respected authority on Japanese classical literature and a poet of some repute; the third son became a successful Western-style painter and essayist; the fourth son was an eccentric unrecognized painter and writer who spent his last days as a chicken farmer in the family village; the fifth son joined the business world and became an executive director of the Japan Pipe Company; and the sixth son ac-quired a doctorate in science and became a professor at Kanazawa University. Hakuchō's eldest sister died before marriage, the second married a man who became a famous university professor in geog-raphy, and the third married into a family of Shintō priests. The fami-ly's artistic leanings were influenced on the paternal side by Hakuchō's grandfather and granduncle, who had been scholars in the "National Studies" (kokugaku) scholarly tradition,[2] and on the ma-ternal side by his mother's father, the official instructor of Chinese lit-erature for the Tadotsu domain.

The striking array of accomplishments also reflects the drive of the family's entrepreneurial father; the nurturing support of the mother; the potential rise in status of rich peasants who, in the early Meiji period, were no longer confined by Tokugawa class restrictions; and the opportunities that abounded for talented youths around the turn of the century.

Hakuchō's birth, like that of all first sons and future heirs, was a

2. "National Studies" was a Tokugawa school of thought that stressed indigenous classical works and was used as the ideological underpinnings of emerging nationalism.

cause for celebration within the family, but it also coincided with other less happy circumstances. Before he was born, Hakucho's paternal grandfather had left the family to live with his mistress, stating that his decision was due to his wife's barrenness. The grandfather soothed ill feelings his move created by splitting the wealth under his control in half, leaving his wife in the main family and setting up his own branch family. His wife, as further consolation, took on the main responsibility for raising the family's next heir, young Hakuchō. She had no children of her own and became particularly attached to the young boy. The elderly woman, steeped in the supernatural beliefs of her time, first exposed Hakuchō to the world of spiritual imagination through the Buddhist sutras and tales of the underworld and to the world of the community through stories about the family and the village.

Hakuchō's first childhood memory involved intense anxiety over separation from his grandmother. He recalled that his grandmother punished him at the age of three by placing him outside the house:

Either from anger or fear I cried and shrieked at the top of my voice and banged on the wooden shutters. I have no idea how long it was. But the fact was I had been thrown outside the house by Grandmother. I was being punished. This, it may be said, was the first step of my life.

(*Masamune Hakuchō zenshū*, vol. 12, pp. 401–02).

The terror of abandonment is also the first step toward autonomous existence. The grandmother is perceived as both tyrannical and the nurturing source. When Hakuchō later left home he missed her more than his mother or father. But generally speaking, the replacement of his mother by this possessive paternal grandmother seems to have contributed to a basic anxiety about life and to an energizing sensitivity to death and its equivalents.

In 1883, at the age of four, Hakuchō entered the village elementary school. He studied diligently and enjoyed reading more than playing outside. By nine, he had read all the storybooks collected in his house, especially the popular novels of the late Tokugawa period, with their picturesque, moralizing fantasies, and romantic tales of superhuman heroism. In particular he liked the long, fantastic adventure stories written by Takizawa Bakin, a leading late Tokugawa novelist of this genre. Thus he first experienced literature through a type of fiction diametrically opposed in length, structure, content, and style to his own later realistic writings. Hakuchō certainly was conscious of Bakin's convoluted style when he later composed his strikingly plain prose. This immersion in Tokugawa fantasy nurtured Hakuchō's literary sensibility; it then became an imaginative structure to react against.

Hakuchō graduated from elementary school in 1892 with an excellent record. His father, immensely proud of his favorite child, urged the thirteen-year-old to continue his studies and to try writing. For example, when a boat capsized in the village that year and seven or eight persons died, Uraji encouraged his son to write an article and submit it to a newspaper. The incident suggests the father's role in motivating Hakuchō toward literary accomplishment and fame. But he also seems to have given his children considerable independence in choosing and pursuing careers, and must have been responding to Hakuchō's literary talent. Although Uraji had no direct access to Western culture, and was totally rooted in rural society, he perceived the opportunity and power associated with the infusion of Western ideas and encouraged his children to explore them.

Soon after graduating from elementary school, Hakuchō entered the former domain school about five kilometers from his home. The school's main course of study was Chinese, but it also offered English and mathematics, reflecting the transition that Japan was undergoing. Hakuchō, however, refused to submit to what he considered to be the coercive pedagogical methods used to teach the Chinese classics. He was already expressing a critical spirit, and also perhaps rebelling against earlier family control. He much preferred current literature, such as the popular magazine *The Nation's Friend (Kokumin no tomo)* published by Tokutomi Sohō, which emphasized social criticism and Western literature in translation.

The journal initially advocated principles of equality and libertarianism, but after the Sino-Japanese War (1894–95) it became increasingly nationalistic on foreign policy issues. Through this journal Hakuchō learned about the emerging Meiji literature and about Christianity. *The Nation's Friend* opened an entirely new world to him. With no other prompting, and at first from curiosity, he began to read the Bible and to succumb to its powerful images. The more he read modern literature and Christian works, the more dissatisfied he became with studying the Chinese classics. In 1893, after about a year of studying, and without completing the course, Hakuchō left school.

Hakuchō's interest in Christianity continued to grow. While recuperating at home from a stomach disorder and general physical weakness, he regularly read the Bible and occasionally traveled to a Christian study group in a neighboring village. He then moved to Okayama City to receive hospital treatment. In Okayama, he entered the Biyō Academy, a private school, managed cooperatively by an American missionary and Abe Iso'o, the principal, who later became one of Japan's first socialists. He studied the Bible and English language, but the school closed less than half a year later. Hakuchō, who was now sixteen, lived at his parents' home for the next year, reading modern literature and about Christianity, toward which he felt propelled by his general state of depression. He regularly attended a nearby Christian seminar center, but felt trapped by a personal dilemma: he wanted to be saved but was unable to believe totally. This ambivalence, which persisted for most of his life, became a source of both conflict and creative energy. But Christianity was central to Hakuchō during adolescence, the time when important constellations of the self take shape in ways that influence the rest of one's life.

In the story "Fantasies and Realities" ("Kūsō to genjitsu"), Hakuchō explained how the Bible helped him resolve his childhood struggle to achieve a sense of vitality:

From childhood on, I had no person with whom to quarrel or compete, but my body was small, my arms weak, and I felt early on the anxieties of living. After graduating from elementary school, I entered a private school that taught the Chinese classics. There, I learned fencing for my weak arms. Later, when I entered a missionary-managed school to learn English, I became involved with Christianity. Both of these were based on my inner demand to overcome the anxieties of living.

(Oiwa, p. 35)

One bright spot in Hakuchō's adolescence was the writings of Uchimura Kanzō, which he read in *The Nation's Friend*. Uchimura exemplified the many young ex-samurai who became fervent believers in Christianity, which as a spiritual structure and symbolization of immortality helped fill the cultural void left by the downfall of the Tokugawa ideology. Uchimura wrote often in *The Nation's Friend* about the need for Japan to adopt values of Christian justice and belief in God.[3] Hakuchō is an example of the extent to which Uchimura and other Meiji westernizers were able to influence young men, even in the countryside, as communication systems expanded. They stimulated many to explore Christianity, if not to follow it throughout their lives.

In February 1896, at seventeen, Hakuchō received permission from his father to move to Tokyo. He wanted to read the new literature where and when it was published, to learn Christianity directly from the great teachers, and to see the plays being constantly performed in Tokyo. Indeed, the evening he arrived in Tokyo he bought the latest copy of *The Nation's Friend* at a newsstand—something he could never do before—and happily read it without delay. Hakuchō moved into the lodginghouse of some friends from his village and began to construct his Tokyo life. He was admitted to the English course of the Tokyo Special School (the predecessor of Waseda University). He also went to many plays and vaudeville reviews, and read a wide variety of books. Every Sunday he visited a different Christian church, sampling the sermons and continuing his personal search for Christianity and God. Finally, he settled on the powerful sermons of the Reverend Uemura Masahisa. Until he graduated from the university in 1901, five years after his arrival in Tokyo, Hakuchō maintained this three-sided pursuit of literature, Christianity, and popular theater.

From childhood Hakuchō was always conscious of his small size and frail physique. Even as an adult he was only about four feet eleven inches tall and weighed eighty-eight pounds. After arriving in Tokyo, he decided to improve himself physically as well as spiritually and intellectually through judo. Despite the daily exercise, or perhaps because of it, he developed a severe illness that was not clearly diagnosed but probably was lung disease. During the hot summer, he returned home for rest and treatment; he was confined to bed for about two

---

3. Among Japanese Christians, however, Uchimura was unusual. He used his belief in the absolute transcendental values of Christianity as the basis of aggressive social criticism, refusing to show allegiance to the emperor, joining social protest movements, and becoming a dedicated pacifist. He is well-known for his "no-church" doctrine, which stressed fundamental Christian principles not compromised by institutional demands of churches or by divisions between different sects. Believing that Japan would lead the world in this movement, Uchimura urged Japanese Christians to break their dependence on foreign churches.

months and came very close to dying. He later wrote: "I constantly thought that human life in this world is of little importance." And, "In such a situation, the only thing I could depend on was God." When he returned to Tokyo, still in a weakened state, he decided to be baptized. He no longer wanted to be a "frivolous believer" (Oiwa, p. 42, 43).

For the next two years Hakuchō dedicated himself to Christianity. He regularly attended Uemura's services, studied with the preacher at his home, and taught Sunday School; apparently he even considered the teaching of Christianity as a profession. But gradually his views changed. According to his later recollections in "About Living," Hakuchō began to feel that Christianity demanded the abandonment of all happiness and pleasure in this world, which the young man who enjoyed theater and literature could not easily accept, and that true believers had to be prepared for martyrdom, which only intensified his fear of death. As he approached graduation, Hakuchō moved away from Christianity and turned more and more to literature. Literature seemed closer to life and Christianity more fictional:

The emotions of literature and drama are more interesting, more truly human. I began to feel that Christianity was like fiction. Therefore, I could not totally embrace Christianity; I felt it was defeated by man's natural instincts. In these feelings originated my reasons for leaving the church.

(Sasaki, p. 36)

A number of Meiji writers around the turn of the century experienced similar encounters with Christianity. Hakuchō was baptized at the age of eighteen and left the church four or five years later. Kitamura Tōkoku, a leading early Meiji "romantic" poet, was baptized in 1882 at the age of twenty and committed suicide six years later. Kunikida Doppo, a poet-novelist, was baptized at twenty and remained with the church for about five or six years. Two other novelists of "naturalistic realism," Shimazaki Tōson and Iwano Hōmei, stayed with the church for five years each after being baptized at ages of fifteen and fourteen respectively. Several well-known authors continued as Christians for longer periods—for example, Tokutomi Roka (baptized at seventeen), Kinoshita Naoe (at twenty-three), and Arishima Takeo (at twenty-two). Thus, from 1882 to 1900, at least eight youths who eventually became prominent authors converted to Protestantism.[4] Of these eight writers, five, including Hakuchō, remained in the church for between four and six years.

In the last two decades of the nineteenth century, Protestantism appealed to young intellectuals, partly because of such eloquent leaders as Uchimura Kanzō, and partly because Christianity was perceived as representing nontechnical or spiritual Western culture. Protestantism also provided creative Japanese with a way of emerging from suffocating group requirements and experiencing through God a direct individual relationship to ultimate principles. Most Japanese Protestant leaders were educated in New England, where they were imbued with an ethically rigorous puritanism. Their ascetic restrictions on curiosity and human impulse clashed with the young writers' inclinations toward imaginative exploration and sensual pleasure. The intense asceticism of early Protestantism in Japan was probably a source of both initial appeal and final incompatibility.

In Hakuchō's youthful interaction with Christianity he relied primarily on Uchimura's interpretations and on his own reading of the Bible. Later, Hakuchō often referred to the Bible, but never to conflicting interpretations of Christianity proposed by different Protestant groups, and certainly not those advanced by the Catholic church, with which he probably had no contact at all. If Hakuchō and other writers had known the Catholic world, they might not have found Christianity so unbearably ascetic, almost to the point of seeming to be an antiart faith. He later wrote, for instance, that Christian prohibitions against going to kabuki plays only heightened his desire to see them. As a student, he seemed to alternate between surreptitiously but enthusiastically attending them, and then for periods of time making himself stay away. Because of these internalized restrictions, he never saw a kabuki performance of the great actor Danjūrō, which he regretted for the rest of life. Only after graduating from the university and leaving the Christian church did Hakuchō begin to attend plays regularly. He felt relieved of a great burden.

When I left the faith I wondered, "Was that fearful God just some illusion of

4. In the late nineteenth century, Protestantism achieved greater influence than Catholicism largely because the model countries for Japan were mostly Protestant and because no charismatic Japanese Catholic leader arose.

mine?" Then, for the first time, I felt the freedom of liberation. Isn't it backward, though, to serve God when young and rebel against God when older?

(*Masamune Hakuchō zenshū*, vol. 4, p. 415)

Like many other writers who embraced Christianity in their youth, Hakuchō found that what initially catalyzed his energies soon became an unpleasant form of restriction.

Among those writers who converted to Christianity and then became nonbelievers, Hakuchō was unique: He alone came back to Christianity at the end of his life. That return resulted from his unusually intense, lifelong preoccupation with death.[5]

Hakuchō was a diligent idiosyncratic university student. One biographer (Oiwa) said he "never missed classes in school, never associated with those who told indecent stories, never discussed theories of law or theories of literature" (p. 41). Hakuchō himself noted that he never competed with other students, but merely read and studied what he wanted to learn. After graduating from the English section in 1898, he entered the newly formed departmant of history, apparently by eliminating other alternatives. He had no desire to learn law or politics and was uncertain about literature since few at the time were able to make a living by writing. But in 1899, when the department of history was eliminated, primarily because of a lack of students, Hakuchō had no choice but to join the department of literature. As part of his serious study of domestic and foreign literature, he became a faithful reader of two journals in particular—*The Weir Papers* and *The Enlightenment Papers*, both edited by Mori Ogai.

Uchimura Kanzō was Hakuchō's first teacher of literature. When he was twenty, Hakuchō regarded the minister-lecturer more as a literary than as a religious man. It was through Uchimura's public talks that Hakuchō learned about Dante, Carlyle, Whitman, Bunyan, and other Western writers. Ultimately literature that was rooted in religion influenced Hakuchō most. Uchimura acted as a bridge between Hakuchō's literary and religious inclinations, and he impressed on

5. This point is illustrated by the difference between the Christianity of Hakuchō and of Uchimura: while Uchimura emphasized judgment according to Christianity's absolute standards, Hakuchō stressed his personal fears about death, an afterlife, and Christian demands for martyrdom. He sought forgiveness without judgment, a kind of *amae*, or total acceptance and dependence. When he realized that Christianity could not provide that sense of total support, and moreover restricted his creative sensibilities, he abandoned the church.

Hakuchō the importance of truth to oneself in living, a theme that runs through much of Hakuchō's writings. Hakuchō adopted Uchimura's belief that literature is important only to the extent that it raises fundamental questions about life—a radical redefinition of literature in Japan, because from Tokugawa times literature had been simply entertainment. Hakuchō's approach to truth, however, significantly differed from Uchimura's. Though Uchimura stressed a transcendent Christian vision as the basis for all faith, Hakuchō conceived of truth as derived from the concrete reality of this world, so that all claim to truth had to be approached with skepticism.

From 1899 to 1901, Hakuchō read widely in both Tokugawa and European literature. Although still studying rather than writing, he was increasingly surrounded by authors with whom he discussed new currents in literature, music, and art. During this period, he met Tayama Katai, a novelist who began as a romantic poet and became enchanted with Zola and Maupassant through English translations. Katai, relatively unknown in 1901, was creating a new style of "naturalist" Japanese writing in which the writer was an objective observer of life's reality and not a purveyor of fantasy or entertainer of the public. Hakuchō might have recognized in Katai's conception of "naturalism" something closer to the Dante introduced by Uchimura than to the Bakin of his childhood, and perhaps a creative resolution to his own struggles around meaning and integrity. "Naturalism" became for Hakuchō a path to immediate truthfulness, which in turn was the best approximation of ultimate truth. Hakuchō's relationship with Katai was his first important literary step along that "naturalistic" path.

In June 1901, Hakuchō at twenty-two graduated from the department of literature at Tokyo Special School (which was renamed Waseda University the following year). Although he had no job he knew he could always return to his parents' home. At the turn of the century, writing was considered an unstable vocation, and only two of the thirteen or fourteen students graduating in literature intended to make their living as writers. Some students' obligations to support their parents further restrained them from taking the risks of the literary life.

Hakuchō's professor, Tsubouchi Shōyō, a leading figure in Meiji literature, one day invited his student to his home to consider Hakuchō's future. Shōyō, after determining that Hakuchō's family posed no obstacles—because of his father's wealth and permissive attitude—approved his decision to become a writer. But the professor gave the first available job to another aspiring writer, because of his more precarious financial situation, and Hakuchō returned home to rest until another chance for employment appeared. At the end of the summer, he was summoned to Tokyo to work at the Waseda University publishing house as an editor, a job he held less than a year before leaving to begin his life as a writer.

After a period of supporting himself as a free-lance translator, Hakuchō was hired in June 1903 by the *Yomiuri shinbun*, then widely recognized as a literary-artistic newspaper. He progressed from researcher to reviewer to page editor, and after two months started to review new literary and dramatic works. In 1904, Hakuchō wrote a few rather mediocre articles on his own, but he was still editing more than writing independently.

His relationship with the growing school of "naturalist" writers strengthened, however; in 1906 Katai invited him to join their group, the Dragonland Society (Ryūdo kai). Hakuchō, almost unknowingly, as he later put it, turned his page in the *Yomiuri* into the main public forum for the "naturalists." He recalled, characteristically, that at first he was not even certain what "naturalism" meant, and selected articles for his page according to the opinions expressed by his friends. By "blindly following the crowd" (*raidōteki*), Hakuchō claimed that he drifted into the literary movement of "naturalism."

In 1906, just after the conclusion of the Russo-Japanese War, "naturalism" emerged as a new style of fiction in Japan. One influential work was *Violating Inhibitions (Hakai)* by Shimazaki Tōson; another was Tayama Katai's *The Mattress (Futon)* in 1907, the beginning of the "I novel." Hakuchō immersed himself in this literary trend. In addition to his work at the *Yomiuri*, he began writing independent essays. In 1907, he was recognized as one of the two most promising young Japanese writers and was compared with Chekhov because of his simple, direct style and combination of humor and pessimism. In 1908, Hakuchō's publication of *Where To? (Doko e)* established him as a leading "naturalist" writer. The novelette described in plain narrative style the daily life of a young journalist caught in a complex network of personal relationships with relatives and friends, disillusioned and not knowing where to go. In 1909, *Chūō kōron*, a prominent popular monthly magazine, devoted a special issue entirely to reviews of Hakuchō's works, indicating his rising reputation.

As Hakuchō's page in the *Yomiuri* became increasingly identified with the "naturalist" movement, his conflicts with the paper's management grew. Articles in the *Yomiuri* frequently attacked non-"naturalists" in bitterly personal tones. Those attacked responded equally bitterly, which brought pressure on the *Yomiuri*, specifically on Hakuchō. Dissatisfaction with his conversion to "naturalism" continued to rise within the newspaper, and in March 1910 the company's president recommended that he take a short vacation. After a two-week stay at home and a brief trip, Hakuchō returned to Tokyo and it was suggested that he resign.

After working at the *Yomiuri* for seven years, during which he suffered from stomach problems and insomnia, Hakuchō became a freelance writer. The transition seems to have caused him great distress. His shift in groups from the church to the newspaper to "naturalism" involved at each step a decrease in formal structure. This gradual increase in his independence was accompanied by greater anxiety, which had both psychological and financial roots and related to doubts about his abilities as a writer. Perhaps his arranged marriage in April 1911, when he was thirty-two, bolstered his sense of stability. For when "naturalism" blossomed into its greatest period of popularity in the Taishō period, Hakuchō—along with Shimazaki Tōson, Tayama Katai, Tokuta Shūsei, and Iwano Hōmei—stood at the center of the movement.

The "naturalist" writers, almost without exception, were sons of relatively well-off farmers or small landowners in rural areas who left their country homes to study at universities in Tokyo, but never completely freed themselves from complex family ties. Japan's rapid industrial expansion during the First World War created an economic boom but did not particularly ease the young writers' lives in Tokyo. Their financial problems sometimes were relieved by assistance from home, but often were aggravated by obligations to care for brothers, sisters, and other relatives. Most of the writers had affairs with women in Tokyo, which often conflicted with family conventions, especially when they thought of marriage. They approached problems related to money and women within the framework of the extended rural family system, the *ie* or "house." As writers, they focused on these personal problems as their major theme, reflecting their common background. In their frequent and explicit literary use of sexuality, the "naturalists" challenged high culture, which tended to formalize and ritualize sexuality and to consider open discussion of such matters as vulgar.

Hakuchō differed from the main current of "naturalists," however, in that he did not write about his sexual relationship with his wife or with any other woman.[6] This connected him more with the educated elite's views of sexuality in pre-1945 modern Japan than with the rebels of the "naturalist" school. On the other hand, Hakuchō agreed with the "naturalists" about the central importance of sexual desires—but for slightly different reasons. In the short story "Desires Are Stronger than Death," he observed that religion as a whole apparently demanded suppression of desire, while literature—by which he meant "naturalism"—would lose its creative force without it, particularly desire for money and women. Hakuchō recognized that desire prevented internal and external deadness, and formed the essence of life. In a half-mocking tone he wrote that it is not love and lust but "rather the desire for money and possessions that overpowers death." More than belief in an afterlife, he wryly observed, this "desire to possess" enabled one "to drive away the shadows of death that haunt the spirit" (*Masamune Hakuchō zenshū*, vol. 9, p. 472). In the end he felt that even the desire to possess was a futile expression of the materialism of the time. All that remained was writing about desire—the literary imagination—which for Hakuchō was a great deal.

Despite the vast social changes after the Meiji Restoration, Tokyo inherited much of the culture of Edo, which by the end of the Tokugawa period had become the center of Japanese literary and artistic life. People born in the capital, particularly those whose families had lived there for at least three generations, were known as *edokko*. In the Meiji period, they lived mostly in the downtown area, spoke the Edo dialect, and maintained certain characteristic tastes and habits. Writers raised in this environment, such as Kōda Rohan, Ozaki Kōyō, and Natsume Sōseki, developed a new urban literature characterized by the elaboration of a highly artificial style, a subtlety of artistic taste,

6. When a young man, Hakuchō apparently had an affair with a geisha, but he never wrote about that relationship.

and a conscious link with Japanese and Chinese literary classics. Mori Ogai, while not an edokko, was raised from childhood in the city and in the environment of the young elite; his writing combined the elaborate style of edokko writers with a strong Western influence.

"Naturalist" writers grew up in the countryside and did not directly experience Edo culture in their childhood. Moreover, none of them studied in the West, because they did not belong to the intellectual elite. For many "naturalists," Christianity and Western literature taught in Waseda University had to replace the experience of going abroad. When the poet Hagiwara Sakutarō wrote the lines

> I wanted to go to France
> But France was too far to reach

he spoke for the great majority of Japanese poets and writers before and after the First World War. Hakuchō also repeated again and again how attracted he was to the West, the model for modern Japan. But he did not directly encounter the West until he was fifty.

Although Hakuchō read English relatively fluently, most "naturalist" writers were weak in foreign languages—none read French or German. They learned about Western literature largely from translations, among which Ogai's were especially important. These limitations partly explain their almost exclusive interest in European naturalism as a form of "objective description" of "truth in life" and their disregard for its stylistic subtleties of prose and its social and historical context. In addition, the Japanese "naturalists" had a far less profound knowledge of the Japanese-Chinese classics than Ogai or Sōseki. This lack of intense connection with any literary tradition, either Sino-Japanese or Western, is reflected in the restricted subject matter of their I novels, but also in an intellectual mobility and openness to new forms that made their I novels a kind of breakthrough. Zola and other Western writers were important as misunderstood models providing prestigious external justification for the Japanese "naturalists."

The themes developed in I novels expressed problems shared by many college-educated young Japanese during and after the First World War: personal dislocations created by industrial expansion, urbanization, the economic depression, educated unemployment, and the suffocating restraints of the traditional family system. The same social situation that produced the leftward shift of intellectuals Kawakami was part of during the Taishō period made the descriptive I novels popular in the literary circles of Tokyo.

From 1913 until 1917, Hakuchō wrote extensively, and most of his work was enthusiastically received. At the same time, he experienced personal physical and psychological distress. In 1915 he was treated for about one hundred days at a hospital specializing in gastrointestinal diseases, and was again hospitalized in 1917. In 1918, Hakuchō at thirty-nine experienced a certain weariness about life and writing. As a popular author he continued to receive many requests for stories, but he was bored by his own unvarying style and increasingly unable to produce the work asked for him. In 1919, Hakuchō vowed to abandon both writing and urban life, and returned to his home village on the Inland Sea. He originally intended to remain permanently in his country home and even sold his house in Tokyo. But after six months, he could no longer endure the slow pace and the isolation of rural life or his own idleness, and returned to Tokyo and to writing.

Although the mid-Taishō years are commonly considered a period of relative ease and pleasure for Japan, particularly in the large cities, Hakuchō experienced severe malaise. His life in Tokyo, too, became quiet and lonely. His writing took the form of I novels, but they were so poorly organized that they seemed more like collections of what the Japanese call "occasional thoughts" (zuisō). Still prone to bodily ailments and creative disruption, during his early forties Hakuchō went through "a particularly lonely time for a writer reputed to be great" (Sasaki, p. 72). For a man long haunted by death anxiety, doubts about his general literary project must have taken their special toll at this time.[7]

By switching from short stories to drama, Hakuchō experienced a limited spurt of creative energy. He thought plays would be easier to write because they used dialogue similar to that in his short stories. It was in 1924, just as the late Taishō revival of interest in "new drama"

7. The timing of Hakuchō's period of depression coincides with what many psychological writers now describe as the mid-life transition—a growing awareness of mortality, of limitation in one's life projects. Those and accompanying doubts about the meaning of one's work and intimate relationships have to do with one's modes of symbolic immortality. Frequently one feels an impulse to make a radical break in these patterns and alter one's way of living. One's sense of the reality and inevitability of death throws into question much of the content of one's life.

occurred—drama that challenged the classical stylized forms of kabuki. The movement originated in the late Meiji period, but only in 1923 after the great Tokyo earthquake was a new drama group able to acquire a playhouse, the Tsukiji Small Theater, for regular performance of its plays. Hakuchō had written two plays, in 1912 and 1914, which were largely ignored. But in March 1924, his newly written third play *The Happiness of Human Life* (*Jinsei no kōfuku*) was performed and acclaimed a success. Over the next few years, Hakuchō concentrated on drama, retaining his basic style while changing his form of presentation. His plays lacked much in subtlety, dramatic climax, action, and attention to the physical movement of characters, but they gave expression to his pervasive despair and sense of nothingness.

The first year of the Shōwa period, 1926, marked another turning point in Hakuchō's literary career. In January, at the request of the magazine's editor, he began writing a monthly column in *Chūō kōron* of literary and drama criticism. His reemergence as a successful critic and concurrent playwriting helped reduce his nagging doubts about his literary capacity. Although most of his creative works were strictly realistic, in his criticism he expressed freely whatever he felt, at times with little apparent logic, as if to mock the very "reality" that ordinarily had such great claim on him. These impressionistic, highly subjective columns covered many topics and were widely read and respected. This turn to literary criticism revitalized him psychologically and helped restore his financial stability. Hakuchō had more confidence in his critical writings than his fiction. This sense of grounding as a critic helped him maintain a degree of inner balance during times of personal confusion.

Yet Hakuchō could not easily rid himself of depressed feelings. In the fall of 1928, he impulsively decided to travel to America and Europe. Since childhood he had always wanted to travel abroad, but had been unable to because of insufficient funds. But at the age of forty-nine, with few obligations and no children, he felt free to leave Japan for a full year. In October he decided to travel around the world with his wife, and in November he left Japan for Los Angeles. He used his savings as well as additional funds he raised by preselling magazine and newspaper articles. The couple traveled through America, France, Italy, England, and Germany. Hakuchō responded with excitement to the visual pleasures he encountered. In a simple but restless way he liked to keep moving, to walk everywhere and constantly take in images. But he felt that the trip came "just too late" in his life to affect significantly his thinking or attitudes. In his *Literary Autobiography* (*Bundanteki jijoden*), he wrote:

One might say that my sensitivities were blunted by old age, but, still, when I first saw the beauty of other countries, my heart throbbed with emotion. . . .I looked at everything with the feeling that "seeing is believing" and was excited by how curious it all was.

(*Masamune Hakuchō zenshū*, vol. 12, p. 131)

The trip was a realization in middle age of the youthful dream of a self-proclaimed admirer of the West—a sentiment typical for many Japanese, but one that few openly admitted. Hakuchō's explicit, unapologetic articulation of his attraction to the West made him somewhat special and reflected his consistent principle of confronting and recording the truth.

Hakuchō's excitement at seeing foreign lands was accompanied by a sense of being left behind by changes in Tokyo literary circles during his absence. Proletarian literature, an outgrowth of Meiji socialist literature, expanded during the Taishō and early Shōwa periods to include a wide range of authors producing self-consciously revolutionary writings for the working class.[8] Countering this trend was the growth of the New Sensibility School (*Shinkankaku ha*) we mentioned in chapter 5. This literary form was influenced by avant-garde European culture, such as Dadaism, and opposed Hakuchō's style of "naturalism." Hakuchō, however, joined neither trend and in that sense was left behind, though he remained a prominent figure in the literary world.

For the next seven years, Hakuchō's writings continued to focus on everyday life while Japan continued on its path to militarism. Then, in 1936, Hakuchō and his wife left Japan on their second voyage abroad. Although he had no sympathy for the Nazi regime in Germany, Hakuchō decided to attend the Berlin Olympics. He also de-

8. Two internationally known novels in this style were published in 1929: *Crab-factory Ship* (*Kanikōsen*) by Kobayashi Takiji, and *A Town Without Sun* (*Taiyō no nai machi*) by Tokunaga Naoshi. In the early years of Shōwa, despite increasing government pressure, many students, writers, artists, and intellectuals began producing proletarian literature. By 1929, the proletarian political parties reached their peak, and Kawakami Hajime, who resigned from his professorship at Kyoto Imperial University the previous year, was actively campaigning for one of them. The government's intensified suppression, however, gave such political opposition little hope.

cided to visit Russia, again not because of any interest in the country's ideology, but mainly to take in impressions, "to have a glimpse of what is there." Hakuchō and his wife also visited Finland, Sweden, Czechoslovakia, Hungary, Austria, and America. While fascism was rising in the world, Hakuchō was sightseeing. His emphasis on nonideological observation fits his conception of literature as simply recording the minute details of daily life. The trip was part of his creative need to take in new images and recreate them in his ostensibly objective fashion. But it also expressed a larger Japanese need for outside impressions.

Few men of Hakuchō's generation shared their Western experiences with their wives. But Hakuchō's wife was indispensable for him at all times and in all places. At the same time Hakuchō had an unusual fear of women, thinking of male-female relations as "ugly and offensive." He wrote in the story "Misanthropy" ("Ningen girai") that he was not particularly attracted to women and that he really did not understand them. His wife, he wrote, was the only woman he could speak with comfortably. His close and dependent relationship with her probably provided him with an island of safety and nurturing, protecting him not only from his fear of "sexual women" but also from the amorphous sense of void and threat of disintegration that haunted his inner life.

In 1937, Hakuchō returned to Japan and could no longer ignore Japan's rising militarism. That year, he was appointed to membership in the Imperial Arts Academy, founded in 1919 with Mori Ogai as its first director. The academy was originally restricted to the fine arts, but in 1935 the government increased the number of artist members, and in 1937 as part of its increasing control over public expression extended the organization to include writers and musicians. Knowing that their names would only be used manipulatively by the government to support the war, Hakuchō and Shimazaki Tōson resigned from the academy. Although in 1937 this sort of passive protest was possible, three years later, Hakuchō was reappointed and was unable to resign. Instead he began to withdraw from Tokyo. In 1940, he started constructing a summer home in Karuizawa and in 1944 moved there with his wife. His withdrawal was only partial, however, because he was mobilized into several semiofficial government positions.

During the later war years Hakuchō withdrew as much as possible from public life. Although he originally intended to reside only temporarily in Karuizawa, he now decided to remain there throughout the year. Hakuchō spent most of his time in Karuizawa gathering food and firewood, reading the few books he had brought from Tokyo, and poring over the skimpy, uninformative wartime newspapers. He wrote surprisingly little for a man who had spent the preceding thirty-five years as a famous author. In the early months of 1945, he struggled through seventeen round trips to Tokyo on the increasingly sporadic and crowded trains, carrying as much as he could of his household goods from Tokyo to Karuizawa. Then in May, the American mass firebombings destroyed Hakuchō's Tokyo house. These years were also a time of personal tragedy, for in 1942 his mother died and in 1943 "naturalist" writers Shimazaki Tōson and Tokuta Shūsei both died.

Although Hakuchō wrote about his father's death and his brother's death, he wrote little, even in his diary, about the deaths during the war years of other relatives and writer-friends—except for a memorial essay on Tokuta Shūsei. He wrote practically nothing about the war itself, in contrast with Nagai Kafū, for example, who later published his wartime diary. There were a number of reasons for Hakuchō's literary silence. The life of a writer who refused to collaborate actively with the government's propaganda campaign was exceedingly difficult, and the elderly couple's struggle to stay alive in Karuizawa left him insufficient time or energy for writing. Moreover, without the confirmation provided by publication, his writing perhaps no longer seemed to him to represent immediate truth. Hakuchō mistrusted all ideological systems, viewing events in terms of personal experience rather than historical evaluation of any kind. He thus resisted the militaristic propaganda concerning Japan's historical mission, but also refrained from taking a clear ideological stand against the war. Kafū in his diary recorded the deaths of Hitler and Mussolini as great events, but Hakuchō in his diary did not even mention them—their significance probably escaped him.

In general, Japanese intellectuals reacted to the war as active collaborators, determined opponents, or as passively uninvolved supporters and opponents. Among active collaborators were the prominent ideologues, such as the supernationalist author Kihira Tadayoshi, who denounced all others not actively working for the war; the literary school of Japan Romantics, promoted by Yasuda Yojūrō, in which Mishima Yukio found his roots; academic rationalizers of the war, particularly at Kyoto Imperial University; and those we might call articulate fellow travelers.

The war's opponents included those inside the power structure, such as career diplomat Yoshida Shigeru who became prime minister after the war; ex-leftist intellectuals who entered the power structure in an attempt to influence government policy (though with little result); intellectuals who opposed the war and secluded themselves from society to avoid cooperating with the government, such as Nagai Kafū, Tanizaki Jun'ichirō, and Miyamoto Yuriko; intellectuals who opposed the war and semiretreated into the relative safety of universities, such as Nanbara Shigeru and Maruyama Masao in Tokyo Imperial University; and those in prison or under strict police supervision, mostly Communists and some Christians, such as Kawakami Hajime and Miyamoto Kenji (who became head of the Japanese Communist party after the war).

The third group, the passively uninvolved, tended to waver between support and nonsupport. It included critics of militarism who supported government policy once war was declared on the basis of doing one's best for one's country; children and childlike adults with little political awareness who were manipulated by the government; mobilized students, some of whom needed to rationalize the war to make their deaths meaningful; and those who passively supported the war to survive.

Hakuchō functioned at the border of passive support and passive opposition. His resignation from the Imperial Arts Academy in 1937 reflected his disillusionment with nationalistic ideals. But in 1943 under strong pressure, he became head of the novelist section of the Japanese Literary Patriotic Society, a government organization formed to propagate militaristic nationalism. His failure to jump on the ultranationalist bandwagon in the face of many opportunities and much pressure, and his retreat to Karuizawa rather than prostituting himself to the government to ensure his material survival, suggest that fundamentally Hakuchō opposed the war. Throughout his life, he tended to flow with historical currents, as suggested by his youthful affair with Christianity, his later joining the "naturalist" movement, and his inability as a mature adult to take a clear stand against the war. But in everything, he struggled seriously, and essentially successfully, to maintain a sense of integrity.

It is instructive on several points to compare Hakuchō with Kawakami. Both were exposed to Christianity in Tokyo about the same time and experienced a similar kind of personal illumination. But Kawakami took a leap of faith into total and literal acceptance of

Christian ideals, while Hakuchō always resisted just that type of impulsive totalistic plunge. Kawakami maintained his ruthless pursuit of absolute truth in religious and intellectual areas, while Hakuchō resigned himself to accepting the events of daily life and frailties of people as the existential limits of truth. Kawakami constantly engaged in equally ruthless self-criticism and pushed himself toward action and risk until he finally joined the JCP and was jailed, while Hakuchō seemed to settle into a complacent disillusionment and to maintain the same style of living, thinking, and writing over the nearly sixty years of his adult life. Kawakami struggled to survive the war in large part to vindicate his ideological beliefs, while Hakuchō sought to outlast the war apparently just to survive and to return to the life he had been leading before the interruption. Kawakami, as a believer who constantly sought a version of truth, represents the relative exception in Japanese society; Hakuchō, as a skeptical nonbeliever, or even antibeliever, approaches the more common pattern.

The postwar revival of literary journalism during the occupation created a sudden demand for authors untainted by fascism. This demand stimulated the emergence of a new generation of writers and put pressure on a few older writers who had no record of wartime collaboration to join in reviving Japan's free press. Among the noncollaborationist prewar authors, Nagai Kafū and Shiga Naoya were no longer creative, and Tanizaki Jun'ichirō, always aloof from changing environments, concentrated on his books about sexual desire in old age and on his translation of *The Tale of Genji* into modern Japanese. Only Hakuchō responded to the editors' requests by writing more than 250 articles, short stories, and novels for magazines and newspapers between 1946 and 1950. He never stopped writing until just before his death in 1962.

Hakuchō felt relief at Japan's surrender, but also apprehension about his own role in the new Japan. He wrote that he did not expect "an old decaying author like myself" to become part of the literary world. But with an impressive capacity for literary survival, Hakuchō resumed his familiar style of realism. In January 1946, as Kawakami Hajime was dying, Masamune Hakuchō resumed his habit of recording the daily life details of Japan. The war created a hiatus in his career and disrupted his personal life, but when it was over, Hakuchō returned to the style of living and writing he had always followed.

Hakuchō's prodigious literary revitalization in old age was related to several factors. First, he needed money. The bombings had destroyed his Tokyo house and possessions, and postwar land reform stripped him of most of his family's assets in Okayama. Inflation combined with a food shortage to exacerbate his financial problems. He also had to support his wife and their adopted son, who was still too young to support himself and was living with Hakuchō and his wife in Karuizawa. Hakuchō's goal was to earn enough money to build a new house on his Tokyo site, which he was able to accomplish and move into in 1957. To that end, he traveled frequently to Tokyo on crowded trains, which required hours each way, to meet editors and publishers.

Writing was also an integral part of Hakuchō's life. For decades he had pursued only writing—without any hobbies, without drinking, without smoking, without much communication with his many brothers, without any serious involvement with women outside his family. And when he ceased writing almost entirely for three years during the war, as he put it, "I felt I had forgotten something, even though I had nothing particular to write about" ("Notes in an Autumn Wind" ["Shūfū ki"], 1961). Hakucho's resumption of writing in 1946 was a return to the rhythm of his life and to a certain amount of inner satisfaction. His sense of revitalization must have been further enhanced by liberation from censorship, from social pressure, and probably from his own isolation in wartime society, which even in Karuizawa was somewhat hostile toward a noncollaborating old man.

Hakuchō also had something to say. As one of the few writers of his generation to survive much beyond the war, he became the sole witness to a complete half-century of Japanese literature. This status of accidental but honored survival, in effect, guaranteed Hakuchō a literary audience. But while strongly motivated to recall and describe his past, both personal and professional, he was increasingly concerned about his future: his death.

In "The Agonies of War Victims," he focused characteristically on concrete daily problems of his life in the fall of 1945, and made no particular comment on the war just lost or on the postwar era just beginning. He and his wife were then lamenting the destruction of their Tokyo house to which they might otherwise have been able to return before the severe Karuizawa winter. Many others who had escaped to Karuizawa from the city during the war now left for Tokyo and other parts of the country where postwar life was expected to begin. Hakuchō, with no place to go, envied those who could leave. He helped his wife with household tasks, but was too depressed to read or write. He napped often, feeling that it must be a sign of old age to sleep well. We feel in this essay the heavy aura of stasis and loss that he struggled with at the end of the war. Yet the writing itself helped restore for Hakuchō a sense of movement, and, we suspect. a sense that life had meaning beyond the immediate moment on which he always focused.

Hakuchō's creative activities after the war can be divided into two periods, before and after 1949, the year he became seventy. Almost all his major works of the postwar era appeared by 1950: *The Rise and Fall of Naturalism (Shizenshugi seisui shi)* in 1948, a loosely chronological presentation of literary events that included portraits of "naturalist" authors with critical accounts of their works, through the Meiji, Taishō, and Showa eras; "Uchimura Kanzō" in 1949, a long essay on the ideas and personality of the Christian invocator, in which Hakuchō reconfronted the man who had so profoundly influenced his life; and *Chikamatsu Shūkō* in 1950, a study of the "naturalist" writer who lived from 1876 to 1944.

Chikamatsu differed markedly from Hakuchō in the way he wrote and lived, but Hakuchō speaks of him as the person he knew best in this world. Previously Hakuchō had written little about the past other than his recollections of childhood, but he now seemed to want to record for posterity his knowledge of events. At the same time, Hakuchō the keen observer of trivial day-to-day events did not disappear: there was the same direct style, down-to-earth realism, and cynical tone. In "Misanthropy" in 1949, Hakuchō plainly described his observations in Karuizawa: "Here too the postwar fashions are baseball, Christianity, and dance." His adopted son was interested in baseball, and his wife in Christianity. Hakuchō, however, did not even know the rules of baseball, had no interest in dancing, and no longer believed in Christianity: "I knew that this imported religion might have a dreamlike appeal in one's imagination, but has no charm at all in reality" (*Masamune Hakuchō zenshū*, vol. 4, p. 414).

If "Misanthropy" represents the continuity of Hakuchō's writings before and after the war, another major work, an unfinished novel also begun in 1949 and continued in 1950, reveals a new dimension. *Escape from Japan (Nihon dasshutsu)* was a rather sudden and radical departure from his old style. Hakuchō called it a fairy tale. The story takes place in different fantastic foreign settings, visited by two lovers escaping from Japan, riding on a magic horse. Since his youth Hakuchō had unfavorably compared the Japanese literary tradition, from Chikamatsu to his own contemporaries, with great Western literary works, from Dante to Dostoyevsky. He had twice visited the West he so admired in the interwar period but knew that he never really became acquainted with Western society. He described his style of traveling as "passing through without becoming involved" (*Masamune Hakuchō shū*, p. 369). Yet as an observer of human truth, Hakuchō could not easily set aside his driving desire to know a human reality other than the Japanese. At the end of his long career as a "realistic" writer, he finally expressed this desire as an imaginative escape from Japan to wonderlands based on his images of the West. He wrote the novel in the form of a fairy tale partly because he could not describe the West with his familiar "realistic" approach. But also involved was a conflict between dreamlike pleasure and painful reality. *Escape from Japan* was a dream shared by many Japanese intellectuals, and per-haps—unconsciously—by most Japanese.

Japanese are more integrated into groups than Westerners, and in some ways more secure, but they are also more deprived of individual freedom. The feeling of latent revolt against the community is especially intense in community-oriented societies. And since Japanese society has been engaged in a far-reaching process of westernization, images of liberation have come from that direction. Intellectuals with great book knowledge of the West have long harbored dreams of escaping there from Japan.

After 1949, Hakuchō undertook no long essays or novels, but published only short articles in which he expressed more explicitly than ever his ambivalent feelings and thoughts about death and about Christianity. "The Bible is nothing but a dreamlike story," but also "I would like to believe the Bible literally" ("About Living," 1954). And about life after death (in "Notes in an Autumn Wind," 1961), he wrote: "All living creatures—human beings, birds, and animals—are the same. They all strive to live as long as they are alive, and are all reduced to nothing after death. I feel this way, as most common people vaguely feel." But earlier, in "Desires Are Stronger than

Death" in 1954, he had written, "I am thinking of something beyond death. Iwano Hōmei might laugh at me, but I cannot help feeling that this is my destiny."[9]

These ambivalent feelings appear also in his description of his father's death. Hakuchō described the event, which occurred in April 1934, in his essay "Desires Are Stronger than Death" written in 1954 when he was seventy-five and thinking a great deal about his own death:

My elderly father, when he was ready to be liberated by death from a long illness, raised his right hand and wrote in the air, "I want to die." He probably died comfortably. One might even say that he died happily. It was a warm spring day in April and the cherry trees were just blooming. Even now I can recall the events of that day. I think that I would like to die that way, but at the same time I feel quite seriously that I could not rest content dying like that. After living a long life, my father was able to feel, "I want to die," and then died satisfied. And that was the end. But I have fantasies about something that transcends death.

(*Masamune Hakuchō zenshū*, vol. 9, p. 472)

Hakuchō admired and even envied his father's self-control and acceptance of death. He could only contrast his father's sense of the continuity of culture and family with his own profound uncertainties. He could neither believe nor surrender his "fantasies about something that transcends death." But he could live with that tension by putting it to work for him in his writing.

We need to look more closely at Hakuchō's vague "nostalgia for Christianity" in the postwar period, long after he had "abandoned without any regret those blessings imported from the West" ("Uchimura Kanzō," 1949). In an essay that explains his inability to accept Christian doctrine, the seventy-nine-year-old man admitted the persistence of a "strange trust in Jesus as our Lord" ("About Living"). This "strange trust" can be interpreted as his feeling, or wish, for the unlimited benevolence of Jesus who might save him in his most difficult moment—at his death.

Now Hakuchō's understanding of Christianity focused on Jesus,

9. Iwano Hōmei (1873–1920) was one of the most famous and most controversial writers of the "naturalist" group.

whose unlimited benevolence would take care of anyone at death no matter what he may have done in this world, including even blasphemy, even denying God, even total absence of faith. In other words, for Hakuchō this relationship to Jesus resembled that of many Catholics to the Virgin Mary and many Buddhists to Amida. All these religious beliefs are deeply infused with a sense of *amae*, of passive expectation of love and nurturing, an attitude psychiatrist Doi Takeo has placed at the heart of Japanese cultural experience. We can say, then, that Hakuchō died an "amae-death." He returned to Christianity in his last days, with a hope, if not conviction, that he would be taken care of, that things would not go too badly for him even beyond death.

Hakuchō's wife, the object of so much of his amae in life, played a very important part in his amae-death. She attended Bible classes every Sunday during the last few years of his life and certainly affected his decision to ask for a Christian funeral in a church. Always exceptionally close to his wife, on his deathbed he worried about how she would live on after him. In dying as he did, then, Hakuchō affirmed and symbolically extended his loving and dependent tie with his wife around primal emotions that take original shape in the mother-child relationship. But in his choice of Uemura Tamaki, whose father had opened Hakuchō's mind to the world, to perform his funeral services, he was also reasserting the broader formative power of Christianity in his life.

Hakuchō's death was not only an amae-death, however, but also, more than in any other case, an "old man's death." He raises the question of what is sometimes called an "appropriate death," a death that is relatively acceptable to the dying person as a more or less proper end to a long, realized life (see Weisman, 1972, pp. 36–41). With Hakuchō there is the further question of the person who has, in his own eyes, lived too long—the "historical survivor" who has outlived not only almost everyone in his generation but his original era. The first, the appropriate death, is relatively ideal; death anxiety, if never fully overcome, is likely to be minimal. The second, the overdue death or inappropriately prolonged life, can often be tinged with despair. The decisive inner question has to do with self-judgments about the authenticity of one's life and its continuing connections beyond itself. Those judgments are rarely absolute. And when Hakuchō tells us that he received his country's honorary Cultural Medal at seventy-one because he had survived all other eligible writers and "was like something picked up by the side of the road," we sense in his irony elements of both pride and despair.

We should not forget the pride that can result from merely surviving into one's ninth decade—and Hakuchō did that by living for twelve more years after that award to the age of eighty-three. Very old people can convey (and share) a feeling of more-than-natural power which has to do with death-linked imagery, the sense that they have for an exceptional duration both held off and maintained special closeness or access to death. Those feelings about the very old probably enter into traditional Japanese expressions of reverence, though they can be present in other cultures where such tradition is weak or absent.

But Hakuchō's life also extended seventeen years into the post–Second World War period, during which such attitudes toward the old in Japan have become unstable and ambivalent. As cultural symbolizations of all kinds were undermined, resentments that probably always underlay those expressions of cultural reverence could be mobilized. Both sides of the ambivalence intensified. The old represented the mythic prewar harmony, pleasure, and honor, as opposed to recent confusion, suffering, and dishonor. But they were also a burden from the past, with little or no capacity to contribute to the collective struggle to assimilate disturbing and exciting new ways. All age groups take on different meaning in the midst of pressures toward change, the old perhaps most poignantly.

Hakuchō lived with various contradictions, and, indeed, the contradictions were his life. Part of him really seemed to believe the Christian message of something beyond death, despite his usually stronger skeptical voice that said there was no such thing. Though the two beliefs were often in conflict, one is impressed with Hakuchō's capacity to maintain them both in his particular version of what we might call psychic blending. Rather than attempt to analyze the contradictions, Hakuchō accepted and channeled them to the events and emotions of his literary work. When his struggle with his contradictions ceased, he was ready to die.

COMMENTARY / S. Katō

Hakuchō's postwar statements about Christianity are often ambiguous and even contradictory. He often mentioned his "swinging back and forth between skepticism and belief" on the one hand, while he emphatically called Christianity a daydream on the other: "Today I am not skeptical about what Saint Paul said, but merely interested in a theory based on nothing but a daydream." The real question is not whether Hakuchō in his last years really believed in Christianity, but what he saw in and through Christianity.

What strikes me most in reading Hakuchō on Christianity is that he wrote so many times the same two words: fantasy *(kūsō)* and dream *(yume)*, in contrast to reality *(genjitsu)* and truth *(shinjitsu)* in human life. In one sense, he was a self-appointed observer of reality in general and of his own life in particular. In another sense, in finally recognizing his nostalgia for Christianity, he realized his aspiration to believe in something unreal as a part of the reality of life. Thus, finally, the unreal as well as the real became part of the sphere of his concerns.

What was the unreal, yet important and compelling thing for Hakuchō? It can be reduced, I believe, to one point: whatever one might do, ultimately one would be saved—not by oneself, but by an all-forgiving, benevolent power, be it mother, be it Jesus, be it Amida, be it the ultimate world order, natural or divine. This optimism has something in common with Dante's *"esperanza"* in the Inferno and with Shinran's "Even a good man will be received in Buddha's Land, how much more a bad man" (Earhart, p. 48). And Goethe's Lord in Heaven: "Man strays, so far as he strives for life" (in "Prolog im Himmel," *Faust I*). An all-embracing forgiveness is here also prominent. What Hakuchō believed in Christianity is not necessarily specific to Christianity. In other words, what was decisive was not Christianity, but the common denominator. Hence the recollection of an illness in his youth: "A sick person feels like appealing to any God or any Buddha. The reason why I wanted to pray to the Christian God was simply that I happened to be in contact with Christianity at that time." Also, "I don't know whether I will pray to Amida or Jesus Christ, when I am dying." He said further that all would depend on his internal balance between Japanese tradition and foreign culture. Clearly the point was not the choice of Jesus or Buddha, but the fact that he needed one of them.

One might say that Christianity didn't change Hakuchō as much as Hakuchō changed Christianity. I think this beautifully parallels the history of Japanese Buddhism. Buddhism as an other-worldly belief system did not change the this-worldly mentality of the Japanese people; on the contrary, the Japanese people made Buddhism this-worldly as part of the process of japanizing Buddhism. Hakuchō accepted Christianity only by japanizing it. In this sense, he represented a common Japanese cultural pattern.

Does all this imply that Hakuchō's life and works might have been much the same regardless of whether he was Christian, Buddhist, or something else? I don't think so. Becoming a Christian in Japan meant and still means a deliberate decision to belong to a very small minority. Unlike Buddhism, and somewhat like Marxism, Christianity is a system of ideas, values, and beliefs, which could only consciously be adopted by an individual willing to resist social pressure to conform. This conscious commitment to a religious system, even if he later gave it up, certainly made Hakuchō in his writings often approach such problems as the ultimate meaning of life and afterlife, which no other modern Japanese writer has so persistently or clearly formulated. In this sense, Christianity made him a unique writer.

Hakuchō's amae feelings in dying are shared by a great many contemporary Japanese. He was a mirror of modern Japan, as he wished to be, in his life and in his death alike.

COMMENTARY / R. J. Lifton

Hakuchō lived and died on a border of integrated achievement and perpetual despair. The presence of despair is suggested by the extent of his continuing fear of death. That fear, of course, had origins in the separations and other death equivalents of his childhood. I do not think that the grandmother's Buddhist chant itself initiated these fears, as he himself thought, so much as it articulated them in a special imagery of a Buddhist afterworld. Perhaps the chant could not contain those already existing fears and was itself perceived by the young boy as strange and separate from the rest of his experience, as what an adult would consider anachronistic. Yet whatever the origins of that anxiety, nothing in Hakuchō's considerable life achievement enabled him to overcome it—to evolve immediate and ultimate forms of connection and meaning that might enable a man to move toward his death more calmly—if not in a sagelike fashion, at least with the ordinary Japanese capacity to "float into death" as one floats with the tide.

Was his final embrace of Christianity, then, a matter of hedging his bets, a small tenkō in relationship to his prior renunciations of Christian belief? Perhaps, in the amae fashion we discussed. But Christianity meant much more to Hakuchō and to many other creative

Japanese. Hakuchō's death anxiety seemed to draw him to Christianity, which in turn further mobilized that anxiety but at the same time gave it something of a structure within a system of belief and practice. In that way his very death anxiety was transmuted into a source of energy, curiosity, and formative struggle. That is, Christianity opened up the possibility to Hakucho that there was, as he put it, "something beyond death"—which, in a narrow sense, means a concrete afterlife, but more broadly a sense of merging with a principle or set of principles so enduring as to provide one with a feeling of endless life.

Hakuchō and so many others of his generation wavered in their Christianity perhaps in part because they perceived its principles as too specific in structured supernatural claim and too demanding in practice. Yet their relationship to it suggests that Christianity played a more important role for Japanese at the forefront of the modernizing experience than many have realized. Christianity's "immortality system," in Rank's phrase, made its strongest appearance in Japan precisely at the time when traditional immortality systems had lost much of their power. Those Japanese who made the leap into Christianity did so primarily because of its powerful imagery of death and revitalization, the kind of imagery that had been so very important in samurai and emperor-centered tradition. In Christianity Japanese could experience passionate feelings of death immersion and transcendence, feelings that vivified all levels of experience. For writers and artists particularly, that vivification of experience probably had special importance. One feels that strongly in Hakuchō, a man who seemed to swing back and forth from that "Christian vivification" to a more quiet, naturalistic skepticism.

That kind of back-and-forth pattern, while common enough everywhere, seems especially prevalent in modern Japan. The more quiet, skeptical side—the "naturalism" of everyday life and of the I novel—has its own immortalizing dimension. It can, that is, contain an implicit sense that ordinary life, with all of its defeats, small victories, and contradictions, is part of an indestructible human flow. But at a time of shifting value systems, there are bound to be doubts about that too. What Hakuchō suggests to me that is so characteristic of modern Japan is an impressively varied psychic (or psychohistorical) constellation of that skeptical everyday naturalism, periodic Christian revivification, doubt and despair about the significance or lasting quality (symbolic immortality) associated with either, imagery of being bound to and nurtured by the Japanese group as well as of escaping totally from its oppression—along with a survivor's sense that one can quietly carry on with that contradictory, supportive, and despair-laden admixture.

7 / MISHIMA YUKIO (1925–1970)

The Man Who Loved Death

Mishima Yukio

FROM THE WRITINGS OF MISHIMA YUKIO

There is something that even now strikes me as strange. Originally I was not possessed by gloomy thoughts. My concern, what confronted me with my real problem, was beauty alone. But I do not think that the war affected me by filling my mind with gloomy thoughts. When people concentrate on the idea of beauty, they are, without realizing it, confronted with the darkest thoughts that exist in this world. That, I suppose, is how human beings are made . . . .

"If the people of this world," I thought, "are going to taste evil through their lives and their deeds, then I shall plunge as deep as I can into an inner world of evil." . . .

"Now that the war has ended, people are being driven about . . . by evil thoughts . . . and in their nostrils is the smell of the deed that is like death, *which already is pressing directly on them . . . . Please let the evil that is in my heart increase and multiply indefinitely, so that it may correspond in every particular with that vast light before my eyes! Let the darkness of my heart, in which that evil is enclosed, equal the darkness of the night, which encloses those countless lights."*

(The Temple of the Golden Pavilion [Kinkakuji], pp. 48, 69, 71)

Manifesto: Leader of the Shield Society, Mishima Yukio

We, the Shield Society, have been raised by the Self-Defense Forces, so that the SDF is our father and our brother. Then why, with our duty to repay our obligations, are we acting so ungratefully? I, for the last four years, and the students for three, have trained within your ranks as quasi–self-defense officials and have received a totally selfless education. We fully love the SDF. Here we dreamed of the "true Japan" that does not exist outside these fences; here we knew men's tears that have not been known since the war. The sweat we shed was purity, as comrades running together in the fields of Mount Fuji and sharing the spirit of patriotism. In this there is not a shadow of doubt.

The SDF is our birthplace, the only place in today's lukewarm Japan where bracing air can be breathed. We received immeasurable devotion from SDF teachers and assistants. Now, what led us to embark on this project? I insist, though it may seem sophistry, that the foremost reason is love for the SDF.

We watched postwar Japan become infatuated with economic prosperity, forgetting the basic principles of the nation, losing the national spirit, engaging in superficialities without correcting the foundation, falling into helplessness and hypocrisy, and sinking into an empty soul. Gnashing our teeth, we have had to watch politics become reduced to contradictory makeshift acts and self-

233

serving egos, greedy for power and fully of hypocrisy, while the state's great future was entrusted to foreign countries, while the humiliation of defeat in war was not wiped clear but only glossed over, and while Japanese themselves defiled the history and traditions of Japan. We dreamed that the true Japan, the true Japanese person, the true samurai spirit remained in the Self-Defense Forces. We saw that because in legal theory the SDF is unconstitutional, because the basic national issue of defense is being covered up by opportunistic legal interpretations, and because the army doesn't use the name army, the Japanese spirit has rotted and morals have become decadent. The army, whose glory ought to be most respected, has been ignored through the most pernicious deception. The SDF has continued to bear the postwar state's cross of disgrace. The SDF is too weak to be a national army, is denied the true meaning of a founding army, and is nothing more than a physical extension of the police. It has not been clearly made an object of loyalty. We resent Japan's very long postwar sleep. We believe that when the SDF awakens, Japan will awaken. We believe that if the awakening never comes to the SDF, then it will never come to sleeping Japan. And we believe that the people's greatest duty is to exert every effort to make the SDF follow the principle of a founding army through constitutional reform and to bring the day when it will be a true national military.

Four years ago, I entered the SDF with determination and in the following year formed the Shield Society. The basic doctrine of the Shield Society was, when the SDF earnestly awakened, to transform the SDF into a glorious national army through the determination to lay down our lives. Constitutional reform, so difficult under a system of representative government, can only be achieved through a mobilization to restore public order. We wanted to become the vanguard and risk our lives, serving as the cornerstone of the national military. The military defends the national essence and the police defends the polity. When police power can no longer protect the polity, then for the first time the military can be mobilized and the national essence can become clear, restoring the basic principles of the founding military to the military. The only basic principle that exists for the Japanese military is "to defend the history, culture, and tradition of Japan centered on the emperor." We few persons have trained ourselves and volunteered our lives for the mission of straightening out the twisted essence of our country . . . .

We have scrutinized the SDF minute by minute. If, as we have dreamed, the Self-Defense Forces contain the remaining samurai spirit, how could they neglect this situation? To defend something that negates oneself is a logical contradiction. As a man, how can a man's pride tolerate this? Though you may endure one trial after another, when you cross the last line that must be defended, you must rise up with determination. That is the way of the man and of the samurai. We have listened intently. But nowhere from within the Self-Defense Forces have we heard the voice of a man cry out against the humiliating order to "protect the constitution that negates yourself." While understanding that the only way is to correct the nation's distorted logic by realizing its power, the SDF has remained silent, like a canary that has lost its voice.

Despairing and angry we finally stirred into action. The officers say nothing can be done without an order. But, tragic though it is, the orders given officers do not come from Japan. Civilian control is said to be the basis of a democratic military. In the case of England and America, civilian control means control over the military budget. But not so in Japan, where the military has been castrated to the point of losing control over personnel decisions, has been manipulated by unprincipled politicians, and has been taken advantage for party benefit and policy.

Is the spirit of the SDF so corrupted that it bows to the politicians' flattery and follows a path of even deeper self-deception and self-desecration? Where has the spirit of the samurai gone? Where will the SDF go now that it is a huge weapon warehouse with a dead spirit? Some textile dealers in the recent negotiations called the Liberal Democratic party traitors. But when the nuclear non-proliferation treaty clearly revives the unequal 5-5-3 treaty, not a single SDF general protests by slitting his belly. What is the Okinawa reversion? What is responsibility for defense of the mainland? It is self-evident that America would welcome a truly independent Japanese military to protect the Japanese land. Within two years, if independence is not restored, the SDF, as the leftists say, will be finished forever as nothing more than an American mercenary force.

We waited four years. The last year we waited passionately. We can wait no more. We cannot wait for those who defile themselves. But we will wait thirty minutes more, the last thirty minutes. Together we pursue this just cause and together we die for it.

Restore Japan to its true form and then die. Can life only be respected and the spirit allowed to die? What is an army that has no values greater than life? Now we will show you where to find values greater than respect for life. It is neither freedom nor democracy. It is Japan. It is the nation whose history and traditions we love—Japan. Is there no one willing to attack the constitution that has disgraced these traditions, to attack with his body and die? If there is, then rise with us, and for righteousness and honor, die with us. We produced this manifesto because of our ardent desire that those of you with a spirit of purity be resurrected as individual men and as samurai.

(Okuma, *The History of Seppuku* [*Seppuku no rekishi*], pp. 270–74)

On November 11, 1970, the photographic essay "An Exhibit of Mishima Yukio" opened at the Tōbu department store in the Ikebukuro section of Tokyo. Mishima himself designed the exhibition, combining pictures portraying his real life from childhood on with photographs literalizing his fantasy life. The odd juxtaposition of images created a bizarre caricature of the life story of one of postwar Japan's most celebrated authors. One picture from a series for which he was then posing, "Death of a Man" ("Otoko no shi"), showed Mishima as Saint Sebastian, strung on a tree and pierced by arrows, visually representing his preoccupation with eroticized death. Other photographs of Mishima naked emphasized his homosexuality and Hollywood-style idealization of the male body. The exhibition left an overall sense of a man who wished to display the full range of his personal mythology in the most extreme way possible.

Mishima divided the photographs into four sections or "rivers"— the river of books, the river of the theater, the river of the body, and the river of action—which converged and flowed into the *Sea of Fertility*, the title of the tetralogy he was then completing. In a real way, this photographic recapitulation of his life's four most important themes was part of his life-review process, exemplifying his remarkably methodical preparations for death. The black-draped gallery walls intensified the aura of death, as if framing—or anticipating—a memorial exhibit.

"An Exhibit of Mishima Yukio" also suggested strong feelings of creative vitality around images of death. We may now suspect that its combination of family album pictures with special poses staging grotesque forms of dying reflected Mishima's loss of inner boundaries between actuality and fantasy, between self and exhibit of self. But few even among his closest friends imagined that Mishima Yukio was about to stage his actual death.

Mishima's plans for his death, like the plots in his novels, were elaborately drawn. He meticulously put all his affairs in order. In the half year before November, he gradually fulfilled all his literary and other obligations. He completed the last installment of his novel, *The Decay of the Angel (Tennin gosui)*, in time to present it to his publisher on the agreed date: Mishima never missed a deadline. He also carefully selected and prepared several members of his private army, the Shield Society (Tate no kai), to participate in the event. The special group even held a rehearsal to ensure a smooth performance. Then, on the evening of November 24, one week after the exhibition closed and one week after selecting the final proofs for his book of imaginary death photographs, Mishima made the final arrangements. He contacted two reporter friends and wrote a number of farewell letters, including his last thoughts and instructions to two of his American translators and to surviving members of the Shield Society. The next morning, he gathered his military sword and an attache case with two daggers; placed the conclusion to his long novel, packaged and addressed to his publisher, in the main hall of his house; telephoned his friends in the news media, requesting they wait for a message in the lobby of a particular building; and left with four Shield Society members.

Mishima and his young followers, all wearing the society's specially tailored uniforms reminiscent of Meiji military styles, drove to the Tokyo base of Japan's Self-Defense Forces in the Ichigaya district. Mishima had secured an appointment with the base commander, General Mashita, for eleven that morning, and on arrival the group was promptly ushered into his office. After a few minutes of conversation, and according to a prearranged signal, Mishima's followers suddenly attacked and bound the unsuspecting general and barricaded the office's entrances. They slipped a list of four demands under the door to startled soldiers on the other side. Mishima threatened to kill the general and commit seppuku if the demands were not followed. Twice a group of confused, unarmed officers pushed their way into the room to see what was going on, and each time Mishima first threatened and then slashed at them with his long sword, injuring several and driving them from the room. Convinced that the author-turned-rebel and his group were serious, and fearful for the general's life, the officer in charge acceded to the demands. He agreed to assemble the entire eastern division of the army at noon for a speech by Mishima and promised not to interfere with the activities until ten minutes past one.

Just before noon, Mishima stepped onto the balcony outside the commander's office. He paced back and forth, waiting for the precise moment, as Morita Masakatsu, Mishima's assistant and rumored lover, unfurled a banner with the demands written on it. At twelve sharp, Mishima turned to the soldiers and growing ranks of newsmen gathered on the assembly ground beneath him. Shouting and gesticulating excitedly, he exhorted the soldiers to join his rebellion against Japan's impotent army.

Copies of the group's manifesto—denouncing the constitution for prohibiting a Japanese military force, [1] and calling on members of the Self-Defense Forces to "rise with us, and for righteousness and honor, die with us"—were tossed over the balcony, but none of the soldiers moved to Mishima's side. Much of his appeal was never heard because of the drone of police helicopters overhead, and the remainder was ridiculed and rejected by the crowd of jeering, raucous soldiers. What was planned as a thirty-minute speech became a seven-minute scene of absurdity. Mishima and Morita shouted the traditional "Long live the emperor!" (*Tennō heika banzai*) three times and reentered the commander's office.

Mishima took off his boots, unbuttoned his jacket, lowered his trousers, and knelt on the floor with his legs tucked under his buttocks. He then plunged the sharp dagger into his abdomen and strained to cut horizontally to his right side. Morita stood behind his chief in the honored post of *kaishakunin,* [2] with sword raised, waiting to sever Mishima's head and end his life. As his intestines spilled onto the floor, Mishima collapsed forward. Morita unleashed two clumsy chops, which failed to accomplish the deed. One of the larger cadets grasped the long sword and, with a third, more powerful and accurate swing, completed the beheading. Morita then knelt beside Mishima's bloody body and slit his own abdomen, but only superficially, not piercing the layers of muscle and fat. He was in turn beheaded with a single, expert stroke. The three remaining members of the group, by then in tears, released the general, arranged the bodies and heads, bowed deeply, and turned themselves over to the authorities. The bloody event was over. Or was it?

Mishima's dramatic death shocked Japanese as much as it did Americans and Europeans. Although he had been "practicing" his death more and more explicitly in the late 1960s and had spoken often about suicide, no one seriously believed he would actually commit seppuku. Undeniably, samurai imagery has remained important in postwar Japan, but mainly in cultural mythology sustained by movies, television, and literature, and in relation to certain psycholog-

1. Article 9 of the 1947 constitution, also known as the "peace" clause, states that the Japanese people "forever renounce war as a sovereign right of the nation" and that the state will never maintain "land, sea, and air forces, as well as other war potential." The existing Japanese military is therefore termed as "self-defense" force.

2. The kaishakunin assists the person committing seppuku by performing the beheading that results in death after the abdomen has been cut.

ical tendencies. Mishima's acting out the samurai ritual death in the context of 1970 was perceived as extraordinarily bizarre.[3]

Mishima's media-event death unleashed a flood of attempts by various commentators to explain why he committed seppuku. Different theories emphasized insanity, aesthetic completion, exhausted talent, love suicide, and patriotic self-sacrifice. There is probably some truth in all of these theories, as we shall try to demonstrate. His suicide expressed many of the central themes in his life: his eroticization of death, his homosexuality, his obsession with the military, his sense of himself as a survivor, his restorationist impulse, and his acute sensitivity to the mass media. Nor were those themes his alone.

Mishima's life, as that of no other contemporary author, symbolized the transition between wartime and postwar Japan. His highly commercialized relationship with the mass media and his calculated efforts to cultivate his image in the West were characteristic of postwar Japan and almost nonexistent in prewar society. At the same time, his increasing concern with traditional values, particularly as advocated in wartime Japan, conflicted with his radically experimental postwar sensibility. His suicide reflected, in a distorted mirror to be sure, the struggles of his generation around the issues of Japan's military defeat, American occupation, and rampant materialism.

Mishima was both a talented writer and an early postwar literary star. He was nominated three times for the Nobel Prize. His first important novel, *Confessions of a Mask* (*Kamen no kokuhaku*, 1949), established Mishima as a gifted young author. He wrote forty novels, eighteen plays, and many short stories and literary and cultural essays. His complete works fill thirty-six thick volumes. He wrote primarily for a popular audience, sometimes with brilliance and beauty, and is the most translated of all Japanese authors.

As the new type of postwar celebrity who was predisposed to stunts, or what biographer Scott-Stokes called "buffoonery" (p. 16), Mishima had no rivals. Starting in the mid-1950s, he engaged in a series of activities totally atypical for writers. He struggled persistently at body building, tried his hand at boxing, constructed a luxurious imitation rococo house, formed a private militia, acted in gangster films, posed for photographs in the nude, espoused a rightist

3. It would be somewhat analogous to an American author of today, like Norman Mailer, adopting the garb and vocabulary of cowboy mythology in a hopelessly suicidal semipolitical shoot-out (from the right hip) with the American military.

political philosophy, simulated death in a number of ways, and finally performed his dramatic seppuku. These activities maintained Mishima's symbiotic relationship with the media by periodically reactivating his commercialized public image. In a paradoxical way, Mishima's suicide was his ultimate proof of existence.

Mishima was born January 14, 1925, as Hiraoka Kimitake, the eldest son of a middle-level bureaucrat in the Ministry of Agriculture.[4] His paternal grandfather, Hiraoka Jōtarō, came from a peasant family near Kōbe. But with Meiji Japan's social mobility, Jōtarō entered the law department of Tokyo Imperial University and then proceeded to the central bureaucracy. Soon after graduating from the university, he married Nagai Natsu, the eldest daughter of an aristocratic samurai family related by marriage to the Tokugawa family. This match across social classes was facilitated in part by Jōtarō's membership in the educated bureaucratic elite and in part by the Nagai family's desire to marry off their somewhat unstable eldest daughter.

Jōtarō, however, after reaching a position of some importance, was forced to resign from the bureaucracy because of a political scandal in which he diverted public revenues into campaign funds. He then became a businessman, but again with little success. His wife resented the poverty into which the family had fallen and continued to live extravagantly. After the marriage of their only son, Azusa, to Hashi Shizue, the daughter of a Tokyo middle school principal, Natsu took to tyrannizing her son and daughter-in-law. The birth of Kimitake in some ways heightened the conflict between Azusa's mother and wife, but it also provided a means for appeasing some of the elder woman's demands: she was entrusted with, or rather seized, responsibility for raising the family's heir.

Just before he became two months old, Kimitake was removed from his mother's care and placed in his grandmother's chambers. His grandmother claimed that it was too dangerous to raise a child on the second floor of a house. Like a nursemaid, Shizue continued to breastfeed the infant, but always under Natsu's watchful eyes. Natsu not only separated the baby from his mother, but confined him to her own quarters. In his largely autobiographical novel, *Confessions of a*

4. Mishima is best known by his pen-name, Mishima Yukio. We refer to him during childhood as Kimitake, and then during adulthood by his chosen surname, Mishima.

Mask, Mishima recalls, "My bed was placed in my grandmother's sick-
room perpetually closed and stifling with odors of sickness and old
age, and I was raised there beside her sickbed." Kimitake's younger
brother and sister were allowed to remain with their mother, but the
eldest son was to become his grandmother's possession, a prisoner of
her rooms during childhood and of her world for many years thereafter. Natsu's pathological protectiveness permeated every aspect of the
boy's life. He always had to choose among the alternatives of obeying
the orders of his grandmother, the unspoken desires of his mother, or
his own needs and feelings. While his grandmother was alive, and
after her death, he strove to fulfill her expectations. Mishima's strong
aristocratic, samurai, and worldly ambitions were closely linked to his
grandmother's determination to restore the family's honor through
him.

Natsu's concept of how to raise the young boy was eccentric in the
extreme, but she ruled absolutely and was rarely contradicted.
Kimitake was not permitted to play outside or with boys, but only
with three specially selected girls, and his toys were greatly restricted.
Even walks with his mother had to be approved by Natsu. The aging
woman completely controlled Kimitake throughout his early formative years. He was her connection to the world of the living and to her
own immortality. This connection was not only symbolic; as Natsu
became increasingly ill, Kimitake administered her medicine. As John
Nathan writes:

Natsu would take her medicine only from her "little tiger," as she called him;
Kimitake had to sponge her brow and massage her back and hip; it was
Kimitake who led her by the hand on her frequent trips to the toilet. The
worst times were at night. When Natsu's pain was bad she would cry and
tear her hair, imploring Kimitake to comfort her. At least once she seized a
knife and held it to her throat screaming she would kill herself.

(P. 19)

Natsu was afflicted with sciatic neuralgia, which is terribly painful,
and she gradually developed stomach ulcers and kidney disease. Yet
Kimitake continued to sleep in his grandmother's room until he was
twelve, when she abruptly consented to his return to his natural
mother.

Much of Mishima's acute sensitivity to death can be traced to his
aberrant and intense relationship with his long-dying grandmother.

Indeed, she is described in *Confessions* as his "true-love sweetheart, aged sixty." Their relationship contributed to his association of death with sexuality, producing an early model of eroticization of death. As his grandmother's child-nurse, he suffered with her through her agonizing, painful disintegration—tears, hair-tearing, and threats of suicide.

A frail, weak, exceedingly sensitive child, Kimitake was surrounded by death in many forms. Around the age of five he suddenly became so ill that he was expected to die. For the next year, until he began to attend school, he continued to have periodic attacks of "autointoxication." Thus through his grandmother and in his own body Kimitake directly experienced pervasive and constant contact with death imagery, from just after birth until early adolescence. He was to use this death imagery as a source of creativity, but it inevitably took its toll.

As Kimitake's fantasy life developed, his death imagery began to take particular contours. In *Confessions*, Mishima remarked that as a child he "delighted in imagining situations in which I myself was dying in battle or being murdered." He described playing war with his girl cousins and ending the game with his death: "I was enraptured with the vision of my own form lying there, twisted and fallen. There was an unspeakable delight in having been shot and being on the point of death." Yet he also stated he had "an abnormally strong fear of death." These were early expressions of the intense duality of Mishima's lifelong *danse macabre*: death attracted him irresistibly and at the same time terrified him.

His feelings about death were also linked with early homosexual fantasies. His viewing the beautiful dying figure of Saint Sebastian, as portrayed in Guido Reni's Renaissance painting, was the occasion for his first ejaculation. His homosexuality and eroticized feelings about death converged in his general sexual arousal in response to "death and pools of blood and muscular flesh." By hiding these feelings, masking his real self, and playing the male role expected of him, he felt that "what people regarded as my true self was a masquerade." *Confessions of a Mask* was, in this sense, the debut of both a talented novelist and a death-obsessed homosexual.

In April 1931, because of his grandmother's stubborn insistence, Kimitake entered the elite Peers School, although his middle-class family was clearly not part of the nobility. About a third of the school's pupils had nonaristocratic backgrounds, but they were mostly from wealthy families. Not surprisingly, Kimitake experienced difficulties in adjusting to his schoolmates. His physical weakness, commoner background, and middle-class economic standing all contributed to feelings of inferiority. Moreover, his continuing psychological and physical confinement by his grandmother prevented him from feeling comfortable with boys. His grandmother still exercised nearly dictatorial control over Kimitake, closely monitoring his diet and activities, and he missed many school days because of actual or alleged physical debility.

In 1937, at the age of twelve, Kimitake advanced to the middle school at Peers, and his grandmother finally released him to join the household of his parents and younger brother and sister. Natsu, whose health was steadily deteriorating, still required that her grandson stay with her one night a week and telephone her daily. Still, the move liberated Kimitake considerably from his grandmother's repressive control. But now he was subject to the despotic authority of his father.

Azusa was a fairly typical petty bureaucrat in his obsessive adherence to social rules. He was intent on making his son into the same, though perhaps at a higher level. Kimitake, however, was already demonstrating writing talent. He joined the literary club and began contributing regularly to the school magazine. Azusa fiercely opposed this literary interest, which according to his Confucian moralism was a form of decadence. Though working in Osaka between 1938 and 1942 and spending only a few nights a month with his family in Tokyo, Azusa created constant scenes with Kimitake about his writing. Several times he burst into Kimitake's room and destroyed his son's manuscripts. Though undoubtedly feeling himself annihilated with his manuscripts, and conflicted about defying his father, Kimitake's passion for writing never wavered.[5]

Kimitake's struggle with his father provided an early model for his later defiance of social norms. Probably, both his writing and his enthrallment with death had elements of rebellion against Azusa's oppressive conformism. This rebelliousness continued throughout his life in a combination of outrageous grotesqueries around death, kill-

5. It is also possible that Kimitake at some level sought this annihilation and played a part in provoking these incidents.

ing, and dying; a purist-extremist emperor-centered ideology; and various forms of "subversive" expressions in his writings, his public escapades, and certainly his sex life. Yet in a paradoxical way Mishima also fulfilled his father's instructions and desires, becoming a kind of postwar aristocrat. He even enrolled his own children in Peers School. His marriage too was a concession to middle-class propriety, though it also provided Mishima with an important area of stability. In sum, he both passionately fought and significantly internalized the conventional values represented by his father.

A more fundamental source of stability for Kimitake was his relationship with his mother. Shizue provided both emotional and intellectual support in early battles with his father over writing. Raised in a family of teachers and Confucian scholars, she appreciated literature and recognized the talent of her precocious son. Moreover, Shizue probably would have directly or tacitly supported almost anything Kimitake wanted to do, perhaps with the sense that whatever her son was attempting was commendable, even "pure." Although this response is related to the sense of amae in the relatively undifferentiated mother-son unit in Japanese culture, related patterns may be much more widespread, in fact almost universal.

In Kimitake's case, the grandmother's extreme intrusion added intensity to the mother-son relationship. His lifelong habit of presenting his mother with his completed manuscripts before submitting them for publication suggests her all-encompassing importance to him. The mother-son relationship thus became a crucial psychological anchor that had much to do with keeping Kimitake's psychic process relatively intact in the face of the terrifying imagery that dominated his life.

Under the sponsorship and encouragement of one of his middle school Japanese language teachers, Shimizu Fumio, Kimitake prepared for the first publication of a long story titled "A Forest in Full Flower" ("Hanazakari no mori"). From September through December 1941 it was serialized in one of the few literary magazines operating during the war, *Literary Culture (Bungei bunka)*. With Shimizu's help, he selected the nom de plume Mishimo Yukio and continued to publish stories in *Literary Culture*.

Through his relationship with Shimizu and the literary journal, Mishima came under the influence of the Japan Romantic School, a literary circle that embellished the war, promoted cultural nationalism, and dominated Japan's wartime literary world. The movement combined style and content to create a special form of politicized romanticism. They wrote in a style that drew heavily on a Chinese vocabulary, was highly decorative and often pompous, and tended to be intellectually and logically ambiguous. They emphasized Japanese traditions interpreted in terms of an emperor-centered culture and an exaggerated aesthestic to which all ethical questions, political action, and social content were reduced. For example, in portraying the twelfth-century samurai wars in Japan, they had no interest in their social context, but only in their aesthetics: the beauty of the armor, the beauty of self-sacrifice, the beauty of songs praising the warriors.

Their writings also frequently stressed the "royal literary tradition." One leading member of the Japan Romantic School, Yasuda Yojūrō, published an extremely popular book during the war. Yasuda's theme in *The First National Poet, the Throne* was that the emperor resembled a poet and was a kind of arbiter of Japanese aesthetics. These writers laid great stress on a literary and cultural nationalism. Like German Nazis before the Second World War, the Romantics never actually compared cultures, but simply asserted that Japan's was superior to all others. These elements of the Romantics—emperor-centered super-nationalism, aesthetic renditions of social and historical problems, and a highly mannered, obscure, vague, and emotive style—influenced all of Mishima's subsequent writing, particularly during the last ten years of his life. Perhaps more than any other postwar writer, he carried the legacy of the wartime Romantics.

Mishima was also deeply affected by Japan's romantic fascism and its emphasis on the spirit of the soldier and on absolute self-sacrifice. In March 1942, he graduated second in his class from Peer's middle school and advanced to the literature department of the upper school. As an adolescent at the height of the war, he intensely embraced the wartime ideology, probably even more than the adults promulgating it. The ideology's structured death obsession, propagated by the educational system, the military, and newspapers and radio, gave a framework and rationale to his personal preoccupation with death. Mishima "sensuously accepted the creed of death that was popular during the war" and hoped for his own early death. As Nathan writes:

Although death cast a shadow on the stories he wrote in 1941 and 1942, it is not until the middle of 1943, when the tide of battle suddenly turned against Japan, that he consciously began to define his destiny as the attainment of beautiful death. The point is that by the end of 1943 death was for all Japanese an inescapable reality.

(P. 50)

In his writing which blended with the historical and literary atmosphere, this sensitive youngster found expression for the vivid, grotesque fantasies dominating his mental life. Unlike most other authors, Mishima retained this literary and personal glorification of death long after the war was over. But in peacetime Japan it became for him a constant source of conflict.

Toward the end of the war, Mishima was presented with the opportunity to realize the call to self-sacrifice, but he could not follow his beliefs. In September 1944 he graduated at the head of his class at Peers School and received a silver watch directly from the emperor. In May of that year he had received his draft notice. His induction was postponed, however, and in October he entered the law department of Tokyo Imperial University in compliance with his father's demand that he prepare for his career as a bureaucrat. In the same month, his first book, a collection of short stories, was published, a remarkable feat at that late point in the war, and all two thousand copies were sold within a short time.

In February 1945, Mishima was ordered to report for duty. But when he appeared at the rural induction center in his father's home area, the military doctor misdiagnosed the frail, sickly Tokyo boy's mild respiratory ailment as tuberculosis. Whether he deliberately lied to the doctor about his physical condition, as described in *Confessions of a Mask*, is impossible to say, but it is clear that he did not contest the doctor's conclusion. Rather than dying nobly in battle, Mishima avoided military service. He returned to factory work, as part of the mobilization of students, and continued to write. His inability to accept the military death he was offered left him with feelings of guilt, weakness, and failure and had much to do with his later suicide.[6]

6. At that time, the combination of ideology and casualty rate led people to equate induction with a glorious death sentence. Mishima, in customary fashion, had left his personal will and nail clippings with his mother before going off for induction.

The end of the war sealed Mishima's identity as a survivor. Many of his generation had perished in battles in the Pacific and bombings at home, while he had, by dubious means (he undoubtedly felt), survived. He also lived through the abrupt, traumatic, and near-total Japanese transition from chauvinistic military aggression to submissive foreign occupation. To Mishima this meant he no longer could die a death of heroic glory and was condemned to live in peace. Many of his literary and nonliterary activities were directed toward giving some meaning and mission to his and to Japan's survival. Like all Japanese, he felt acutely the discontinuities imposed by defeat and occupation. But not until the 1960s did he clearly articulate what those discontinuities meant to him.

In the first years of the postwar period, Mishima lived a double life. During the day he studied law at Tokyo University as Hiraoka Kimitake; at night he wrote stories as Mishima Yukio. Seeking aid in publishing his short stories, the precocious twenty-year-old asked the prominent writer Kawabata Yasunari to be his patron. Kawabata consented and helped the young man publish a story entitled "Cigarettes" ("Tabako"), Mishima's little-noticed entrance to the postwar literary world.

In November 1947, Mishima graduated from the law department and successfully passed the highly competitive civil service examination for the central government. He was accepted for a position at the elite Finance Ministry, which immensely pleased his retired father. Throughout 1948 Mishima wrote furiously at night, publishing at least one work a month. Then, in September, he resigned his post, no longer willing to endure the demands of being day-bureaucrat and night-author. He turned his full efforts to writing, and two months later, on November 25, began his autobiographical novel, *Confessions of a Mask*. On that same day twenty-two years later he killed himself.

The occupation almost totally transformed the Japanese publishing world. Because writers who had collaborated with the militarists were not allowed to publish, a sudden demand arose for authors who had not published or had not supported the war effort in their writings. Some established authors, such as Hakuchō, helped fill the publishing void left by purged writers. But the main body of the postwar literary circle were writers who had been unable to publish during the war, because they had been in high school, college, or the army. The new generation wrote about wartime experiences that differed from those of the older generation. In 1946, Noma Hiroshi wrote *A Dark Painting (Kurai e)*; Nakamura Shin'ichirō published *Under the Shadow of Death (Shi no kage no motoni)* in 1947; Ooka Shōhei's first successful work was *Memory of a Prisoner (Furyo ki)* in 1948; and Hotta Yoshie began his career with *Solitude in the Marketplace (Hiroba no kodoka)* in 1951.

Among these writers was Mishima, who in July 1949 published *Confessions of a Mask*, his crucial literary breakthrough. In describing the main character's childhood, Mishima blended his urgent personal fantasies with disciplined imagination and unsparing self-scrutiny to produce a lucid and compelling novel. In that book, his original purpose of analyzing his preoccupation with death became complicated by the powerful emergence of his sexuality. Nathan writes:

> Reliving his life in *Confessions of a Mask* through his first-person hero, Mishima drove himself remorselessly to the recognition that he was a latent homosexual and, worse, a man incapable of feeling passion or even alive except in sadomasochistic fantasies which reeked of blood and death.
>
> (P. 95)

Mishima's extraordinary self-discovery provided him with the beginnings of a workable, if bizarre, adult identity.

Confessions achieved immediate success and catapulted Mishima from literary obscurity to popular frame. The book is one of his best—bold, brilliant, and direct—perhaps in part because he was not famous when he wrote it. Mishima's later works differ subtly because they were attempts to maintain rather than achieve success. Although *Confessions of a Mask* bore some features of wartime romanticism, Mishima managed to strip away the frills of that movement and evoke genuine childhood and adolescent experience.[7]

Mishima simultaneously entered adult and literary life. By transforming his childhood into literary form and combining fact and fan-

---

7. Mishima's style of exploring and portraying his childhood sexual life differs significantly from Ogai's *Vita Sexualis*. Ogai evoked a more or less normal sexuality in an objective, cold, clinical, and somewhat mocking form; Mishima's bizarre sexuality was rendered in a style that also had elements of mockery but was at the same time involved, emotional, serious, and elaborately descriptive. One reason for the book's soaring success was its originality: Mishima was the first in Japanese literature to depict the development of homosexuality from childhood, especially in combination with bizarre death imagery and a kind of self-analysis. The book also set a pattern in Mishima's writing of direct and extensive use of personal experience as source material.

tasy, he gave meaning to his extreme personal images. By making his homosexuality public, he somewhat detoxified it and turned sexual shame into creative pride. Partly because Mishima was too young to discuss Japanese history, the emperor or the occupation, he focused on personal experience.

Like almost all writers—indeed most Japanese—between 1944 and 1950, Mishima lacked continuity in values and found it extremely difficult to assess Japan's wartime and postwar events. (Leftists who had opposed the war, on the other hand, felt justified by Japan's defeat and had a consistent ideological vantage point from which to understand immediate social transformations.) Another reason Mishima did not speak out on Japanese nationalism during the occupation is that it would have meant certain investigation and possible blacklisting. He dealt with the sense of political and historical malaise by writing about his idiosyncratic death fantasies and his homosexuality. Many writers in the same period similarly transformed dark personal struggles into literary virtues. Dazai Osamu recorded his fall from an established family into decadence and deterioration. Others wrote about alcoholism, drugs, and self-disintegration. This major turn in literary creativity focused on individual struggles, which came to represent the larger sense of Japan's moral collapse—and the atmosphere of defeat and extreme poverty.

In the early 1950s Mishima enjoyed a period of relative stability while his social life became increasingly complex. In 1949, at the age of twenty-four, *Confessions of a Mask* brought him recognition as one of Japan's leading writers. He published something every month and in 1949 his first play, *Fire House (Kataku)*, was performed by a well-known theatrical group. The next year he published his second major novel, *Thirst for Love (Ai no kawaki)*, and again received favorable reviews from the critics. The book embodied themes discussed in his previous novel, particularly in the heroine's anxieties exploding into bloody violence, and included a homoerotic presentation of the heroine's peasant lover. In this period, Mishima ventured out more openly into the homosexual world of Tokyo, frequently visiting gay bars patronized by Japanese men of different backgrounds and by American businessmen and soldiers. The pretext for his visits was to investigate the homosexual scene for his next book, but Mishima was exploring ways to live with his newfound identity and discovering that his homosexuality was not unique. When his book describing To-kyo's homosexual society, *Forbidden Colors (Kinjiki)*, appeared late in 1951, it received mixed reviews, and Mishima himself had mixed feel-ings about its quality.

In an effort at revitalization, he obtained through his father's con-tacts accreditation as a special foreign correspondent for the *Asahi shin-bun* to travel to North and South America and Europe, which was difficult to obtain because of tight restrictions imposed by the occupy-ing forces. On the journey his homosexuality apparently became more explicit. But after his return to Japan in mid-1952, he continued to date young women, with his mother often joining the outings. Characteristically, he balanced strict, even extreme, adherence to so-cial rules with the open flouting of convention.

At the same time, Mishima was beginning to create a media image. He had active contact with prominent figures from the literary, homosexual, and kabuki worlds, as well as with university students (whom he met when he returned to Tokyo University to study Greek). He would stroll about Tokyo in a fifties' Japanese version of American hip fashion, but with his own eclectic imprint:

He wore loud shirts, often alohas, black "pegged" trousers, and pointy black shoes. He wore the shirts open halfway to the waist to expose a chest which for a Japanese was hirsute; around his neck he hung a golden chain and a variety of medallions he had bought in Italy and Greece. He was never with-out dark glasses, and, literally to top it off, he affected a crew cut, considered in Japan in 1953 to be "the latest Hollywood fashion."

(Nathan, p. 119)

Even as a child Mishima had enjoyed outlandish costumes, often bor-rowing his mother's clothing to fit his dreams, fantasies, and sexual confusion. The pattern continued through to his final costume, the caricature of Meiji military. These were not simply vain games at "dressing up," but part of Mishima's perpetual, often desperate, effort to feel alive. And to a limited degree they succeeded.

In 1955, at the age of thirty, Mishima began a body-building pro-gram. His frail, sickly physique had been a constant source of embar-rassment and humiliation, even self-contempt, since childhood. Once he began weight lifting he continued the regimen with almost religious dedication for the fifteen years until his death. Body building in Japan was a postwar phenomenon, an imported ideal of publicly displayed physical attractiveness. For Mishima it provided a sense of power, erotic feelings toward himself and other men, and a group to which he could belong. And it may have also been a physical means of holding off constantly threatening feelings of disintegration at a time when he was beginning to question his literary creativity. Artists often feel an ebbing of creative power before the critics perceive and announce it, as they did with Mishima in the late 1950s, and before sales of their works decline, which occurred to Mishima in the mid-1960s. Body building was the first of Mishima's shifts from internal-private to external-public spheres.

From 1955 on, photographs of Mishima in various weight-lifting postures appeared in weekly magazines and received much popular attention. Both the publicity and weight lifting itself probably served to demonstrate to him the reality of his existence—of body and self—in a way that his writing no longer could. Finally, body-building helped create both the physical and psychological strength needed for seppuku, the strength he had lacked as a young man during the war. Mishima made clear in his later writings that he needed to make himself beautiful before he could destroy himself.

In 1956, Mishima published one of his most successful novels, *The Temple of the Golden Pavilion* (Kinkakuji). The novel was based on the true story of a young acolyte living at the famous Zen temple in Kyoto who burned down the Golden Pavilion and then attempted suicide. Mishima transformed the news item into a problem of aesthetics, powerfully evoking the principle of beauty in destruction. That principle had been articulated by the monk during his court trial, but it was also a central part of Mishima's own psychology and a significant theme in Japanese culture. His novelistic young monk has a bad stutter, is frustrated by his isolation, sexual blocks, and inability to communicate, and focuses his total impairment on the temple, his ultimate symbol of beauty and also of oppression. Only after he has destroyed the temple can he feel—as Mishima wrote at the close of the book—"I want . . . to live."

The book is not without power, but Mishima's style is mannered, his prose overly decorative and baroque, and his metaphors somewhat grandiose. It lacks the directness and authenticity of *Confessions of a Mask*, perhaps because the author mixes cultural themes with clichés, aiming the book specifically at a mass audience. It was a huge popular success. As in *Confessions* Mishima strongly identifies with the main

THE MAN WHO LOVED DEATH / 253

character, the stuttering monk, and expresses his own preoccupation with the necessity of destroying beauty for his sense of vitality. Like the monk, Mishima also was obsessed with his own ugliness, sexual conflicts, and inability to relate to others. But instead of destroying external symbols of beauty, he rechanneled his destructive impulses into his death-haunted writing and finally directed them at himself.

In 1957 Mishima made his second trip abroad at the invitation of the American publisher Alfred Knopf. After lecturing at the University of Michigan, he traveled to New York, where he waited several months for a staging of his recently translated *Five Modern Nō Plays*, which never occurred. To pass the time, he attended many theater productions and continued with his body building. But he became increasingly depressed and when he finally realized that the producers would never be able to stage the plays he departed for a quick trip through southern Europe, returning to Tokyo in January 1958.

Once back home, Mishima agreed to be married—a promise he had made his parents before leaving Japan. His decision was influenced by his desire to maintain public propriety but also by the sudden hospitalization of his mother and the diagnosis of her illness as terminal cancer, although that diagnosis was later found incorrect. In March 1958, after several arranged introductions in the traditional style of *omiai*, Mishima selected for his wife Sugiyama Yōko, a college sophomore studying English and the daughter of a well-known traditional painter. They were married in June with Kawabata Yasunari, the famous novelist and Mishima's postwar literary mentor, acting as the formal go-between.

Mishima's marriage epitomized his striving for the perfect image of propriety in family matters. He strictly compartmentalized his public escapades from his family life. But at the same time, he was notedly modern, or we might say Western, in his relationship with his wife. He made special efforts to include Yōko in conversations, traveled with her on several trips abroad, and held luxurious international dinner parties at his home at which she cooked elegant Western-style meals. Their marrage outwardly exemplified postwar trends in husband-wife relationships, while retaining certain traditional features.

In January 1959, with Yōko pregnant, Mishima decided to construct a new home that would include a wing for his parents. The design he chose was a collage of various Western styles, reflecting his gaudy eclecticism and the superficiality of some of his aesthetic sensibilities, but also expressing his energy and courage. Removing various architectural styles from their historical contexts, Mishima stuck together fragments of rococo interiors to create a jarring effect that he himself called "anti-Zen." His house was in some ways consistent with the equally radical and disjointed eclecticism in his literary symbolism. Mishima struggled to integrate these different elements into his life, but never really could. They were masks that he would wear, deriving satisfaction both from the actual wearing and from public reactions, from his outrageous house and from public uproar about it and him—but as he repeatedly wrote, underneath the masks there was terror and pain.

In 1959, three years after *Temple of the Golden Pavilion* appeared, Mishima wrote a long novel, *Kyōko's House (Kyōko no ie)*. He had been brilliant and convincing when he directly identified himself with the hero, as in *Confessions of a Mask*, and partially convincing when he transformed himself into a slightly different person, as in *Golden Pavilion*. But he was utterly unconvincing when he assigned different aspects of himself to different persons, such as the men who frequent Kyōko's home: an angelic painter who feels he should kill himself while his body is still beautiful, a proper businessman who believes the world is doomed, an actor who practices body building, and a boxer who must give up his profession after an accident and becomes a member of an extreme rightist group. These persons reflect Mishima's worlds—or masks—of artist-martyr, conventional entrepreneur, playwright-actor, body builder, and romantic rightist. The novel is pervaded not only with death but with anticipation of the destruction of the world. None of the characters, however, carries the weight or feeling of a real person; each is but a pale shadow of Mishima. Literary critics, who so far had praised Mishima's talent, did not fail to perceive the flaws in *Kyōko's House*.

Kyōko's House marked a turning point for Mishima. It began his transition from powerful, genuine novelist to public showman. His writing became increasingly contrived and drawn from fragments of his own surface imagery. Literary fame abroad—particularly in America—became increasingly important to him. And at home, the need for public display became all the more urgent. Mishima was now in his mid-thirties, a time when one tends to become aware of the actuality of death. Mishima sought to incorporate that actuality into his longstanding fantasies.

In the spring of 1960, the question of renewing the Japan–U.S. Mutual Security Treaty politicized and polarized Japan. Many opposed the agreement, which provided American bases in Japan in exchange for military protection, arguing that it would drag Japan into American military actions in Asia. Proponents claimed that the treaty was essential to protect Japan's national security and to maintain good relations with America, which were important for economic and political reasons. On May 19, Socialist Diet members staged a sit-in in the Lower House in an effort to prevent the opening of the session and police were called in to remove them. The same night, a little after midnight, remaining conservatives, in a dubious parliamentary maneuver, voted to extend the session and then, with no protest, quickly passed the treaty. The government's strong-arm tactics aroused immediate response from the press as well as large numbers of university students and professors, labor leaders, and politicians, who denounced the ruling Liberal Democratic party—and Prime Minister Kishi Nobusuke—as deceitful and antidemocratic.

Protests escalated rapidly, and on June 16, 1,000 demonstrators were injured in clashes with the special riot police and a female student, Kamba Michiko, was trampled and died. On June 19, 300,000 demonstrators gathered outside the Diet and demanded its dissolution, but that midnight, one month after the treaty's unusual approval by the parliament, the agreement automatically went into effect. The demonstrators did succeed, however, in bringing about Kishi's resignation the day the treaty was officially ratified.[8]

The general social agitation during the Mutual Security Treaty rekindled Mishima's political interests. He became totally absorbed in the events and reported his observations in an article in the *Mainichi shinbun* titled "A Political Opinion" ("Hitotsu no seijiteki iken"). But the article took no clear political position and did little more than make the enigmatic observation that both he, Mishima, and Kishi were "nihilists" and that "realists" make better prime ministers. But it was a first step into the political arena, after which Mishima entered it regu-

8. See Lifton's discussion (1970, pp. 81–100) of these events, based on observations and interviews in Tokyo at the time of the large protest demonstration. Beyond immediate political issues, Lifton stresses various psychological sources of protest energies: the extent to which Kishi and the Liberal Democratic party came to symbolize an "evil past"; the overall Japanese resentment of dependency on the United States; and the ambivalent Japanese attraction to social and political revolutions in other parts of East Asia, notably China.

larly and wrote from a more explicitly conservative-rightist perspective. The atmosphere of the 1960 demonstrations served to evoke in him nostalgic feelings for the Second World War and stimulated him to formulate his own political images.

Three works are especially representative of Mishima's politics. "Patriotism" ("Yūkoku"), a story published in 1961 and based on the unsuccessful military coup d'état of February 26, 1936, portrayed in gory detail the seppuku of an army lieutenant during the uprising. Mishima praised the supernationalist military officers' devotion to the emperor and no doubt envied their ability to fulfill his romantic fantasy of self-sacrifice. In 1965 Mishima rewrote "Patriotism" as a screenplay with subtitles in English, French, and German and played the role of the "heroic" lieutenant himself. Then forty, he had begun rehearsing his own bloody finish. The film was a one-man Mishima show: he was author, screenwriter, director, producer, and leading actor. The camera's exaggerated affection for blood and death to the musical back ground of Wagner's dirge from *Tristan* renders the film melodramatic, painful, and, for many, repulsive. Viewing the film after his death, watching Mishima prefiguring his own seppuku, is a particularly bizarre experience, perhaps one that Mishima intended.

Mishima's play *My Friend Hitler (Waga tomo hittorā)*, published at the end of 1968, also has political overtones. It takes place in 1934, the year Hitler eliminated his close comrade Ernst Röhm and a number of others who had helped him come to power. Hitler is at the center of the drama, constantly making pompous speeches. But the play is unconvincing, because everything is simply too Mishima-like. For example, Röhm, leader of the Nazi storm troops or SA, talks about his men's golden hair shining in the sunshine and their strong breasts proudly set against the morning wind. This is clearly the transplanted language of Japan's wartime Romantics (and of Mishima's rather than Röhm's homoeroticism). Gustav Krupp, the industrialist, speaks in flowery phrases to Hitler about how his company is led by a will of steel and motivated by a heart of iron—hardly the language of a German capitalist. Finally, Hitler at one point states that it is important for him to know why he is so great and powerful. Röhm, says Hitler, is a soldier, but the Führer will be a great artist. In a sense, Röhm and Hitler represent the two images of soldier and artist-dictator toward which Mishima aspired.

His title, *My Friend Hitler,* thus had a double meaning. On the one hand, it expressed in an ironic way Röhm's feeling of friendship to-ward Hitler which was betrayed. On the other, it expressed Mishima's own ambivalent feelings of admiration and identification toward Hitler. The play merged Mishima's two levels of romanticism, one revolving around self and the other centered on fascist politics.

"The Defense of Culture" ("Bunka bōei ron"), published in 1968, was a political essay on culture in the idiom of restorationism. In seeking to defend or restore Japanese culture, he was reacting against Western influences or impurities, in himself as well as in postwar society. Mishima believed that Japanese culture could be divided into artistic expression and traditional action. The latter culminated in the samurai warrior's killing himself with his sword. The authority of Japan's culture, he asserted, is symbolized by the emperor—defense of Japanese culture requires defense of the emperor. To restore the integrity of Japanese culture in the postwar era, the emperor's original function had to be restored. In this sense, Mishima linked the emperor not only with Japanese poetry, as had the romanticists, but directly with the army, as had the militarists.

This essay is argued loosely; its words and concepts are vague and some facts are wrong. For example, Mishima states that because historically Japan has had a single language and cultural tradition, it has since ancient times experienced political unity. But the fact is that despite this cultural homogeneity, in ancient times as well as in feudal times, political unity did not exist in Japan.

When he felt his literary talent beginning to fail, Mishima declared that man's real world existed not in words but in warriorlike behavior. He found support for this view in the teachings of Wang Yang-ming, an early sixteenth-century Chinese philosopher who stressed thought with action. Restorationist politics gave Mishima a new raison d'être, that of purifying and revitalizing postwar Japanese society, as well as himself. We are reminded of Kawakami's need to prove his thoughts and beliefs through concrete deeds. But unlike Kawakami, Mishima felt driven by personal and ideological impulses to prove himself by suicide, by a version of seppuku stamped with his own personal flamboyant style and timed to meet the deadlines of the evening papers.

The rightist politics he expounded more frequently and concretely after 1960 connected him with the wartime ideology he absorbed during his formative years. And passions around the emperor cult lay just beneath the surface of Japanese society. Mishima's rightist political ideas and actions have created problems of interpretation for everyone, including his Western biographers and translators. John Nathan interprets Mishima's infatuation with the right primarily as a means for achieving heroic death:

It appears, I mean, that Mishima wanted *passionately* to die all his life, and that he chose "patriotism" quite consciously as a means to the painful "heroic" death his lifelong fantasy prescribed. I don't believe necessarily that the ardent nationalism of his final years was a hoax. But it does seem to me that his suicide was in essence private, not social, erotic, not patriotic. I do not claim that my account is whole truth. I do believe it to be true.

(Pp. x–xi)

Nathan also refers to Mishima's 1968 autobiographical statement in *Sun and Steel*, in which Mishima

accounted for his actions past and future more persuasively than anywhere else, and in a context that had nothing to do with the constitution, the Emperor, or anything social. The context was his knowledge that he would obtain the incontrovertible "proof of existence" he required to feel alive and real only in the moment of death.

(P. 237)

We admire Nathan's biography and agree with his understanding of Mishima's suicide as an affirmation of existence. But it does not follow, as Nathan claims, that the act had "nothing to do with . . . anything social." Recognition of Mishima's use of ideology to express profound personal conflicts should not blind us to the significance of the particular ideology he chose. Mishima was struggling to overcome personal feelings of deadness and unreality but his actions were associated with—and shaped by—specific historical and political themes in Japanese society.

In his quest for symbolic immortality, Mishima was constantly trying to place himself within different historical continuities, within different worlds: literature, art, and the cult of the warrior. The historical moment was so characterized by dislocation and unlimited cultural fragments—and Mishima was so energetic, gifted, and propelled by extreme fantasies—that virtually anything and everything was available to him. In his politics, as in his writing and public poses, he took bits and pieces from a wide variety of Japanese and Western cultural currents. He was very much a postwar eclectic who felt driven toward

constructing his own social universe, which to a considerable extent
he finally accomplished. He could have killed himself in various other
ways such as swallowing sleeping pills, slashing his wrists, or jumping
in front of a train. His decision to die by seppuku in a spectacularly
public manner was not random. It linked him with that peculiarly
Japanese cultural tradition. By imitating military seppuku he sought
to associate himself with the deaths and suicides of celebrated samurai
of the past and more specifically with the deaths of soldiers twenty-
five years earlier—with the heroic, personal death he had so vividly
imagined but had been unable to achieve.

Ivan Morris, another Western student of Japan and translator of
Mishima, associates him with the phenomenon of the "failed hero" in
Japanese history. Morris evokes various figures of the past to illustrate
his thesis that Japanese choose as heroes those who die a "splendid
death" and thereby display a quality of absolute "sincerity" that can
only be demonstrated on behalf of a lost cause. Morris does not include Mishima in his biographies as a failed hero, but refers to his
ideas and actions, and in fact dedicates the book, in friendship, to
Mishima's memory. But Morris minimizes the importance of Mishima's political views and criticizes the "oversimplification of motives
and distortion of objectives that has allowed Mishima to be dubbed a
'fascist.'"[9]

But we would insist once more on the importance of the ideological
content, as well as the behavioral form, of Mishima's way of living and
dying. Regardless of whether one considers Mishima a fascist, he was
certainly an extreme rightist, albeit an idiosyncratic, romantic, self-
schooled, and creatively gifted rightist. In sum, he did make his politics a vehicle for his death and would-be immortalization. But the
vehicle itself—the idea-structure that framed his actions—was also
central to his moral and psychological existence. The principle holds
for all of us.

Mishima explained much about himself in *Sun and Steel* (1970). With
retrospective wisdom, we can see this statement as proposing the concrete program for his death and building toward the reality of his
suicide. It was another form of Mishima's rehearsing his death. Mishi-

9. Though we disagree on this point we consider Morris's study to be a very important one.

ma remarked that he believed in two contradictory elements, words
and body. Initially he concentrated on the language of words. But later, "thanks to the sun and the steel, I was to learn the language of the
flesh" (p. 12). In the beginning of the book, Mishima defines his fundamental problem as a survivor:

> Longing at eighteen for an early demise, I felt myself unfitted for it. I lacked,
> in short, the muscles suitable for a dramatic death. And it deeply offended
> my romantic pride that it should be this unsuitability that had permitted me
> to survive the war.
>
> (P. 28)

His goal, particularly in the 1960s, was to revive in himself and society the traditional ideal combination of two fundamental aspects of
culture: letters and the martial spirit, or art and action. Mishima
romantically explained that

> to combine action and art is to combine the flower that wilts and the flower
> that lasts forever, to blend within one individual the two most contradictory
> desires in humanity, and the respective dreams of those desires' realization.
>
> (P. 50)

Mishima perceived both art and action as struggles for symbolic
immortality, but as "no more than pathetic efforts of resistance against
death and oblivion" (p. 54). A blending of the two seemed to hold out
greater promise: "Somewhere within me, I was beginning to plan a
union of art and life, of style and the ethos of action" (p. 47). Perhaps
this is why Mishima's rightist political statements have an unnatural
feeling. They were contrived to serve his personal project of uniting
art and action. He created a script with various characters and
speeches and acted it out. Did he believe his own lines? We can at least
say that he believed he should believe them, and that the lines themselves were from an old and familiar drama—on which he and his
country had long been nurtured, even if some elements were a bit
anachronistic. He surely felt himself to have much at stake in carrying
out his seppuku.

His mother understood her son well. At Mishima's memorial service at the family home, when someone brought white roses signifying
sadness, she said: "You should have brought red roses for a celebration. This was the first time in his life Kimitake did something he always wanted to do. Be happy for him" (Nathan, p. 281).

In 1965, the year Mishima turned forty, his death plan was probably taking shape. He began work on his last major literary work, the tetralogy known as *The Sea of Fertility*, including *Spring Snow*, *Runway Horses*, *The Temple of the Dawn*, and *The Decay of the Angel*. These books are difficult to summarize briefly, but the whole story is framed by the Buddhist concept of reincarnation. The hero has three moles on his body, which is the sign of his reincarnation from book to book. The subplots include every variety of violence, vile action, and sexual aberration, themes that are found in his earlier writings. But compared to *The Temple of the Golden Pavilion*, for example, the tetralogy is much longer and its philosophical framework much weaker.

Still more significant is the fact that Mishima constantly repeats in these novels things he has already said in others. Self-imitation comes close to self-caricature. This represents the artist's loss of his capacity for inner transformation, which must be accompanied by feelings of inner deadness. In Mishima's case the literary critics did notice what was happening, and the consensus among them was that Mishima's tetralogy represented a definite creative decline. The general impression was that his attempt at a huge synthesis failed because he lacked a viable framework for integrating his diverse elements. To make matters worse, it was clear that Mishima's popularity with the reading public was declining. Mishima probably experienced considerable despair on all these counts, the sense that his literary mode of immortality was collapsing. His suicide, like all suicides in different ways, was a desperate attempt at revitalization.

An earlier effort at revitalization was Mishima's open campaign to win the Nobel Prize for literature. The tetralogy may have been his last-ditch effort to impress the West that he was Japan's greatest living author, by combining all sorts of exotic themes in an eclectic tour of Buddhism and reincarnation, South East Asian princes and princesses, and the Japanese samurai spirit. He actively lobbied for influence, on several occasions traveled to Stockholm to look over the city where the prize was offered, and always worked hard to get his works translated into English, a prerequisite for the Nobel. The 1968 selection of his mentor, Kawabata Yasunari, as the first Japanese to receive the coveted award was undoubtedly more than merely a blow to Mishima's pride.[10] It provided external corroboration for his internal doubts

10. In 1972, two years after Mishima's suicide, seventy-two-year-old Kawabata ended his life by gas asphyxiation.

262 / MISHIMA YUKIO

about literary immortality, and a further incentive for his shift in psychological emphasis, already well underway, toward the warrior mode.

In the latter half of the 1960s Mishima often discussed politics and martial arts, emphasizing the sword and fighting. He proclaimed repeatedly that Japanese culture is not simply kabuki theater, flower arrangement, and tea ceremony, but also bushidō, the way of the samurai. He made a sharp division between the two spheres. One was literary and "feminine," soft, gentle, delicate, and elegant, like *The Tale of Genji*. Mishima expressed contempt for this literary culture— "feminine" was his most pejorative adjective. The other side of Japanese culture, the warrior cult, was "masculine" and highly admirable, even sacred.

The inclination toward this kind of male-female polarization of imagery and behavior is probably universal—its American counterpart is the John Wayne ethos.[11] In extreme form it becomes both a "biologization" of ethics and an application of "male chauvinism" to ultimate dimensions of experience. It probably always contains an important compensatory element—the male's fear of both his own weakness or "feminine" traits and of the power of women—all the more so when the polarizing voice is that of a man whose own sexual identity is so confused and bizarre, and who is, among other things, a homosexual.

Mishima's equation of feminity with weakness and deadness, and masculinity with vitality and life-power, had an additional compensatory function for him. It was a way of coping with his literary decline—of debasing that which was declining—and of finding a larger cultural rationale for his shift to the "masculine" world of the warrior. He could enter a world of swords, physical and spiritual conditioning, and self-sacrifice, bring to it his mimetic talent and impressive capacity for self-discipline, and with the help of the media once more emerge as a "star." But while he attempted to portray the process as a struggle against general Japanese weakness and decay, the evidence suggests that the decay of the angel was the decay—the sense of inner disintegration—of Mishima.

Mishima had begun to emphasize masculine culture when he

11. See the discussion of the John Wayne ethos and its bearing on personal and cultural polarization in Lifton (1973), pp. 217–63.

launched his body-building project in 1955 at the age of thirty. He continued weight lifting on a regular basis, but also tried other forms of physical discipline more active and closer to violence, such as boxing, kendō (Japanese fencing), and swordsmanship. Then, in 1966, just after turning forty, he approached Japan's military forces for permission to train with them. Although his initial request was refused, Mishima persisted and in early 1967 was admitted to basic training. For one month and a half in that spring, he left his writing table to join teen-aged volunteers in a series of physical trials. He was proud that he could do everything they did and overcome the more than two decade's difference in age. Publicly, Mishima announced that he undertook his military training out of patriotic concern for Japan's national security and to help restore national pride in the way of the warrior. Privately, the project fulfilled his unrealized soldier fantasy and placed him closer to becoming a modern postwar samurai, which for Mishima meant one step closer to death. Mishima himself said as much—and more—in *Sun and Steel*:

Nothing gives the armed forces so much attraction as the fact that even the most trivial duty is ultimately an emanation of something far loftier and more glorious, and is linked, somewhere, with the idea of death. The man of letters, on the other hand, must scratch together his own glory from the rubbish, within himself, already overfamiliar in every detail, and refurbish it for the public eye.

(P. 72)

Here is Mishima's starkest contrast between the genuine, death-linked glory of the warrior and the futile individual constructs of the literary man bored by his own repetition and offended—perhaps also terrified—by his "rubbish within." The first could rescue him from the second—and having just turned forty, Mishima believed he had to act quickly.

In late 1967, Mishima took another step. He proposed to a group of ultraconservative university students that they form a private militia as an additional force that could assist Japan's army in supressing leftist uprisings. At a melodramatic ceremony in the office of a right-wing student journal, Mishima and his followers signed a pledge in blood, and in March 1968 he accompanied the first small group to train with Japan's Self-Defense Forces. Because of difficulties in raising funds from other sources and, we may assume, to have the group available for his purposes, Mishima decided to form his own private militia. He also provided its name, Shield Society, which was drawn from the ancient Japanese patriotic image of becoming "the emperor's shield."[12] Mishima justified this goal of providing protection for the emperor in numerous political essays, notably his convoluted "Defense of Culture." However odd this minimilitary organization seemed to most Japanese in 1968, its members were using the words Japanese warriors had used for centuries—each pledged himself to fight to death to defend the emperor.

Mishima's little army served various functions. Most obviously, it made him closer to an actual soldier and officer, even if in Don Quixote-like fashion. He enjoyed dressing up in his special uniform—another mask—and engaging in various kinds of physical drill. During training exercises Mishima thrived on feelings of solidarity, simplicity of purpose, and common discipline. The Shield Society also created an all-male world which in itself had appeal for Mishima, and he found a close relationship, by some accounts one of sexual love, with a younger student member. He could thus live in a way that fulfilled many of his fantasies, while remaining the director of the group's drama. That drama included constant assertion of the restorationist theme of revitalizing postwar Japan around a strengthened emperor. The Shield Society gave Mishima a group to identify with, a cause to fight for, and above all a way to die.

In the late 1960s Mishima moved more explicitly toward death as his only goal. He could readily switch to the warrior hero as his immortalizing mode because that image had been a powerful one all through his life, and during adolescence had taken on lasting ideological form. Similarly, his principle that "Death is the only erotic concept," while part of his bizarre self-system, also connected with a traditional Japanese cultural emphasis on the perfect death. Even the urgency he felt about killing himself before he became too old was associated with the Japanese version of the near-universal romanticization of dying young. One thereby immortalizes youth, beauty, and life-power, and circumvents—even eliminates—old age, deterioration, and in a sense death itself. Our point here is that each of Mishima's most idiosyncratic images and actions related to universal

12. The image is from the classical eighth-century anthology of early Japanese poetry, the *Manyōshū*, and was used actively in slogans and songs during the Second World War (see Morris, p. 346).

psychological struggles, as mediated by specific, mainly Japanese, cultural traditions. It is never a question of either-or—for him or any of us, in dying or living.

In Japan, as in many countries around the world, 1968 was the height of intense, sometimes violent student uprisings. Mishima joined the political battle by holding a series of dialogues with students at three different universities. Despite angry disagreements a certain sympathy existed between Mishima, the vociferous proemperor, rightist ideologue, and the student advocates of the antiemperor extreme left. That sympathy arose from a shared belief in risking all for one's cause and from a similar approach to emotions. Mishima, like the students, emphasized the nonrational, the *quality* of emotional experience.

Once, when discussing assassination, he stressed the significance of the "voltage" of one act and the difference between "assassinations of high quality and assassinations of low quality" (Nathan, 1974, p. 247). Certain leftist students spoke similarly of the quality of their emotional experience when "on the barricades," in violent confrontation with the police. The moment of unity between these romantic revolutionaries of the left and the romantic apostle of the right was brief. But as we know, that worship of pure feeling, especially when associated with destruction, has roots in Japanese cultural tradition, was very strong in Mishima as an individual, and is a basic characteristic of fascism.

Finally, we may summarize the social and historical context of Mishima's death by comparing his performance of seppuku with Nogi's. Nogi committed suicide in the quiet privacy of his home in a way that was anachronistic, but he lived in an age when a real connection with feudal traditions still persisted in Japan. Mishima flaunted his suicide in a sensational public media-event, as if the balcony of the army headquarters building were a stage, and at a time when feudal death ritual was limited to films and plays. Nogi's seppuku expressed the conflicts of his generation around the transformation of the Meiji Restoration and was an attempt to revitalize early twentieth-century society with an act recalling Tokugawa Japan; Mishima's seppuku symbolized the struggles of his generation with Japan's defeat, occupation, and prosperous commercialism, and was an attempt to revitalize the society of 1970 with an act recalling wartime Japan.

COMMENTARY / R. J. Lifton

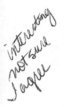

Mishima's life and death almost seem to have been written for our study. Everything in his excessive existence suggests imagery of death and of the struggle for continuity. He is so excessive, in fact, that some have been tempted to sequester him in a realm of psychopathology, and perhaps genius, apart from other Japanese and other men in general. I think we must do the opposite and find in his very excess connections with the ordinary. Nothing Mishima experienced, however intense or bizarre, is alien to the human condition, to the struggles of living and dying.

To understand better both Mishima's specific struggles and the application of our paradigm, I would like to examine his evolving death imagery, efforts at vitality, immortalizing quest, and moral and political aspirations. We have already said quite a lot about his death-haunted childhood and his early and consistent eroticization of death. His attraction to death was in part a manifestation of his terror of it. He could not assimilate death to the life process. The death in his imagery had little to do with larger human rhythms of continuity, of endings and beginnings. Rather, it was death as a grotesque destroyer—and that image of death became something close to his primary personal source of vitality. That kind of process has to be inwardly reworked during adolescence. And at that time it could join with the military and political glorification of transcendent forms of death on behalf of emperor and nation. In the face of such symbolism, Mishima's retreat from military service and the death it offered him suggests again the extent of his death anxiety, and undoubtedly left him with a sense of profound shame over his failure to carry through his own highest principle. That failure probably gave his affiliation with the Japan Romantic School all the more psychological importance. Death-centered romanticism (then politicized in Japanese writers but later less so) became his métier, his way of maintaining his early death imagery and at the same time giving it broader, aesthetically disciplined expression, thereby gaining immediate group belonging and wider recognition.

This takes us to the second area, efforts at vitality, and here Mishima's literary work takes precedence, especially during his early adulthood. *Confessions of a Mask* is the crucial novel, and Nathan quotes him as commenting while writing it: "I am desperate to kill a man; I want to see red blood. An author writes love stories because he isn't popular with women; I began writing novels so I wouldn't end up with a death sentence" (p. 103). In his writing he could transmute his related impulses of grotesque dying and killing. The autobiographical structure of *Confessions of a Mask* enables him to make his most direct contact with his own death imagery in all its luridness. The work that enabled him to achieve what we could call vital identity as a writer was at the same time, in his words, an attempt to "turn upon myself the scalpel of psychological analysis . . . to dissect myself alive . . . to achieve a scientific accuracy, to become, in the words of Baudelaire, both the condemned and the executioner" (p. 94).

Mishima was frightened by the extent of his destructiveness, as well he might have been: "I had taken secretly to jotting down epigrams such as 'Whether another A-bomb falls or not is no concern of mine. All that matters to me is whether the shape of the globe would become even a little bit more beautiful as a result'" (p. 97). But I believe the artist in him was less interested in overcoming this psychopathology—the sadomasochistic imagery that dominated his mind—than in transmuting that imagery into personal and literary energies. In *Confessions* he did just that, brilliantly. But his structure of imagery and vitality was much more fragile than anyone could know. The transmutation was never again to be as successful, and in fact became increasingly problematic with each subsequent novel. His sense of inner deadness—derived from profound early currents of separation, disintegration, and stasis—would never quite go away.

This view of him helps us understand a bit more about his homosexuality and body building. Though he revealed quite a bit of anxiety about his emerging homosexuality in *Confessions of a Mask*, in the end it too became subsumed to those transmutations. The body building took on increasing importance, we suspect, as he felt his imaginative-symbolizing power to be weakening. Eventually he came to a simplistic male-female dichotomy: only in cultivated masculinity, Japanese warrior-style, could one find a true mixture of vitality and transcendence; the rest, including literature, was "female," inwardly dead, weak, contemptible. In all this he was undoubtedly fighting his own *self*-contempt at what he must have perceived as the "woman" in himself. But sexual behavior itself, homosexual or otherwise, became quite secondary to these struggles around vitality and deadness, and in another sense absorbed by the lust for blood and death.

As inner deadness becomes more difficult to overcome, Mishima turns to the creation of public happenings. In American letters, this phenomenon has been represented by Norman Mailer. As the symbolizing capacity becomes blunted, or at least insufficient for what the artist seems to require, he may substitute direct public impact— public happenings—for art itself. The problem is not so much becoming too public or social as the fundamental solipsism which interferes with the artist's efforts at psychic transformation and connection with others. Mailer has managed the problem by partial retreat from fiction, substituting instead a brilliant form of personal journalism that enables him to make full use of his own imagery but always in some relationship to events outside himself. But while Mishima tried many forms of writing (and many public happenings) his sense of himself remained that of the artist. He might denigrate the "femaleness" of art, but he would, quite literally live or die with the novel.

Those immediate struggles with vitality were of course inseparable from his ultimate struggles with symbolic immortality, our third area. However Mishima negatively compared literary efforts with warrior achievements, he wrote with demonic energy. He was always extraordinarily conscientious, and when the writing was going well it was a source of direct transcendence: "It is like saddling this globe of ours, leaping astride, and with one crack of the whip making it gallop through the blackness of the void." Another important indication of the ultimate importance of his writing to him and its relationship to his sense of immortality was the care he took, before his suicide, not only to complete his tetralogy but to arrange for its English translation. These efforts undoubtedly were related to imagery about the unending and expanding life his novels would have following his own death. In that light, we can begin to understand the kind of despair he must have experienced when not only his critics but he himself sensed that he was essentially repeating himself, that his creative power was waning. Then he was, so to speak, naked before his own terrifying fantasies—no longer able to absorb or transform them into fiction. Thus exposed to his own bloody constructs and uncertain about the larger connection literature had afforded him, he took concrete steps toward making the blood his own.

Because of the prominence of his restorationist impulses, commentators have tended to underestimate Mishima's protean side. In addition to his wide array of traditional and postmodern involvements, Mishima varied enormously in psychological level and personal style. At times he seemed complex, profound, fascinating in his talent and grotesquery. At other times he seemed quite superficial, manipulative, almost uninteresting, blatantly "putting on" just about everyone without even an attempt at subtlety. Certainly he was dazzlingly protean, and when he seeks fiercely to defend or restore Japanese culture, he is simultaneously struggling to defend himself from protean impurities (whether Western, literary, or whatever) and restore an earlier sense of purity of purpose and commitment that he had known as an adolescent during the war, and perhaps as a very young child before that.

The extraordinary array of possibilities presented by postwar Japan in its very dislocation, when combined with his gifted protean energies, made virtually anything available to him in his visions of destruction and revitalization. Everything was available, but nothing quite worked. And when he did finally commit seppuku, it was a modern seppuku, combining traditional features with contemporary absurdities—the presence of the media, the balcony scene, and above all his own earlier comparison of himself as a warrior with Don Quixote. He both sought and mocked the persistent Japanese cultural aspiration toward the perfect death. He did after all realize his impulse "to kill a man" and became literally "the condemned and the executioner" (Nathan, pp. 103, 94). His mother quite accurately said that his death was the only thing he ever did that he really wanted to do. But the fact he was so extreme did not mean that others have not also felt most alive in destroying themselves—and many more in imagining their self-destruction.

Mishima's self-immolation, then, was a combination of personal despair and a culturally influenced orchestration of dying on behalf of a larger purpose. That purpose, the kind of revitalization sought by Mishima, brings us to our fourth area, that of moral and political aspirations. The main point I would make is that the paradigm of death and continuity, with its emphasis on symbolic immortality, is in no way a substitute for moral and political judgments. Rather it provides a context for and a psychological approach to moral and political questions. Mishima by no means killed himself solely out of despair—he also expressed in dying a vision of cultural revitalization. But that vision was so dominated by solipsistic needs that it was rendered highly amorphous and quite disconnected from most of contemporary Japanese life. Yet it was by no means *totally* removed from collective currents, present and especially past.

We hear much these days about male chauvinists, cultural

chauvinists, and class chauvinists—and Mishima was all of these. But more than anything else I would call him a "death-chauvinist," one who, through embrace and worship, lays claim to death and thereby associates himself with totalistic ideologies that grant only the select—the fellow death-worshipers—the full right to life. For such people the historical continuity of symbolic immortality is centered around such death worship and therefore denied to those outside of the ideology or cult. It becomes all too easy to contrast the heroic death being worshiped (which enables one, psychologically, to live forever) with the demeaning death taint one assigns to others (and where victimization proceeds further, is implemented via mass murder).

Mishima was no murderer, and he was hardly alone in his murderous fantasies. But he was, in effect, a romantic fascist. His evocation of "my friend Hitler" was not the mere political idiosyncracy of an essentially literary man; it was a strongly felt, even if in some ways superficial, identification with the romantic death-worship and associated revitalizing claim of Hitler and the Nazi movement. One reason why Mishima's brand of restorationism was so repulsive to many of his Japanese contemporaries was its throwback not so much to a genuine samurai ethos but to the muddled militaristic romanticism—the whole state of mind that entered into Japan's homegrown twentieth-century fascism—precisely the politics and cast of mind that enlightened Japanese have struggled to cast off during the entire post–Second World War period.

fascism - totalitarian, dictator, aggressive nationalism + often racism

COMMENTARY / S. Katō

Immediately after the end of the Pacific War, I used to meet Mishima on various occasions, always together with other writers of the postwar generation. At that time he was very small, rather thin, with big eyes, nervous and somehow rigid in attitudes, and almost stubborn, concentrating on his own problems which the others present did not share. Dazzled by enormous social changes under the occupation, most writers of that time were largely concerned either with their war experiences or with reappraisals of Japanese history and society. Not much involved in any of such problems, however, Mishima started his literary career as a young novelist by exploring his own inner sensual and psychological world.

When others were extroverted, he was introverted; when others were preoccupied with social situations, he was definitely self-centered. He was unique and unusually gifted. Mishima, in *Confessions of a Mask*, combined determined self-exploration, keen sensitivity, and original style. Then came Mishima, as a creative writer, who brilliantly transposed his personal experiences to the imaginary world— notably in *The Golden Pavilion, After the Banquet*, some short stories, and a series of modern nō plays.

Mishima, however, was a controversial man: a good observer of himself with a limited ability to understand other personalities, a sensitive aesthete with no profound cultural background, an intelligent writer without intellectual discipline at an abstract level. He always had difficulty, I believe, in moving beyond the interiority of his sensual-emotional self toward the exteriority of history and society—a difficulty which he apparently never managed to overcome. In his imaginative world of novels, stories, and plays, Mishima's characters, even during his best years, risked becoming mere mouthpieces of the author, a tendency culminating in *Kyōko's House*, which clearly marked the beginning of his decline in creativity.

Mishima, who so often considered himself an aesthete, was no connoisseur of either European or Japanese art, in sharp contrast, for example, with the writer Kawabata Yasunari, who loved and knew the world of pottery. Mishima's taste was at times so banal that his pompous style produced the effect of tourist post cards. Choosing the Golden Pavilion as the symbol of architectural beauty in Kyoto was no more original than choosing the Arch of Triumph as the symbol of Parisian architecture. In his novel, erotic sensation within the hero is quite convincing; aesthetic presentation of the temple is commonplace. The same may be said about history. He was original and convincing when he wrote about his personal reactions, for instance, to Racine's *Britannicus*, even if in effect he removed the work from its seventeenth-century French context, about which he knew little. He was often sensitive and provocative when he made personal comments on the *Hagakure*, though he singled that work out from the large body of eighteenth-century writings on samurai discipline, most of which he apparently did not bother to read. His references to his own experiences are interesting; his generalizations often make no sense at all.

Mishima was neither a Christian, nor a Buddhist, nor an atheist, nor an intellectually sophisticated skeptic. In at least that respect, he was not much different from the majority of the people on the streets in modern Japan, and indeed radically different from all other writers in our study, from Nakae Chōmin, Mori Ogai, Kawakami Hajime, and Masamune Hakuchō. Nogi, the general, was closest to Mishima, but Nogi had a comprehensive set of samurai principles to follow. As a writer, Mishima had no larger religious or philosophical system as a general frame of reference. His impassioned but fragmentary emperor-centered rationalism did not suffice. Yet he needed just that for the construction of the long story of his last work, the tetralogy. Although he had never made any serious reference to Buddhism in his previous writings, he rather abruptly adopted a Buddhist concept of rebirth *(samsara)* as the guideline for the tetralogy.

Certainly conscious of his waning creativity, Mishima during his last days was trying to reestablish his literary fame. He mobilized all the cards in his hand: the Peers School, survival themes, extreme nationalism, homosexuality, eccentric erotic scenes. The tetralogy became a kind of summation of all his previous creative works, a literary testament. The Buddhistic framework, however, was shallow. Its story of rebirth is rather absurd: one of the two friends at the Peers School dies young; the other, who survives, later meets a princess from Southeast Asia, who is disclosed to be his reborn late friend as a beauty spot on the thigh proves.

Interestingly, Mishima wrote about Buddhistic rebirth and Kawabata talked about Zen philosophy when both tried to appeal to the Western public—Mishima in lobbying for the Nobel prize, Kawataba in accepting it. Both references to Buddhistic concepts only demonstrated that Buddhism in any serious sense was quite beyond their scope and that it didn't help much to revitalize their exhausted literary inspirations. Mishima's and Kawabata's suicides shared one aspect: both were related to a sense of despair about their future as creative writers.

Mishima was a restorationist. Unlike Nogi, however, he was a restorationist without a past to restore—hence his vague, romantic, convulsive nationalism, which I believe led him to an almost logical consequence: death. Born to a middle-class family, Mishima aspired to be a member of the upper class; for heroes and heroines in his fiction he liked to choose the aristocrats, princes, and princesses who peopled the Peers School of his youth. Because he couldn't inwardly affirm his belonging in any concrete social group, either the middle class or the ruling elite, he tended to emphasize his imaginative ties with the West, particularly with America as well as with what he considered the true Japan. But the Western society that he knew mainly through literature was very remote, indeed—not only for Mishima, but also for most Japanese of his generation. And the more remote the Western world was for him, the more polarized his sentiments toward the West: admiration and resentment, cultural ethnocentrism and sentimental nationalism.

As a reaction to temptations of the Occident, his nationalism was not based primarily on the affirmation of genuine Japanese traditional values. Rather, Mishima was searching for a true Japan, which he could find only in the belligerent Japan of his youth. In his immediate environment, he tried to identify with the Self-Defense Force, a part of the accommodationism of postwar Japan. The Self-Defense Force certainly regarded him as a desirable spokesman, but was appalled by his anachronistic idea of an imperial army. As a cultural nationalist, Mishima had no supporting historical substance; as a political nationalist, he had no group association other than his own paramilitary band. His nationalism trapped him into a dead end, so to speak, and he knew it.

Mishima's political ideas might have been his mask, as some observers have suggested. But everyone chooses a mask suitable for himself. Mishima might have felt an erotic ecstasy at his own death. But in any case his political ideas allowed him no exit other than death. It would be one-sided to explain Mishima's suicide only by his erotic death wish. Yet even if we could depoliticize him as a person, it is obviously impossible to depoliticize his role in Japanese society—not because the extreme rightists have been celebrating the anniversaries of his suicide, but because being nonpolitical in postwar Japan was, and is, a political action. No protest against the war may mean a tacit approval of the war; silence about the abuse of power under the name of scientific or artistic neutrality may imply a passive support for that power. Mishima as a political propagandist was favored only by small groups on the extreme right. Mishima as a nonpolitical aesthete, however, was, and still is, a perfect model of all writers who accept by silence values prevailing in society and support by implication the established power structure. He preached for the restoration of the emperor's sacred status, which, after all, is the goal that all recent Japanese governments have been striving for in a more subtle and more realistic way than Mishima.

I feel, in Mishima's case particularly, that death was the end rather than the interruption—the end of declining creative force, the end of impossible forms of political engagement, the end of exhausted showmanship. His spectacular suicide was probably a form of ecstasy for himself, but for the public a strange scream from the distant past. Nogi's postmortem history will not be repeated. Japan will make no powerful symbol out of Mishima's seppuku, the Japanese will instead, I believe, bury once and for all the sad memory of the wartime mentality. *Is this in fact true or is Kato + overly optimistic?*

8 / DEATH
AND SOCIAL CHANGE

DEATH AND POLITICS

Societies, like individuals, deal with threats of annihilation by maintaining images of continuity with both past and future. In times of rapid change, existing symbolic forms tend to break down, and societies often experience an outpouring of cultural death imagery—that is, feelings and ideas, art and literature, associated with death or its equivalents. Death imagery, in turn, can become part of a process of rebirth, helping to reassert sacred cultural visions that contribute to social integration and make change possible. We have observed both tendencies in the Japanese modernizing process. But it is fair to say that the culture has placed particular stress on the revitalizing functions of death imagery and also that this form of revitalization carries special dangers.

Rituals associated with death exist in all cultures and have important functions. They transform the private character of death into a sacred public event, provide the structure for survivors' mourning experiences, and turn a potential disturbance into a functional expression of social continuity. But sharp tensions can arise between an individual's quest for a personal death and a society's efforts to socialize that death. In Japan, as elsewhere, funeral ceremonies tend to support the existing value system by providing the pomp and ritual appropriate to social status and class. Mori Ogai tried to break out of that convention by prescribing the elimination of all such ritual and honor in his funeral. His refusal, and the strong language in which he expressed it, shocked people in official circles. But the army ignored his testament and reclaimed his death for "history" as the military defined it. Even in dying Mori remained part of the military community and, in important symbolic ways, continued to serve that community. The private man Mori Rintarō reaffirmed his deepest personal connections to natural and biological origins, but the public figure merged with the glory of the imperial army.

Manipulation of death symbolism by the political authorities is particularly dramatic in the case of Nogi. In committing junshi, Nogi sought to overcome his inner deadness and despair and to achieve, for himself and others, a feeling of revitalization and identification with Emperor Meiji and samurai ideology. But the state focused entirely on Nogi's devotion to the emperor and transformed it from an expression of personal loyalty to an individual emperor into a symbol of general loyalty to a system. The state created from his death and his life an image of the ideal samurai, a kind of military god, devoted to the imperial cause. The manipulation of Nogi's image into a powerful symbol of Japanese militarism and nationalism was effective not simply because of the government's intensive propaganda but also because his ritualized death reinforced connections with cultural values that were still compelling for large numbers of Japanese.

Until the end of the Second World War, Japan used the death symbol of Nogi and its evocation of a "traditional" Tokugawa samurai glorification of death to motivate and mobilize students for the military, particularly for the kamikaze suicide brigades. In this sense, Nogi's seppuku was a bridging image between the "traditional" samurai and the modern imperial soldier. Nogi's historical transformation shows how violent death can be to energize social and political movements.

It is too soon to judge the extent of political manipulation of Mishima as a death symbol or to predict its long-term social impact. But Mishima's death clearly has become a rallying point for a small group of extreme rightists who identify with the restorationist politics of his death. His suicide at least partially inspired a small-time pornographic movie actor to don a kamikaze pilot costume and crash his plane into the home of underworld magnate Kodama Yoshio. He felt Kodama should have committed suppuku to accept responsibility for his wrongdoing in the Lockheed scandal. We thus have a sequence linking the bizarre death imagery created by Mishima's suicide, first to the extreme rightists who use Mishima as a death symbol, and then to one of them who recaricatured and reformulated Mishima's death imagery to connect with a new historical political crisis. In this sense, Mishima's seppuku was a bridging image between the extremes of imperial militarism and the extremes (and absurdities) of postwar rightists.

The way an individual constructs death is likely to be shaped, if not dictated, by society or specific groups which may then reclaim that death for their own purposes. Moreover, the meaning of a death may change as old symbols are reshaped and used for new functions. Thus, we can understand a lingering uneasiness in many Japanese that sometime in the future the death symbolism around Mishima might be redefined and used in the service of violent forms of restorationism. That fear is based on an awareness of the malleability, persistence, and potential power embodied in symbols around dramatic deaths. The struggle to control the meaning of symbols associated with particular deaths and ways of dying has great political importance for all cultures and has special significance for Japan.

Japan, of course, is not alone in its use of the warrior's death to symbolize military and political virtues of valor, loyalty to superiors, and dedication to group or country. Other societies also propagate death imagery of warriors in funeral and commemorative ceremonies, political exhortation and demogogary, as well as such literary works as epics, folklore, and drama. In the West, these forms of death symbols flow through Homer, Chanson de Roland, and Corneille, and extend to John Wayne cowboy and war movies.

A range of death symbols in Japan has also been used to oppose the political authorities: from Oshio Heihachirō in the premodern period, a Tokugawa Confucianist of the Wang Yang-ming school who led a peasant rebellion and died in battle with government forces, to Kamba Michiko in postwar Japan, a woman college student who died in the violent clash between police and student demonstrators against renewal of the Japan–U.S. Security Treaty in 1960. Death imagery of victims has also been central in Japanese protests against nuclear weapons and against environmental pollution.

Among our six cases, Yamamoto Senji's death exerted a crucial influence on Kawakami. And Kawakami's own death, although not dramatic, became a symbol of a political warrior in his long, consistent devotion to the Communist cause in Japan. Though opposition groups have used particular deaths as motivating political symbols, we have seen how established political powers with their vast resources and media control can more effectively exploit as symbols the deaths of both "heroes" and "enemies."

Japan's death-centered romanticism, and eroticization of both death and violence, may be considered products of its cultural split between public rationality and private emotions. Germany experienced a similar phenomenon as an outgrowth of the rapid modernization process itself, especially the exaggerated focus on technology as a means for dealing with the death of an old culture and the birth of a new.[1] When

1. In the late nineteenth century, Germany, like Japan after the Meiji Restoration, experienced a rapid modernization. Its use of French and British models created a split between intensely rationalized institutions and suppressed internal passions and a divorce between public and private values. Instead of a *giri-ninjo* dichotomy between obligation and human feeling, however, Germany had a *Zivilisation-Kultur* dualism between the materialistic world of *Zivilisation*, which includes *Realpolitik*, and the spiritual world of *Kultur*, which includes literature and philosophy. Both Japanese and German cultures generated an extreme romanticization of death. The split in Germany between an abstract, rational system of technology that excels in efficiency without being hampered by human feelings, and an exaggeratedly and passionately

this split occurs, the individual's intense passions can be fulfilled only by transcending the inevitable clash with the rationality of the social order—through romantic imagination or, in the extreme case, through self-destruction. Private emotions, when no longer held in check by public rationality, can generate various kinds of artistic and literary symbolizations around death. But for ordinary people, such symbolization can be especially impaired by the split, and passions may then be directed toward forms of experiential transcendence that depend on violence. The malevolent forms that death-centered romanticism took in Japan and Germany will remain two indelible tragedies of human civilization.

SUICIDE AND JAPAN

Suicide is in itself a political act and can be aimed at a collective beginning no less than an individual end. Suicide is the most extreme and literal way of taking hold of one's death. Indeed, the deaths of Nogi and Mishima demonstrate, contrary to many psychological theories, that suicide can be a controlled enactment of a vision of revitalization. But the meaning of suicide is much influenced by historical context and social change.

The self-immolations of Nogi and Mishima reflected a mixture of personal despair and commitment to the larger purpose of restoring past values. Yet there was an important difference. Nogi could connect his death with actual life experience in Tokugawa samurai society, while Mishima, in the very uniform he wore, caricatured the death of a distantly imagined Meiji ex-samurai. Nogi sought to seal his membership in an existing but dying community of the last real samurai, while Mishima attempted to join a fabricated community of warriors at a time when no actual samuarai existed.

In recasting a traditional death form, both engaged in ritual anachronism. Yet their very use of seppuku—and later responses to their deaths—suggest some of the continuing symbolic power of such a form, long after it has ceased to be culturally manifest. For both could evoke in others (Nogi much more than Mishima) imagery similar to

---

romanticized literary and artistic tradition with tendencies toward loss of control and balance, contributed to the Nazi combination of Auschwitz technological slaughter and Wagnerian glorification of death.

their own around the drowning of "traditional" values by "modern" ways and the necessity to reverse this tide.

Modern Japan inherited from Tokugawa society a second form of immortalization by suicide—*shinjū*, the double suicide of lovers. Shinjū has been a consistent and deeply compelling theme in kabuki and puppet theater and at times during the Tokugawa period became associated with something close to death worship. But that death served as a completion of love, an affirmation and immortalization of erotic life. Lovers kept apart by unyielding social obligations evoked a moment and an eternity of ecstatic union. Death itself became erotic—and erotic realization was achieved only in death. This tradition probably played an important part in Mishima's lifelong eroticization of death, as well as in his actual suicide, which had elements of homoerotic shinjū.

Tokugawa Japan thus provided two systems of death-centered revitalization which existed in parallel and sometimes in conflict: the one ascetic and warrior-centered, the other romantic and centered on erotic love. From the seventeenth-century the rising chōnin class had to adopt aspects of the dominant samurai culture, but also sought increasingly to affirm its own values. Chōnin respected the imposed samurai principles of rational social order and suppression of emotions, but did not internalize these as much as the samurai themselves. With the dissolution of formal Tokugawa class structure following the Meiji Restoration, however, samurai and chōnin constellations of death imagery and related values merged and were popularized among all classes. The new combination contributed to a sense of continuity and of national "essence" on which the institutions of a modern nation-state could be built.

The blending of samurai and chōnin death imagery also gave rise to modern forms of suicide, including family suicide, youth suicide, and versions of double love suicide. They differ considerably from Nogi's and Mishima's own modern renditions of seppuku in that they involve much less structured ritual and use no samurai weapons. Yet contemporary suicides can share certain characteristics with seppuku and its modern versions. We observe this continuity with both seppuku and shinjū in the frequent association of contemporary suicide with fulfilling obligations to the group—be it family, company, *yakuza* (gangster) group, or nation. One such expression is the resolution by suicide of an otherwise insoluble situation for one's group—a love affair threatening family or families or an irreconcilable impasse within a company. The motivation here is related to certain premodern examples: Tokugawa women who kill themselves to resolve triangular love affairs, men who kill themselves to remove the cause of social friction permanently from the community, the suicide of general's wives (often with their children) held hostage in a camp during the civil wars of the sixteenth century to give their husbands freedom of action in battle.

A second group-centered motivation for suicide is to redeem failure or "apologize by dying" *(shinde owabi o suru)*. A failed student by killing himself not only expresses his personal shame and guilt but also resolves conflicts with family, teachers, and peers. Or an employee commits suicide to express his company's apology for a gross error, and thereby overcomes otherwise unmanageable resentments of company authority (which might well have been a factor in causing the error). A recent celebrated example was the suicide of the director of a food supply section of Japan Air Lines after an outbreak of severe food poisoning among a planeload of passengers had been traced to the contaminated hangnail of an employee under his supervision. In such cases there is a continuity of premodern expressions of suicide as a way of assuming ultimate responsibility, restoring various kinds of group harmony (in this case between company and passengers, and between Japanese and foreigners), and of perpetuating the good name of the group (Japan Air Lines in this case).

Such group-centered forms of suicide can be found in many societies. In ancient Rome, for instance, defeated generals preferred suicide by sword to disgrace at the hands of the enemy, and Lucretia killed herself to preserve her chastity. But Japan has perhaps gone farther in institutionalizing the idea of killing oneself for the sake of one's group, thereby rendering suicide acceptable and plausible.

This contrasts dramatically with the revulsion toward virtually all forms of suicide in the Christian West. In medieval Europe the bodies of suicides were usually mutilated and then buried in unsanctified ground, often at crossroads. These measures were meant to symbolize the absolute denial of immortality to those who had sinned against God by taking their own lives. God alone, it was felt, could be the arbiter of life and death. But Christianity nonetheless provided a suicidal equivalent in martyrdom; one could indeed agressively seek one's death, if in the service of God. The larger principle, for both samurai warrior and Christian martyr, is that of taking hold·of one's death on behalf of the prevailing collective vision of immortality.

Particularly striking in Japan is the phenomenon of collective suicide—of a mother and her children, an entire family, or two lovers. Collective suicide dramatically illustrates the precedence of group-centered values in death no less than in life. It also involves coercion: the group forces individuals to participate in the irreversible project—as in family suicides involving young children, who may be actually killed by parents in the latter's struggle with their own death imagery. Involved in the act is the powerful Japanese cultural image of the mother and child as something close to a single organism, so that the mother or both parents may well be convinced that family death is considerably less cruel than leaving children without parents to care for them. Darker emotions may also contribute to family suicide, such as a parent's feelings of resentment and jealousy toward any family members—even young children—who might survive one's own death.

Yet whatever its pathos and degradation, collective suicide of this kind is also likely to contain an element of protest: lovers expressing their rage at society's restrictions, a family venting its anger toward whomever or whatever has reduced it to its presuicidal state of hopelessness. In this protest there is a glimmer, however faint, of an alternative vision of existence—an affirmation of the very life principle the group or its leader feels deprived of.

In the experience of kamikaze pilots during the Second World War, certainly a form of collective suicide, feelings of affirmation were inextricably bound up with those of coercion. Though these pilots sought to connect with immortalizing principles related to emperor and imperial state, their "decisions" were enormously influenced by psychological pressures within their immediate military units and the extreme sense of humiliation they anticipated if they returned alive. A similar combination of immortalizing affirmation and coercive potential humiliation may well be present in the suicidal-homicidal actions of young Japanese—as well as European—terrorists.

More generally, these Japanese patterns remind us that there is no such thing as a "simple suicide," that suicide is never merely a matter of ending one's life. Suicide is a form of self-expression around immediate psychological conflict and ultimate concern. The immortalizing principles so explicit in certain forms of Japanese suicide can also be found in the contemporary West: in the self-immolation by fire of an American girl in Washington and of a young student in Czechoslavakia, each seeking to affirm a vision of peace or of freedom. And the suicides of individual Jews in Treblinka, the notorious Nazi death camp, were important forms of self- and group-assertion. By taking death out of the hands of the murderers and forcing other inmates to confront their fate, these suicides contributed to a prisoner uprising in which many Nazis were killed and a small group of inmates escaped to bear witness.

In most ordinary suicides, both in Japan and the West, immediate conflicts predominate, often suffused with depression and other forms of psychiatric disturbance. Ultimate meanings may hardly be discernible, but in our view have considerable importance nonetheless. For the suicidal act, however desperate, aims at radical alteration and expresses what Hillman (p. 73) has called "the urge for hasty transformation." The most ordinary suicide in any culture is somehow connected to group relationships and images beyond the self, and bears some relationship to the more flamboyant suicides in which public symbolizing dimensions are more clearly articulated. Suicide is an attempt at purposeful control over one's life and one's death, even if expressed around one's own degradation and misery.

MODERN JAPAN: DEATH AND CHANGE

The six men we have studied were separated from the masses, and often from other members of the elite, by the intensity of their personal encounters with new ideologies and cultures. Insofar as they expressed the elite tendency to take hold of death, they did so in a shifting historical and psychological field, within which existing arrangements for living and dying had come under external attack and inner doubt. Each approach to death was constructed from both the Japanese past and from immediate psychic and moral schisms accompanying radical change.

Their Japanese "death roots" were evident in their sharing with the common people a stress on this-worldliness, a sense of merging with the cosmos, and an emphasis on the group. These longstanding Japanese tendencies maintained connections between the world of the living and that of the dead rather than separating them—as stressed in the West. Even the pantheon of spirits and ghosts that has always been prominent in Japanese popular culture (some of which undoubtedly affected these six members of the elite) is neither organized by a systematic theory nor cut off from daily life. Death is perceived less as an enemy than in the West because it belongs to the same cosmos as life.

These perspectives are not unique to Japan—something like them can probably be found in most non-Western and premodern societies. But the Japanese may well have been the first to carry the imagery of dying into the cosmos into a modern, industrialized, secular society. This has in part been accomplished by the structuring of institutions and groups to provide so nurturing an embrace as to function like a premodern cosmos. We have in mind the combination of pervasive control and cradle-to-grave security provided by the contemporary large business firm or company. But psychologically, the replacement only succeeds partially. The company cannot quite instill emotions equal to premodern confidence in the cosmos. The result is pain, confusion, and creative energy. We could in fact observe these three change-related tendencies in the lives and deaths of these six men, whether or not their modified cosmos was defined in relationship to some such institution.

Like many Japanese, they showed considerable flexibility in altering their sense of the cosmos without abandoning the basic Japanese relationship to it. Consider Ogai's dedication to completing as much of his opus as possible before dying, while insisting on being buried as a commoner of his native place. This sophisticated "Meiji-Renaissance man" was able to combine modern artistic assertion with an image of merging with the cosmos in the simplest, most fundamental way. And Chōmin, in his image of reducing the self to an insignificant part of the materialistic universe, resembled someone as different from him as Kawakami, whose reduction of self was in terms of "selfless love." Both patterns were consistent with the popular Japanese view of death, and with a more general principle in East Asian philosophical and religious traditions of dissolving into the cosmos.

We are not suggesting that the Japanese are without fear of death. But they may well have a stronger sense than Westerners of being part of a single, encompassing human group that survives, perhaps forever, the "flow of events beyond individual influence" (see chapter 1). Even in the midst of change, then, a sense of being Japanese can be perceived as something given, on the order of nature itself. We can thus speak of the Japanese tendency toward deification of the human group.

Japanese symbolization of immortality is thus extremely strong in relationship to the human group but weak in connection with the individual immortal soul. It includes formed connection to a specific group within a formless connection to the inclusive cosmos. Each of these connections has been threatened and altered by social change, but versions of the combination persist.

In times of rapid change certain deaths become important symbols of social struggle, and thereby lead to intense forms of survivor experience. When one belongs to a tight, cohesive group in conflict with the rest of society—such as a young samurai unit in Chōshū before the Meiji Restoration, like Nogi, or a Marxist-socialist activist group in the interwar period, like Kawakami—the death of a member can give rise to a powerful survivor mission. Much of one's subsequent existence—including the risking or taking of life—can be organized around the impulse to bear witness and the commitment to carrying out the work of a dead colleague.

Similar conflicts can occur around surviving the end of an era, where conflicts around change have been particularly painful. Nogi exemplifies one type of survivor of the Tokugawa period. He participated in killing, physically and metaphysically, the remnants of samurai society, and then later in life he embraced samurai values with extreme intensity, perhaps in part as a means of attenuating his guilt over what he had "killed" and survived. Hakuchō, by living as long as he did, survived most of his generation, and gave meaning to his life by focusing on the continuity of Japanese everyday cultural experience. Mishima felt himself a survivor only as a result of cultural dislocations and actual widespread death during the war. He tried to cope with imagery of annihilation and loss, first by his bizarre combinations of psychic and cultural elements, and later by reasserting the values originally embraced by his wartime generation. The experiences of Nogi and Mishima particularly suggest the impact that the abrupt end of an era can have on young adults, with its combined survivor emotions around actual and social death. Surely large numbers of modern Japanese experienced a similar impact from the abrupt, violent, and radically dislocating experience of the Meiji Restoration and the defeat in the Second World War.

For survivors of such radical upheaval the path of accommodation becomes difficult to follow, and many embrace patterns of restoration or transformation. The restorationist turns to the past for ultimate standards of how society ought to be shaped, while the transformationist looks to an equally ultimate future vision. But the accommodationist must hold to an uneasy balance of conflicting values and images of past and future.

Actual lives rarely fit neatly into a single category and usually combine elements of the different modes. The most efficient Westernizers—for example, Ogai in literature and medicine and Chōmin in human rights—had a profound knowledge of Tokugawa culture. Their transformationist ideas and actions were not based on a simple dualism of "Japanese spirit and Western technology" but expressed subtle interactions between elements of the two cultures. Indeed the transformatist requires, both publicly and intrapsychically, considerable "tradition" to legitimate his visions of radical change.

Restorationists can call forth similarly complex cultural combinations. Nogi and Mishima, for example, spoke on behalf of perpetuating old values, but by invoking a past that was either illusory or unviable, they imposed their own historical discontinuity on the present. One can say that they made a psychological attack on the actual sequence of history—though in Nogi's case, the connection with recent experience was sufficiently great to enable him to contribute significantly to historical change.

Ogai, in contrast, was the exceptional accommodationist able to equilibrate the most disparate and threatening historical pressures—his focus on both Western scientific developmens and traditional Japanese forms of experience in the service of cultural and national continuity. If Ogai was a positive accommodationist, in that he believed in both Western and Japanese values, then Hakuchō was a negative one who doubted the validity of either. That difference was revealed in the manner in which they approached death—Ogai with confident, formed images about who he was and where he was going, and Hakuchō with uneasy questions about the fate of the individual self and the possibilities of an afterlife.

None of the six men plunged suddenly into his approach to social change or to death. Each struggled with these fundamental images for many years. Many commentators have noted the shifts in allegiance to groups that occurred with the emergence of a modern Japanese state, in both immediate small groups as well as loyalties around the larger, impersonal nation-state. We would stress that these shifts created survivor constellations of profound individual pain and conflict and of extensive social impact.

We have witnessed conflicts in our six men between nation-centeredness and universal principles. The development of the modern state required people to identify with a larger national community that was unfamiliar in its abstract, impersonal, and distant nature. But the shift could be accomplished because Meiji leaders skillfully manipulated the emperor-centered symbolism that was both transcendent and rooted in Japanese ties to the human group.

The resulting Japanese nationalism gained such pervasive power that even those few intellectual leaders who embraced universal values continued to regard the nation-state as the focus of their principles. Chōmin and Kawakami, for example, respectively expressed their advocacy of human rights and Marxism within a nationalistic framework. This tension between nation-centeredness and universal principles is fundamental to emerging nations, and for that matter continues to confront all nations. The compelling need is to blend ideas that liberate in their very universality with cultural patterns that provide anchorage for those ideas, and to find in the blend symbolic power and meaning for people at all levels of society. The lives of our six men suggest that, at least for Japan, that goal could be only approximated—and that in the symbolic gaps that remain we encounter potentially dangerous psychological and political possibilities. There is the modern temptation to call forth the immortalizing vision of the state, which is the essence of all nationalism, on behalf of a sacred and consolidating mission.

The human power of that kind of call to Japanese essence is expressed in the phenomenon of tenkō, ideological backsliding. In the late 1930s and 1940s a considerable number of Christians, liberals, Social Democrats, and Communists disavowed their beliefs in favor of ultranationalism. The conversions occurred under police torture, physical threat, and excruciating psychological pressure. But also involved was the susceptibility of Japanese to the pull of the human group—that of the inclusive nation-state and the institutional and family units successfully integrated within it. There were of course notable exceptions, including Chōmin and Kawakami. But the prevalence of tenkō suggests—in Japan and elsewhere—the vulnerability of innovative ideas that deviate from the dominant symbols of human connection. (A related phenomenon occurred among some American Communist intellectuals of the 1930s who, through combinations of disillusionment, accommodation, and coercion, surrendered their beliefs in favor of right-wing Americanism.) The experiences of our six men suggest the possibility for achievement and change in the midst of that vulnerability. But they also suggest the extent of residual Japanese dislocations and the unpredictability of their consequences.

Japan is sometimes referred to as a death-haunted culture, but this tendency is not without a modern paradox. Death symbolism has not only mobilized forays of romantic destruction but has also been a source of vitality and continuity in connection with necessary social transformations. Here too the Japanese experience has universal implications. For in our era of holocaust, experienced and threatened, we have all become part of a global death-haunted culture, with similar possibilities of destruction and revitalization. Inundated by death imagery posed by threats of environmental catastrophe, worldwide famine, and nuclear war, how can we avoid confronting that imagery in the hope of gaining further understanding of our condition and a measure of control over our destiny? We have much to learn from the experience of modern Japan.

The traditional way to end a biography is for the subject to die on the last page. Our case studies reversed this order by starting with death and then moving through life. We examined individual deaths and lives as a way of exploring issues of history and social change. Our arena has been Japan, but the questions we have raised could be asked anywhere.

BIBLIOGRAPHY

CHAPTER 1: APPROACH

Ariès, Philippe. *Western Attitudes Toward Death: From the Middle Ages to the Present*, trans. Patricia M. Ranum. Baltimore: Johns Hopkins University Press, 1974.

Becker, Ernest. *The Denial of Death*. New York: The Free Press, 1973.

———. *Escape from Evil*. New York: The Free Press, 1975.

Bellah, Robert N. *Tokugawa Religion: The Values of Preindustrial Japan*. Boston: Beacon Press, 1970.

Benedict, Ruth. *The Crysanthemum and the Sword*. Boston: Houghton Mifflin, 1946.

Bowlby, John. *Attachment and Loss*, vol. 1: *Attachment*. New York: Basic Books, 1969.

Earl, David Magarey. *Emperor and Nation in Japan*. Seattle: University of Washington Press, 1964.

Eliade, Mircea. *Cosmos and History—The Myth of the Eternal Return*. New York: Harper Torchbooks, 1959.

Erikson, Erik H. *Gandhi's Truth*. New York: Norton, 1958.

———. *Young Man Luther*. New York: Norton, 1969.

Freud, Sigmund. *Moses and Monotheism, Standard Edition of the Complete Psychological Works of Sigmund Freud*, ed. James Strachey. London: Hogarth Press, 1953–66, vol. 23, pp. 3–137.

Gorer, Goffrey. "The Pornography of Death," in *Death, Grief, and Mourning*. New York: Doubleday, 1965.

Ishida Takeshi. *Japanese Society*. New York: Random House, 1971.

Lifton, Robert Jay, edited with Eric Olson. *Explorations in Psychohistory: The Wellfleet Papers*. New York: Simon and Schuster, 1974.

———. *The Life of the Self*. New York: Simon and Schuster, 1976.

Maruyama Masao. "Rekishi ishiki no kosō" ("The ancient structure of historical consciousness"), in *Rekishi shisō shū (Selections on Historical Thought)*, ed. Maruyama Masao. *Nihon no shisō 6 (Japanese Thought 6)*. Tokyo: Chikuma shobō, 1972, pp. 3–42.

Nakane Chie. *Japanese Society*. Berkeley: University of California Press, 1970.

Plath, David, "Where the Family of God Is the Family—the Role of the Dead in Japanese Households," *American Anthropologist* 66 (1964), pp. 300–17.

Rank, Otto. *Beyond Psychology*. New York: Dover, 1941.

Van der Leeuw, G. *Religion in Essence and Manifestation: A Study in Phenomenology*. New York: Harper & Row, 1963.

World Health Organization. *World Health Statistics Annual*, vol. 1: *Vital Statistics and Causes of Death*. Geneva: World Health Organization, 1977.

CHAPTER 2: NOGI MARESUKE

Nogi Maresuke. *Nogi Maresuke nikki (The Diary of Nogi Maresuke)*, ed. Wada Masao. Tokyo: Kinen sha, 1970.

Ohama Tetsuya. *Nogi Maresuke*. Tokyo: Yūzankaku, 1967.

Washburn, Stanley. *Nogi, A Man Against the Background of a Great War*. New York: 1913.

Background Material

Ashmead-Bartlett, Ellis. *Port Arthur, The Seige and Capitulation*, 2d ed. London: William Blackwood and Sons, 1906.

Craig, Albert. *Chōshū in the Meiji Restoration*. Cambridge: Harvard University Press, 1961.

Lifton, Robert Jay. *Thought Reform and the Psychology of Totalism*. New York: Norton, 1961.

Nitobe Inazō. *Bushidō, The Soul of Japan*, rev. and enl. ed. Rutland, Vt.: Charles Tuttle, 1969.

Okamoto Shumpei. *The Japanese Oligarchy and the Russo-Japanese War*. New York: Columbia University Press, 1970.

Tanaka Akira. *Bakumatsu no Chōshū (Chōshū in the Bakumatsu Period)*. Tokyo: Chūkō shinsho, 1965.

White, John Albert. *The Diplomacy of the Russo-Japanese War*. Princeton: Princeton University Press, 1964.

CHAPTER 3: MORI OGAI

Hasegawa Izumi. *Mori Ogai ronkō (Study of Mori Ogai)*. Tokyo: Meiji shoin, 1962.

———. *Ogai "Vita Sexualis" ko (Study of Ogai's "Vita Sexualis")*. Tokyo: Meiji shoin, 1968.

———. *Zoku Oagi "Vita Sexualis" ko (Sequel to Study of Ogai's "Vita Sexualis")*. Tokyo: Meiji shoin, 1971.

Katō Shūichi. "Mori Ogai, bungaku no sekai, kagaku no sekai" ("Mori ogai, the World of Literature, the World of Science"), in *Nihon no shisōka 3 (Japanese Thinkers 3)*, ed. *Asahi jyanaru (Asahi journal)*. Tokyo: Asahi shinbun, 1963, pp. 7–18.

Kobori Kei'ichirō. *Wakakibi no Mori Ogai (Mori Ogai's Youth)*. Tokyo: Tokyo daigaku shuppan kai, 1969.

Kojima Masajirō. "Mori Ogai" in *Mori Ogai shū (Selected Works of Mori Ogai). Gendai nihon bungaku taikei 7 (Outline of Modern Japanese Literature 7)*. Tokyo: Chikuma shobo, 1972, pp. 409–27.

Mori Ogai. *Mori Ogai shū (Selected Works of Mori Ogai). Gendai nihon bungaku taikei 7-8 (Outline of Modern Japanese Literature 7-8)*. Tokyo: Chikuma shobō, 1972.

———. *Ogai zenshū (Collected Works of Ogai)*, vols. 1–38. Tokyo: Iwanami shoten, 1971–1975.

———. "The Last Testament of Okitsu Yagoemon" ("Okitsu Yagoemon no isho"), trans. William Ritchie Wilson. *Monumenta Nipponica* 26 (1971), 147–58.

Rimer, J. Thomas. *Mori Ogai*. Boston: Twayne Publishers, 1975.

Yamamuro Shizuka. *Hyoden Mori Ogai (Biographical study of Mori Ogai)* Tokyo: Jitsugyo no nihonsha, 1967.

Background Material

Camus, Albert. *The Rebel*. New York: Knopf, 1954.

Handy, Rollo. "Hans Vaihinger," in *The Encyclopedia of Philosophy*, ed. Paul Edwards. New York: Macmillan, 1967, vol. 8, pp. 221–24.

Katō Shūichi. "Deutschland als Beispiel" ("Germany as model"), in *So sehen sie Deutschland (They Look at Germany in This Way)*, ed. Francois Bondy. Stuttgart: Seewald Verlag, 1970.

———. "Japanese Writers and Modernization," in *Changing Japanese Attitudes Toward Modernization*, ed. Marius Jansen. Princeton: Princeton University Press, 1965, pp. 489–531.

Kōsaka Masaaki, ed. *Japanese Thought in the Meiji Era*, trans. and adapt. David Abosch. Tokyo: Pan-Pacific Press, 1958.

Montaigne, Michel Eyquem de. *Oeuvres Completes de Montaigne*. Bibliothèque de la Pléiade. Paris: Editions Gallimard, 1962.

Pyle, Kenneth. "Some Recent Approaches to Japanese Nationalism." *Journal of Asian Studies* 21 (November 1971): 5–16.

CHAPTER 4: NAKAE CHŌMIN

Dardess, Margaret Beckerman. "The Thought and Politics of Nakae Chōmin (1847–1901)." Ph.D. dissertation, Columbia University, 1973.

Ishikawa Hanzan. "Nakae Chōmin sensei tsuikai ki" (Reminiscences of Nakae Chōmin *sensei*"), in *Nakae Chōmin shū (Selected Works of Nakae Chōmin)*, ed. Matsunaga Shōzō. *Kindai nihon shisō taikei 3 (Outline of Modern Japanese Thought 3)*. Tokyo: Chikuma shobō, 1974, pp. 406-11.

Kōtoku Shūsui. *Chōmin sensei*. Tokyo: Hakubunkan, 1902.

Kuwabara Takeo, ed. *Nakae Chōmin no kenkyū (Studies on Nakae Chōmin)*. Tokyo: Iwanami shoten, 1966.

Matsunaga Shōzō. *Nakae Chōmin*. Tokyo: Kashiwa a shobō, 1967.

Nakae Chōmin. *Ichinen yūhan (One Year and a Half)*, in *Nakae Chōmin shū (Selected Works of Nakae Chōmin)*, ed. Hayashi Shigeru. *Meiji bungaku zenshū 13 (Collected Works of Meiji Literature 13)*. Tokyo: Chikuma shobō, 1967.

————. *Nakae Chōmin shū (Selected Works of Nakae Chōmin)*, ed. Hayashi Shigeru. *Meiji bungaku zenshū 13 (Collected Works of Meiji Literature 13)*. Tokyo: Chikuma shobō, 1967.

————. *Nakae Chōmin shū (Selected Works of Nakae Chōmin)*, ed. Matsunaga Shōzō. *Kindai nihon shisō taikei 3 (Outline of Modern Japanese Thought 3)*. Tokyo: Chikuma shobō, 1974.

————. *Zoku ichinen yūhan (Sequel to One Year and a Half)*, in *Nakae Chōmin shū (Selected Works of Nakae Chōmin)*, ed. Hayashi Shigeru. *Meiji bungaku zenshū 13 (Collected Works of Meiji Literature 13)* Tokyo: Chikuma shobō, 1967.

Yamaguchi Kōsaku. *Itan no genryū, Nakae Chōmin no shisō to kōdō (Source of Heterodoxy, the Thought and Behavior of Nakae Chōmin)*. Kyoto: Hōritsu bunka sha, 1961.

Background Material

De Vos, George, and Wagatsuma, Hiroshi. *Japan's Invisible Race*, revised ed. Berkeley: University of California Press, 1972.

Ike Nobutaka. *The Beginning of Political Democracy in Japan*. Baltimore: Johns Hopkins Press, 1960.

Illich, Ivan. *Medical Nemesis*. New York: Pantheon, 1976.

Jansen, Marius. *Sakamoto Ryōma and the Meiji Restoration*. Princeton: Princeton University Press, 1961.

Medzini, Meron. *French Policy in Japan During the Closing Years of the Tokugawa Regime*. Cambridge: East Asian Research Center, Harvard University, 1971.

Pyle, Kenneth. *The New Generation in Meiji Japan*. Stanford: Stanford University Press, 1969.

CHAPTER 5: KAWAKAMI HAJIME

Bernstein, Gail. *Japanese Marxist: A Portrait of Kawakami Hajime, 1879–1946*. Cambridge: Harvard University Press, 1977.

————. "Kawakami Hajime: A Japanese Marxist in Search of the Way," in *Japan in

Crisis: Essays on Taishō Democracy, ed. Bernard S. Silberman and H. D. Harootunian. Princeton: Princeton University Press, 1974.

Itō Shōshin. "Muga en to Kawakami hakase" ("The Garden of Selflessness and Dr. Kawakami"), in *Kawakami Hajime no ningen zō (Portraits of the Person Kawakami Hajime)*, ed. Amano Keitarō and Noguchi Tsutomu. Tokyo: Tōshō shinbun sha, 1968, pp. 60–65.

Kawakami Hajime. *Gokuchū nikki (Prison Diary)*, vols. 1 and 2. Tokyo: Iwanami shoten, 1947.

———.*Jijoden (Autobiography)*, vols 1–5. Tokyo: Iwanami shoten, 1947.

———. *Kawakami Hajime*, ed. Ouchi Hyōe. *Gendai nihon shisō taikei 19 (Outline of Modern Japanese Thought 19)*. Tokyo: Chikuma shobo, 1964.

Nawa Tōichi. "Bannen no Kawakami sensei" ("Kawakami sensei's Last Years"), in *Kawakami Hajime no ningen zō (Portraits of the Person Kawakami Hajime)*, ed. Amano Keitarō and Noguchi Tsutomu. Tokyo: Tōshō shinbun sha, 1968, pp. 247–54.

Ouchi Hyōe. *Kawakami Hajime*. Tokyo: Chikuma shobō, 1966.

Suekawa Hiroshi. "Kawakami no jisei to shūsen" ("Kawakami's Passing and the Postwar Period"), in *Kawakami Hajime no ningen zō (Portraits of the Person Kawakami Hajime)*, ed. Amano Keitarō and Noguchi Tsutomu. Tokyo: Tōshō shinbun sha, 1968, pp. 261–67.

Sumiya Etsuji. "Bōyū Yamamoto Senji kun no bozen ni kataru" ("Speaking before the grave of my deceased friend Yamamoto Senji"), in *Kawakami Hajime no ningen zō (Portraits of the Person Kawakami Hajime)*, ed. Amano Keitarō and Noguchi Tsutomu. Tokyo: Tōshō shinbun sha, 1968, pp. 255–60.

———. *Kawakami Hajime*. Tokyo: Yoshikawa kōbunkan, 1962.

Yasuda Tokutarō. "Kawakami sensei no omoide" ("Reminiscences of Kawakami sensei"), *Kawakami Hajime no ningen zō (Portraits of the Person Kawakami Hajime)*, ed. Amano Keitarō and Noguchi Tsutomu. Tokyo: Tōshō shinbun sha, 1968, pp. 220–24.

Background Material

Beckmann, George, and Okubo Genji. *The Japanese Communist Party 1922–1945*. Stanford: Stanford University Press, 1969.

Silberman, Bernard S., and Harootunian, H. D., eds. *Japan in Crisis: Essays on Taishō Democracy*. Princeton: Princeton University Press, 1974.

Totten, George O. *The Social Democratic Movement in Prewar Japan*. New Haven: Yale University Press, 1966.

CHAPTER 6: MASAMUNE HAKUCHO

Arima Tatsuo. *The Failure of Freedom*. Cambridge: Harvard University Press, 1969, chap. 4.

Masamune Hakuchō. "Dust" ("Jin'ai"), trans. Robert Rolf. *Monumenta Nipponica* 25 (1970), 407–14.

———. *Masamune Hakuchō shū (Collected Work of Masamune Hakuchō)*. *Gendai nihom bungaku taikei 16 (Outline of Modern Japanese Literature 16)*. Tokyo: Chikuma shobō, 1969.

———. *Masamune Hakuchō zenshū (Collected Works of Masamune Hakuchō)* vols. 1–13. Tokyo: Shinchōsha, 1965–68.

Oiwa Kō. *Masamune Hakuchō ron (On Masamune Hakuchō)*. Tokyo: Gogatsu shobō, 1971.
Sasaki Tōru. *Masamune Hakuchō*. Tokyo: Shimizu shoin, 1967.

Background Material

Beardsley, Richard; Hall, John W.; and Ward, Robert E. *Village Japan*. Chicago: University of Chicago Press, 1959.
Earhart, H. Byron, *Japanese Religion: Unity and Diversity*. Belmont, Ca.: Dickenson Publishing, 1969.
Katō Shūichi. *Form, Style, Tradition: Reflections on Japanese Art and Society*. Berkeley: University of California Press, 1971.
Smith, Thomas C. *The Agrarian Origins of Modern Japan*. Stanford: Stanford University
Weisman, Avery. *On Dying and Denying*. New York: Behavioral Publications, 1972.

CHAPTER 7: MISHIMA YUKIO

Mishima Yukio. *Confessions of a Mask (Kamen no kokuhaku)*, trans. Meredith Weatherby. New York: New Directions, 1958.
———. *Sun and Steel (Taiyō to tetsu)*, trans. John Bester. New York: Kōdansha International, 1970.
———. *The Temple of the Golden Pavilion (Kinkakuji)*, trans. Ivan Morris. New York: Alfred A. Knopf, 1959.
———. *Mishima Yukio zenshū (Collected Works of Mishima Yukio)*, vols. 1–36. Tokyo: Shinchōsha, 1975–76.
Nathan, John. *Mishima: A Biography*. Boston: Little, Brown and Co., 1974.
Okuma Miyoshi, *Seppuku no rekishi (The History of Seppuku)*. Tokyo: Yūzankaku, 1973.
Scott-Stokes, Henry. *The Life and Death of Yukio Mishima*. New York: Farrar, Straus & Giroux, 1974.

Background Material

Lifton, Robert Jay. *History and Human Survival*. New York: Random House, 1970.
———. *Home from the War: Vietnam Veterans–Neither Victims nor Executioners*. New York: Simon and Schuster, 1973.
Morris, Ivan. *The Nobility of Failure, Tragic Heroes in the History of Japan*. New York: Holt, Rhinehart and Winston, 1975.
Tsurumi Kazuko. *Social Change and the Individual: Japan Before and After Defeat in World War II*. Princeton: Princeton University Press, 1970.
Vogel, Ezra. *Japan's New Middle Class*. Berkeley: University of California Press, 1963.

CHAPTER 8: DEATH AND SOCIAL CHANGE

DeVos, George. *Socialization for Achievement: Essays on the Cultural Psychology of the Japanese*. Berkeley: University of California Press, 1973.
Doi Takeo. *The Anatomy of Dependence*. New York: Kōdansha International, 1973.
Farberow, Norman, and Shneidman, Edwin, eds. *The Cry for Help*. New York: McGraw-Hill, 1961.

Hillman, James. *Suicide and the Soul*. New York: Harper Colophon, 1968.
Lifton, Robert Jay. *Death in Life: Survivors of Hiroshima*. New York: Random House, 1967.
Menninger, Karl. *The Vital Balance*. New York: Viking, 1963.
Shneidman, Edwin, Farberow, Norman, and Litman, Robert, eds. *The Psychology of Suicide*. New York: Science House, 1970.

INDEX